Palgrave Studies in Creativity and Innovation in Organizations

Series Editor
Roni Reiter-Palmon
Department of Psychology
University of Nebraska
Omaha, NE, USA

This book series presents the latest research on creativity and innovation in the workplace, showcasing the unique contribution that psychology can contribute to workplace innovation studies both now and in future. Addressing individual, team and organizational issues of innovation at work, books in this series offers insight from organizational and social psychology to cover topics with key applications to business and management, design, engineering and other applied domains. Encompassing a broad range of types of organization, it investigates the psychology of creativity and innovation in non-profit enterprises, entrepreneurship, small business, and research and development contexts, among many other domains.

The series brings together research in creativity and organizational innovation to investigate a range of key contemporary issues. Topics addressed include the relationship between creativity, innovation and organizational performance; measuring creativity in organizations; applications of creativity and innovation for top management and senior leadership; and the potentially negative consequences of innovation.

More information about this series at
http://www.palgrave.com/gp/series/16308

Roni Reiter-Palmon · Colin M. Fisher ·
Jennifer S. Mueller
Editors

Creativity at Work

A Festschrift in Honor of Teresa Amabile

palgrave
macmillan

Editors
Roni Reiter-Palmon
Department of Psychology
University of Nebraska
Omaha, NE, USA

Colin M. Fisher
School of Management
University College London
London, UK

Jennifer S. Mueller
School of Business
University of San Diego
San Diego, CA, USA

Palgrave Studies in Creativity and Innovation in Organizations
ISBN 978-3-030-61310-5 ISBN 978-3-030-61311-2 (eBook)
https://doi.org/10.1007/978-3-030-61311-2

Cover illustration: stilllifephotographer/gettyimages

This Palgrave Macmillan imprint is published by the registered company Springer Nature Switzerland AG
The registered company address is: Gewerbestrasse 11, 6330 Cham, Switzerland

A Festschrift for Teresa Amabile: An Introduction

In August 2019, a day-long seminar to celebrate the research and work of Teresa Amabile took place on the campus of Harvard, where Teresa has been a faculty member until her retirement. Teresa Amabile has started her Psychology career in 1977 with a Ph.D. in Social Psychology from Stanford University. During the 40 years she has been a faculty member she has contributed significantly to the research and study of creativity. Her work focusing on the social psychology of creativity is considered foundational to the study of creativity. Students and researchers studying creativity recognize her many contributions to the development of the field. Most notable are the development of The Consensual Assessment Technique (CAT), the componential model of creativity, the development of a measure of creative climate, and the progress principle. The chapters in this volume were written by those that have gathered to celebrate Teresa Amabile's research and accomplishments. They include her students, colleagues, and other creativity researchers. The chapters are based on presentations given at the Festschrift in August 2019.

The first chapter by Justin Berg drills down on a less known paper published by Teresa—"Brilliant but Cruel"—a paper that showed that those who gave negative reviews were perceived to be more intelligent than those who gave positive reviews. He proposes and provides initial evidence to support a fascinating idea: Rather than being critical, being optimistic and benevolent may actually contribute to more accurate evaluations of creative ideas.

The next chapter, by Regina Conti and Brynn April, introduces the concept of inspiration into Amabile's componential model of creativity, focusing on its relationship with intrinsic motivation. In doing so, the authors summarize research linking inspiration, intrinsic motivation, and creativity and detail a new empirical study on how the physical environment can inspire creativity. The chapter is book-ended by Conti's reflections on her work with Teresa Amabile and the inspiration she received from it.

The chapter by Jonathan Cromwell focuses on two aspects of the componential model—intrinsic motivation and creative thinking skills. He posits that Amabile's work has shown that social environment shapes both intrinsic motivation and creative thinking skills, which has led him to investigate how external constraints can enhance creativity (rather than harming it, as prior research has suggested). Building on his own experience working with Teresa, he also recounts how both her ideas and guidance have affected his own development as a scholar.

The chapter by Colin Fisher, Poornika Ananth, and Ozumcan Demir Caliskan elaborates how Teresa's work contributed to theoretical discussions and observations of the creative process. This chapter identifies how Teresa's view of the creative process changed and expanded over time to include more social and dynamic aspects and identifies key questions to guide future scholarly efforts. The chapter ends by describing the first author's own creative process journey with Teresa, and how Teresa's ideas shaped and honed his own contributions to the field.

The chapter by Lucy Gilson lists the many major theoretical contributions Teresa's work has made in no particular order of importance—making the claim that they are all important. In particular, she emphasizes specific contributions which inspired her and her colleagues to publish important insights that extended Teresa's work in the domain of understanding the conceptual definition of creativity, the relationship between motivation and creativity as well as the interactionist perspective on creativity, and the crucial insight that creativity and innovation were separate and distinct parts of a process critically related to organizational success.

Spencer Harrison provides a novel reflection on the influence of Teresa Amabile and her work—in both the content and format of his chapter. Harrison ranges from discussing the role of memes in creativity and science, to reflecting on the influence of Teresa's ideas on scholarship, as well as her personal impact on him. He concludes with expressions of that impact in the form of a poem and figure that we will not spoil for readers by attempting to summarize it here.

The chapter by Beth Hennessy describes her intellectual and personal journey with Teresa which started when entering graduate school and continued until today as she contemplates retirement herself. In particular she describes the development and cultivation of a tremendous intellectual synergy with Teresa and how this synergy contributed to their publishing many pieces together over many years across a range of topics related to creativity. In particular, she describes her journey studying the consensual assessment technique, early studies of intrinsic motivation as well as later "immunization studies" aimed at making school culture more conducive to creativity.

In his chapter, Giovanni Moneta revisits Amabile's componential theory and five-stage process model by considering the concept of flow. Moneta argues that moving toward a flow state in creative work creates disturbances in creators' subjective experiences. These disturbances can help account for dynamism in the creative process and the role that failure plays in going "back to the drawing board."

The chapter by Jennifer S. Mueller focuses on how people evaluate creativity. She describes her interest starting with her work with Teresa Amabile, and identifying that while employees and managers state explicitly that they prefer creativity, this is not always reflected in their actions. She summarizes her research in which she attempts to identify the reasons why this happens. Her research indicates that uncertainty and evaluations from authority figures play an important role. She then proceeds to discuss the implications of this to the componential model. Specifically, the componential model takes the perspective of the employee but not that of the decision-maker.

The chapter by Michael Mumford and Mark Fichtel focuses on the environment in creativity occurs, specifically, a climate for creativity. Amabile was a pioneer in this work and developed a measure of climate for creativity. In this chapter, Mumford and Fichtel highlight the dimensions of creative climate, and apply those to the study of creativity in professionals. They then address the conflicting demands of risk and safety, both important attributes of a creative environment. They argue that the integration of these two aspects is critical, and understanding the mechanisms by which this integration occurs is important for our understanding of creativity and creative environments.

Paul Paulus focuses his chapter also the Social Psychology of creativity and the connection between the work of Teresa Amabile and his own work on group or team creativity. He notes that the componential model, while focusing on the individual creator, provided a roadmap for the study of creativity in groups. The chapter further details how the consensual assessment technique was important in the facilitation of the study of group creativity moving the research beyond just counts of ideas. He then details the implications of Amabile's body for the future of group creativity research.

This chapter by Gregory Fetzer & Michael Pratt drills down into a recent addition to the componential model—in 2016—Pratt and Teresa wrote an article which infused the componential model with theory around meaningfulness. This chapter expands upon this insight to explore two new lines of inquiry: (1) uncovering conditions that motivate different orientations to be creative; and (2) understanding how creative persistence may unfold in the long term.

The chapter by Jill Perry-Smith chronicles her intellectual journey which was strongly shaped by her advisor Christina Shalley—both of whom were inspired by Teresa's componential model. In early works Jill and Christina examined Teresa's idea that intrinsic motivation and resulting creativity might be undermined by evaluation—work which began her focus on examining the "social side of creativity." Today, inspired by Teresa's work, Jill has expanded our understanding of how network and social interaction can help and hinder creative efforts.

The chapter by Gerard Puccio focuses on the crucial contribution polarity thinking, that is the integration of opposite qualities and characteristics, makes to creative achievement. Second, Puccio revisits Amabile's seminal work and integrate the notion of polarities with her componential model. Puccio focuses on four specific polarities that are critical for creativity, with two being specific to the work of Amabile. Task motivation is reexamined from the perspective of intrinsic and extrinsic motivation as a polarity dimension. Finally, the balance between creativity and domain-relevant skills is framed as opposing poles within a dialectic relationship.

The chapter by Roni Reiter-Palmon details the extension and modification of the consensual assessment technique over the years it has been used in research. In her chapter she indicates that modifications were necessary due to the use of everyday problems and the lack of expert judges. She then provides information on the specific modifications such as the use of separate ratings for solution quality (usefulness) and originality (novelty) and rater training.

Next, Mark Runco discusses how Amabile's work has influenced the development of his model of creative cognition to incorporate intrinsic motivation. The chapter examines intrinsic motivation within a larger context where it intersects with cognition. Runco then moves to discuss the consensual assessment technique and the creative product. He raises a concern about the generalization from judges used in the consensual assessment technique, an area that needs further study.

The chapter by Christina Shalley reflects on both the influence of the componential model and consensual assessment technique for the field and her own influential body of research. Specifically, she recounts how the intrinsic motivation principle influenced her work on goal setting, expected evaluation, and competition, which ultimately led her to examine additional motivational and contextual factors involved in creativity.

Dean Simonton recounts in his chapter the genesis of the term "the social psychology of creativity," focusing on the context within social psychology prior to both his and Amabile's pioneering work. Simonton argues in his chapter that, although Amabile and others have credited

Simonton with coining the term "the social psychology of creativity," Amabile deserves the credit for establishing creativity as an accepted area of research in social psychology.

The chapter by Jeff Steiner focuses on Teresa Amabile's more recent work, the progress principle. Steiner highlights the role that this work had in emphasizing the importance of inner working life, an area that has been understudied. He suggests that this work is unique due to its person-centered approach and the use of rigorous methodology to study a difficult area. He further notes that this research provides a unique contribution to practitioners in the field. The chapter concludes by discussing the future of the progress principle, both in terms of its application and additional research.

Robert Sternberg provides an overview of the work by Teresa Amabile as it relates to creativity. He notes that Teresa's work transformed the field of creativity, and discusses a number of major contribution to the study of creativity. First, the new focus on the social psychology of creativity, and the integration of creativity into the wider field of social psychology. Second, the development of the componential model of creativity, which provided a theoretical model for the study of creativity. Third, her study of the role of intrinsic motivation in creative performance. Finally, the development of the consensual assessment technique which allowed for the previous development in a scientifically rigorous way.

Jing Zhou also blends a personal account of Teresa's work with her professional influence. Zhou commends Amabile's research for three main reasons: (1) creating a coherent body of work, (2) being courageous in challenging assumptions, and (3) making a positive contribution to the community. She then details how these commendable aspects of Amabile's work have helped inspire her own research contributions, including the interactional effects of personal and situational variables on creativity, her recent work on the receiving side of creativity, and many valuable reviews of the literature on creativity in organizations.

Teresa Amabile herself then offers an afterword on these chapters. In it, she reflects both on her research career, its roots, and the many people who have offered support and love to her over her 40 years of creativity research. She draws three main lessons from her experience about drawing power from uncertainty, failure, and "confident humility."

Roni Reiter-Palmon
Colin M. Fisher
Jennifer S. Mueller

Contents

Notes on Contributors

Teresa M. Amabile has researched and written about creativity for 45 years. Beginning with a series of empirical and theoretical papers in the 1970s and 1980s, she was instrumental in establishing the social psychology of creativity—the study of how the social environment can influence creative behavior, primarily by influencing motivational state. Originally focusing on experimental studies of individual creativity, Teresa's research expanded to non-experimental, field-based studies that also encompassed individual productivity, team creativity, and organizational innovation. Her more recent research incorporates the study of creativity into broader investigations of two topics: the day-by-day psychological experience and performance of people doing creative work inside organizations, and American professionals' experience of transitioning to retirement. Teresa's scholarly work has appeared in a variety of psychology and organizational behavior journals, as well as her books, including *The Social Psychology of Creativity* (1983), its update, *Creativity in Context* (1996), *Growing Up Creative* (1989), and *The Progress Principle* (2011). Teresa has received the Distinguished Scholar Award from the Society for Personality and Social Psychology, the Lifetime Achievement Award from the Organizational Behavior Division of the Academy of Management, and the Lifetime Achievement Award from the Israel Organizational Behavior Conference, as well as other honors and grants. Teresa holds a B.S. degree in Chemistry from Canisius College and a Ph.D. in psychology from Stanford University.

Poornika Ananth is a Ph.D. candidate at University College London School of Management. Her research explores the challenges, experiences, and practices associated with creativity and sustainability at work. She received her Master of Science in International Strategy and Economics from the University of St Andrews, Scotland. Poornika also has a background in banking, having worked with Citibank in Europe and the Middle East in their Treasury and Trade Solutions Group.

Brynn April graduated summa cum laude from Colgate University in May 2020, receiving her B.A. in both Psychological Science and English. She completed an honors thesis on inspiration in the creative writing process with Regina Conti as her faculty mentor. Brynn also published an article entitled "We Run by the Mirror" in the University of Melbourne Periodical in 2019 and has authored several creative works including personal poems and a novel. She currently works as a Junior Associate at Gasthalter & Co., a New York-based financial communications firm.

Justin M. Berg is an Assistant Professor of Organizational Behavior at the Stanford Graduate School of Business. His research focuses on creativity and innovation. He studies how to successfully develop, evaluate, and implement creative ideas in and outside organizations. This includes research on job crafting, which is the process of employees creatively reshaping their own jobs to better suit their personalities and interests. He received his Ph.D. in Management from The Wharton School, University of Pennsylvania and his B.A. in Organizational Studies and Psychology from the University of Michigan.

Ozumcan Demir Caliskan is a Ph.D. candidate at University College London School of Management. She aims to integrate her experience in the field of design with organizational theory to understand creativity and innovation in organizations. Her research focuses on how new technologies and new forms of organizing affect creative processes and the experience of creative workers. She received her Master of Science and Bachelor's degrees in Industrial Design at Middle East Technical University (METU).

Regina Conti received her Ph.D. in social psychology from Brandeis University in 1995 where Teresa Amabile was her faculty mentor. She is currently an Associate Professor of Psychology at Colgate University. She teaches courses in the areas of human motivation, research methods, and the psychology of work. Her research investigates motivational processes in school, work, health, and family contexts. Most recently, she is exploring how the motivational dynamics of family life are influenced by a diagnosis of autism in a child or children.

Johnathan Cromwell is an Assistant Professor in the department of Entrepreneurship, Innovation, Strategy, and International Business at the University of San Francisco. His research focuses on creative problem-solving in organizations, particularly how individuals and groups tackle vague, open-ended, and ambiguous problems. Through this research, he aims to develop a new theoretical framework called "dynamic problem solving" that explains why, when, and how people change their problem-solving style as they respond to various constraints throughout the creativity and innovation process. He earned an S.B. in Chemical-Biological Engineering from MIT and a Doctorate in Management from Harvard Business School.

Greg Fetzer is a Doctoral Candidate at the Carroll School of Management at Boston College. His research focuses on creativity and meaningful work: what makes work novel, useful, and worth doing. In particular he focuses on the temporal experience of creative work and the social and cultural influences that shape work meaningfulness.

Mark W. Fichtel is a Doctoral Student in the University of Oklahoma's program in Industrial and Organizational (I/O) Psychology. His research interests include leadership, creativity, and ethics. He has worked on grants examining ethical decision-making and technology use during the Covid-19 pandemic.

Colin M. Fisher is an Associate Professor of Organizations and Innovation at University College London. His research explores how people lead, help, and coach teams and individuals in situations requiring collective creativity, improvization, and effective decision-making. His research has been published in leading journals, such as *Academy of Management Journal*, *Academy of Management Review*, *Organizational Behavior and Human Decision Processes*, and *Harvard Business Review*. Colin received his Ph.D. in Organizational Behavior from Harvard University. In his work as a professional jazz trumpet player, Colin was a long-time member of the Grammy-nominated Either/Orchestra, with whom he toured and recorded several critically acclaimed albums.

Lucy L. Gilson is the Associate Dean for Faculty & Outreach and serves as the Faculty Director for the Geno Auriemma UConn Leadership Conference, the faculty advisor to the UConn women's MBA association, a visiting Scholar at Universidade Catolica Portuguesa (Lisbon), and the Senior Associate Editor of *Group and Organization Management*. She is a Fellow of the Southern Management Association, and in 2019 she was named by the Web of Science Group as one of the world's most highly-cited researchers. Her research focuses on creativity, virtual teams, and team effectiveness; in particular, she is interested in examining teams in different organizational settings performing a diverse range of jobs. Specifically, she studies how creativity, employee empowerment, diversity, fairness issues, leadership, and virtual communication influence team effectiveness. Her research has been published in the *Academy of Management Journal*, *Journal of Applied Psychology*, *Group and Organization Management*, *Journal of Management*, *Production and Operation Management (POM) Journal*, *Innovation: Organization & Management*, *Journal of Occupational and Organizational Psychology*, *Journal of Organizational Behavior*, and many other international journals and books.

Spencer Harrison's research is typically an answer to one of three broad questions: 1) Creating: how do managers and leaders help people be creative together? 2) Coordinating: how do groups and teams work together in patterns that lead to optimal outcomes? 3) Connecting: how do people connect with the organizations they work for? He is always on the lookout for quirky settings where he can learn new things.

Beth A. Hennessey received her Ph.D. in Social/Developmental Psychology from Brandeis University in 1986. Before pursuing graduate study, Beth taught at the elementary school level. She was a member of the Wellesley College's Psychology Department from 1985 until her retirement in 2020. Beth served as the Faculty Director of Wellesley's Pforzheimer Learning and Teaching Center from 2007–2011. Across her career, Beth was involved with a number of international investigations of the connection between intrinsic motivation and creativity. She has also worked with the Lego corporation and the government of Singapore to better understand the connection between creativity and play across cultures.

Giovanni B. Moneta is a Senior Lecturer teaching personality psychology, work psychology and research methods. His main research interests are in positive psychology, with a focus on optimal experience (flow), creativity, adaptive metacognitions, and on how these influence performance in occupational and educational contexts. He is Author of *Positive Psychology: A Critical Introduction* and co-editor of *Psychology of Creativity: Cognitive, Emotional, and Social Processes.*

Jennifer S. Mueller (jmueller@sandiego.edu) is an Associate Professor of management at the University of San Diego. She received her Ph.D. from Brandeis University. Her research examines implicit beliefs (e.g., stereotypes, cultural narratives, and lay scripts) that harm effective collaboration, assessments of leadership potential, as well as the recognition of creative ideas.

Michael D. Mumford, Ph.D., is the George Lynn Cross Distinguished Research Professor of Psychology at the University of Oklahoma. He has published more than 400 peer-reviewed articles on creativity, leadership, planning, and ethics. Dr. Mumford has served as senior editor of *The Leadership Quarterly* and the *Creativity Research Journal*. He is a recipient of the Academy of Management's Eminent Leadership Scholar Award and the Society for Aesthetics, Creativity, and the Arts' Lifetime Scholarly Contribution award.

Paul B. Paulus received his Ph.D. from the University of Iowa and is a Distinguished University Professor in the Department of Psychology at the University of Texas at Arlington. He served as the Director of the Industrial/Organizational Psychology program and for 10 years taught the high performing teams course in the executive MBA program. He has published about 160 papers and chapters and five edited volumes related to group processes. About 100 of these papers and chapters are related to group creativity, with much of this research done in collaboration with cognitive and computer scientists in the past 20 years. With Bernard Nijstad he has edited two volumes on group creativity-*Group Creativity: Innovation Through Collaboration* (2003) and *The Handbook of Group Creativity and Innovation* (2019). He has served as Chair of the Department of Psychology and Dean of the College of Science and has been a visiting scholar at nine different institutions.

Jill Perry-Smith is Professor of Organization and Management in the Goizueta Business School at Emory University. She earned her Ph.D. from the College of Management at Georgia Institute of Technology. Professor Perry-Smith researches and writes about creative problem-solving, entrepreneurship, and social networks. She is fascinated by people dynamics and informal relationships that undergird the formal organization. In another stream of research, she explores how family influences work engagement and the role of company policies that help employees integrate life and work. Her research has appeared in leading management journals such as *Academy of Management Journal, Organization Science, and Journal of Applied Psychology*; she also has contributed to several books including Encyclopedia of Creativity, and The Oxford Handbook of Creativity, Innovation, and Entrepreneurship. She has served as an Associate Editor of *Academy of Management Journal*. Prior to her academic career, Professor Perry-Smith worked in the oil and gas industry overseeing large refinery expansion projects across the United States.

Michael G. Pratt (Ph.D. University of Michigan) is the O'Connor Family Professor at the Carroll School of Management at Boston College. In addition to his work on creativity, his recent research focuses on identity processes, meaningful work, trust in organizations, as well as on the writing, evaluating, and publishing of qualitative research. He is an Academy of Management Fellow and currently serves as an associate editor for the Administrative Science Quarterly.

Gerard J. Puccio is the Department Chair and Professor for the Creativity & Change Leadership Department at SUNY - Buffalo State. Dr. Puccio has written more than 60 articles, chapters, and books. In recognition of his outstanding work as a scholar, Dr. Puccio received the State University of New York Chancellor's Recognition Award for Research Excellence, as well as the President's Medal for Scholarship and Creativity. The Teaching Company selected Dr. Puccio as one of America's great lecturers and as such released a Great Course titled "The Creative Thinkers' Tool Kit" that features Dr. Puccio and his work.

Roni Reiter-Palmon is the Varner Professor of Industrial/Organizational (I/O) Psychology and the Director of the I/O Psychology Graduate Program at the University of Nebraska at Omaha (UNO). Her research focuses on creativity and innovation in the workplace, cognitive processes, and individual difference variables that influence creative performance of individuals and teams, leading creative individuals, and development of creativity and leadership skills. She has over 80 publications in leading journals. She is an Associate Editor for the European Journal of Work and Organizational Psychology and Frontiers: Organizational Psychology. She was the former editor of The Psychology of Aesthetics Creativity and the Arts. She serves on the editorial boards of a number of journals, including *The Psychology of Aesthetics, Creativity, and the Arts, Journal of Creative Behavior*, and *International Journal of Problem Solving and Creativity*. She has received UNO's College of Arts and Science Excellence in Research Award in 2013, UNO's Award for Distinguished Research and Creative Activity (ADROCA) in 2014, and the Nebraska University System Award for Research in 2017.

Mark A. Runco earned a Ph.D. in Cognitive Psychology from the Claremont Graduate School. He studied creativity as a student and has kept it since graduating in 1984. He earned tenure at the University of Hawaii, Hilo, and then moved to California State University, Fullerton and in 2008 was awarded an Endowed Professorship at the University of Georgia, where he was also Director of their Creativity Center. He has held adjunct positions at Buffalo State University and the Norwegian Business School. He is currently the Director of Creativity Research at Southern Oregon University (www.soucreativityconference.com), as well as a Fellow and Past President of Division 10 of the APA. He is the Founding Editor of the Creativity Research Journal. His creativity textbook has been translated into 10 languages. The 3rd edition of that text and 3rd edition of the Encyclopedia of Creativity, which he co-edited, are being released in 2020 (www.markrunco.com).

Christina E. Shalley is the Sharon M. & Matthew R. Price Chaired Professor of Organizational Behavior in the Scheller College of Business, Georgia Institute of Technology. Her research interests include investigating effects of various social and contextual factors on employees' creativity. She has published several articles and chapters on ways to structure jobs and the work environment to support the creative capabilities of individuals and teams of employees. She also works with organizations to help them find ways to facilitate employees' creativity. She is a Fellow of the Society for Industrial and Organizational Psychology and the Association for Psychological Science.

Dean Keith Simonton is Distinguished Professor Emeritus of Psychology at the University of California, Davis. His 500-plus single-authored publications focus on genius, creativity, and leadership. Honors include the William James Book Award, the George A. Miller Outstanding Article Award, the Theoretical Innovation Prize in Personality and Social Psychology, the Sir Francis Galton Award for Outstanding Contributions to the Study of Creativity, the Rudolf Arnheim Award for Outstanding Contributions to Psychology and the Arts, the E. Paul Torrance Award for Creativity, three Mensa Awards for Excellence in Research, and the Mensa Lifetime Achievement Award. MIT published his *Genius Checklist* in 2018.

Jeff Steiner is a Doctoral Student in the Organizational Behavior program at Harvard Business School. His research interests lie at the intersection of well-being and work. He is interested in how individuals think about what it means to live a good life, and the extent to which experiences with work helps or hinders the realization of it. Jeff was formerly a Talent Development Director at Morgan Stanley, as well as a Research Associate to Professor Teresa Amabile at Harvard Business School. Jeff earned his B.B.A. in Management and Psychology from the University of Miami.

Robert J. Sternberg is Professor of Human Development at Cornell University and Honorary Professor of Psychology at the University of Heidelberg, Germany. His B.A. is from Yale, his Ph.D. from Stanford, and he has 13 honorary doctorates. He has won the Grawemeyer Award in Psychology and the James and the Cattell Awards from the Association for Psychological Science. According to Google Scholar, he has been cited over 186,000 times with an h index of 208. He is past-president of the American Psychological Association and the Federation of Associations in Behavioral and Brain Sciences. He has been a university dean, provost, and president.

Jing Zhou is Mary Gibbs Jones Professor of Management at Jones Graduate School of Business at Rice University. Dr. Zhou has built a systematic program of research into creativity and innovation, receiving over 25,000 citations for her work (Google Scholar, 2020). Her research interests include antecedents of creativity, creativity receiving, and impact of creativity on organizational innovation and performance. She served as an Associate Editor of *Journal of Applied Psychology*. She is Fellow of the American Psychological Association, Association for Psychological Sciences, and Society for Industrial and Organizational Psychology.

List of Figures

1

Brilliant and Benevolent: The Optimism of Teresa Amabile's Legacy for Creativity in Organizations

Justin M. Berg

In 1982 and 1983, Teresa Amabile almost singlehandedly laid the methodological and theoretical groundwork for studying the social psychology of creativity. This is when she first published her consensual assessment technique (Amabile, 1982) and componential model of creativity (Amabile, 1983a). Paradigm shifts are by definition rare, and it is even rarer to be able to trace a paradigm shift back to a single scholar at a particular moment in time. Yet, we can point to Amabile's work in 1982 and 1983 as the foundation of a paradigm shift that led creativity to be a core area of study in both social psychology and organizational behavior.

During the same two years, she also published two papers that have received comparably less attention (Amabile & Glazebrook, 1982; Amabile, 1983b). From my view, these papers contain profound insights

J. M. Berg (✉)
Stanford Graduate School of Business, Stanford, CA, USA
e-mail: jmberg@stanford.edu

R. Reiter-Palmon et al. (eds.), *Creativity at Work*,
Palgrave Studies in Creativity and Innovation in Organizations,
https://doi.org/10.1007/978-3-030-61311-2_1

that remain understudied, particularly when they are combined with insights from the body of work Amabile has built since then. My goal in this essay is to encourage more research unpacking these insights. To do so, I put forth some initial ideas that I hope will serve as useful fodder for building on the largely untapped gems in these two papers.

The two papers both addressed a common situation in organizations: individuals evaluating others' ideas. The first paper (Amabile & Glazebrook, 1982) used two clever experiments to show that when evaluators were led to feel insecure about their intellectual standing, or they expected their audience to be of higher status than them, their evaluations were more negative and critical in nature. It seems insecure individuals think that criticizing others will make them look smart. But does this actually work—are more negative evaluators perceived as smarter than more positive evaluators?

The second paper (Amabile, 1983b) examined this question, again using two cleverly designed experiments. She took book reviews from the New York Times and adapted them to either be negative or positive, but otherwise the reviews were equivalent. Participants rated the intelligence and competence of the two reviewers, and indeed, negative reviewers were rated as smarter than positive reviewers. She titled this paper "Brilliant but Cruel," conveying that when evaluating others' ideas, cruelty is a way for evaluators to seem brilliant.

Taken together, these two papers point out a potentially huge problem for creativity in organizations. Insecure individuals have a powerful incentive to tear down others' ideas, regardless of how good or bad the ideas may be, as doing so will likely help them obtain the intellectual status they desire. Moreover, given that creativity usually requires considerable effort (Amabile, 1982, 1985), gaining status by tearing down others' ideas likely requires much less effort than gaining status through building one's own creative ideas. From here forward, I will refer to this as the "cruelty incentive." Insecure individuals who leverage the cruelty incentive may reap the benefits of appearing smarter, but at what cost?

Since these two papers, decades of research done by Amabile and others inspired by her suggest that the cruelty incentive may be a very costly impediment to creativity in organizations. A key tenet of Amabile's body of work is that creativity is fragile. People need supportive environments to take the risks and exert the considerable effort that is required to cultivate creative ideas (Amabile, Conti, Coon, Lazenby, & Hermon, 1996). In addition, constructive feedback from others is often critical to creativity in organizations (Harrison & Rouse, 2015). Research has demonstrated that feedback tends to foster creativity when it is framed positively and in an informational way, as opposed to negatively and in a controlling way (Zhou, 1998). This does not mean that negative feedback is always bad for creativity—pointing out flaws and weaknesses in others' ideas may facilitate improvement (Harrison & Dossinger, 2017). But it is unlikely that focusing primarily on negative feedback would be conducive to creativity (Zhou, 2003, 2008). Indeed, recent research suggests that trying to anticipate both the positive and negative outcomes of new ideas fosters more accurate evaluations (McIntosh, Mulhearn, & Mumford, 2019). However, the cruelty incentive may lead individuals to deliver only negative feedback about others' ideas to make themselves look and feel smart, but doing so may undermine the creativity of the subordinates or colleagues who receive the feedback, and perhaps others in the organization who fear similar feedback on their ideas in the future. Harsh criticism may also dampen positive affect in the organization, further stifling creativity (Amabile, Barsade, Mueller, & Staw, 2005).

In my own research, I have found evidence hinting that the cruelty incentive may lead individuals to undervalue others' most creative ideas. One relevant study was in the circus arts industry, with companies like Cirque du Soleil (Berg, 2016). The study was about creative forecasting, the skill of predicting the outcomes of new ideas. Circus professionals forecasted the success of new circus acts with the audience, and the accuracy of their predictions was tested with a large sample of audience members. The key comparison in the study was between creator and manager roles. Like many creative industries, managers' evaluations are all that really matter in the circus industry, as managers select which acts reach the stage and which do not. Creators are expected to generate new acts, but they have no say in which acts get put into shows. Interestingly, the study results showed that creators were more accurate than managers at predicting the success of other creators' ideas. Creators were not good at evaluating their own ideas, however—they thought too highly of their own ideas. But regarding their peers' ideas, creators were more accurate than managers. Managers were statistically no better than an average layperson with no expertise in the circus industry. Creators' advantage over managers was strongest for the most novel ideas, as managers undervalued novel ideas while creators were more likely to accurately spot value in them.

A follow-up experiment suggested that creators' advantage over managers was at least partially thanks to the nature of their respective roles. Specifically, creators may benefit from the emphasis in their role on divergent thinking (idea generation), as opposed to the emphasis on convergent thinking (idea evaluation) in the manager role. Engaging in divergent thinking to generate their own ideas may help creators stay more open minded about others' novel ideas (Runco, 1991; Runco and Smith, 1992; Silvia, 2008). Managers may miss out on the benefit of divergent thinking by specializing in idea evaluation, ironically making them worse at idea evaluation.

In the same vein, managers in the circus study were also harsher critics than creators. In addition to predicting how the audience would respond to new circus acts, creators and managers were also asked to evaluate the quality of each act from their own perspective, using items adapted from Amabile's (1982) classic work. This showed that on average, creators appreciated *all* acts more than managers. One might expect that liking all ideas more would make creators Pollyanna and undiscerning. But on the contrary, appreciating all ideas more was associated with greater accuracy in forecasting success with the audience, especially for the most novel ideas. By seeing the best in all ideas, creators were more likely to correctly identify the best ideas over less promising ideas. Conversely, by taking a more negative perspective, managers overlooked value in novel ideas that creators were able to see.

In this way, the cruelty incentive may be especially problematic for individuals in manager roles, who control which ideas are selected versus rejected and do not have the benefit of divergent thinking to keep their minds open to novel ideas. When managers feel insecure about their status, the cruelty incentive may lead them to unwisely reject their employees' most creative ideas. This may be especially true for highly promising ideas that are still early in their development, as the most creative final ideas often begin as relatively uncreative and incoherent initial ideas (Berg, 2014, 2019). Thus, insecure managers may reject high-potential ideas long before they have the chance to realize their potential.

The cruelty incentive may not only lead insecure individuals to stifle others' creativity, it may also undermine their own creativity. One of Amabile's major contributions is highlighting the positive relationship between intrinsic motivation and creativity (Amabile, 1985; Amabile, Hill, Hennesey, & Tighe, 1994). Grant and Berry (2011) built on this finding by showing that prosocial motivation—the desire to benefit others—strengthens the relationship between intrinsic motivation and creativity. In short, people are most creative when they are working because they enjoy it and want to help others. When individuals are focused on tearing down others' ideas, they may be less likely to come up with creative ideas themselves. Moreover, creativity can be contagious, as working with creative colleagues can help individuals be more creative themselves (Zhou, 2003). When individuals stifle others' creativity, they may also undermine their own creativity going forward.

In sum, the cruelty incentive may act as a self-fulfilling prophecy. Insecure individuals who harshly criticize others' ideas to make themselves look and feel smart may garner the intellectual status they seek. But over time, their cruelty may stifle their own and others' creativity in the organization. In the end, cruel evaluators may prove themselves right, as the ideas generated by them and others around them in the organization may become increasingly uncreative. In contrast, more benevolent evaluators may produce a more productive self-fulfilling prophecy. By resisting the cruelty incentive, benevolent evaluators may strike a more optimal balance of positive and negative thinking that is more conducive to creativity than solely focusing on the negative. In turn, benevolent evaluators may encourage the important drivers of creativity that cruel evaluators are likely to discourage, such as risk-taking, constructive feedback, positive affect, accurate idea evaluation, and intrinsic/prosocial motivation. In so doing, benevolent evaluators may enhance others' creativity and ultimately their own as well.

In this way, benevolence and creative brilliance may be mutually reinforcing over time. When evaluating others' new ideas, cruelty may be a way to appear smart, but benevolence may actually be the smarter approach. This notion is not only supported by Teresa Amabile's body of research, her benevolence and brilliance are a vivid illustration of it. Those of us who have been lucky enough to receive her guidance and mentoring can attest—her benevolence fuels her brilliance, and her brilliance fuels her benevolence. The result can be seen in the monumental impact she has made and inspired throughout her prolific career.

To help frame her research question, Amabile (1983b) opens her aforementioned "Brilliant but Cruel" paper with the following quote: "Only pessimism sounds profound. Optimism sounds superficial (Blotnick, 1979, p. 229)." Indeed, in evaluating others' new ideas, pessimists may seem more profound than optimists in the short run. But in the long run, both pessimists and optimists may end up surrounded by the level of creativity they expected.

References

Amabile, T. M. (1982). Social psychology of creativity: A consensual assessment technique. *Journal of Personality and Social Psychology, 43*(5), 997–1013.

Amabile, T. M. (1983a). The social psychology of creativity: A componential conceptualization. *Journal of Personality and Social Psychology, 45*(2), 357–376.

Amabile, T. M. (1983b). Brilliant but cruel: Perceptions of negative evaluators. *Journal of Experimental Social Psychology, 19*(2), 146–156.

Amabile, T. M. (1985). Motivation and creativity: Effects of motivational orientation on creative writers. *Journal of Personality and Social Psychology, 48*(2), 393–399.

Amabile, T. M., Barsade, S. G., Mueller, J. S., & Staw, B. M. (2005). Affect and creativity at work. *Administrative Science Quarterly, 50*(3), 367–403.

Amabile, T. M., Conti, R., Coon, H., Lazenby, J., & Herron, M. (1996). Assessing the work environment for creativity. *Academy of Management Journal, 39*(5), 1154–1184.

Amabile, T. M., & Glazebrook, A. H. (1982). A negativity bias in interpersonal evaluation. *Journal of Experimental Social Psychology, 18*(1), 1–22.

Amabile, T. M., Hill, K. G., Hennessey, B. A., & Tighe, E. M. (1994). The work preference inventory: Assessing intrinsic and extrinsic motivational orientations. *Journal of Personality and Social Psychology, 66*(5), 950–967.

Berg, J. M. (2014). The primal mark: How the beginning shapes the end in the development of creative ideas. *Organizational Behavior and Human Decision Processes, 125*(1), 1–17.

Berg, J. M. (2016). Balancing on the creative highwire: Forecasting the success of novel ideas in organizations. *Administrative Science Quarterly, 61*(3), 433–468.

Berg, J. M. (2019). When silver is gold: Forecasting the potential creativity of initial ideas. *Organizational Behavior and Human Decision Processes, 154,* 96–117.

Blotnizk, S. (1979, September 17). Things are ruff all over. *Forbes,* 228–229.

Grant, A. M., & Berry, J. (2011). The necessity of others is the mother of invention: Intrinsic and prosocial motivations, perspective-taking, and creativity. *Academy of Management Journal, 54*(1), 73–96.

Harrison, S. H., & Dossinger, K. (2017). Pliable guidance: A multilevel model of curiosity, feedback seeking, and feedback giving in creative work. *Academy of Management Journal, 60*(6), 2051–2072.

Harrison, S. H., & Rouse, E. D. (2015). An inductive study of feedback interactions over the course of creative projects. *Academy of Management Journal, 58*(2), 375–404.

McIntosh, T., Mulhearn, T. J., & Mumford, M. D. (2019). Taking the good with the bad: The impact of forecasting timing and valence on idea evaluation and creativity. *Psychology of Aesthetics, Creativity, and the Arts.*

Runco, M. A. (1991). The evaluative, valuative, and divergent thinking of children. *Journal of Creative Behavior, 25*(4), 311–319.

Runco, M., & Smith, W. (1992). Interpersonal and intrapersonal evaluations of creative ideas. *Personality and Individual Differences, 13*(3), 295–302.

Silvia, P. J. (2008). Discernment and creativity: How well can people identify their most creative ideas? *Psychology of Aesthetics, Creativity, and the Arts, 2*(3), 139–146.

Zhou, J. (1998). Feedback valence, feedback style, task autonomy, and achievement orientation: Interactive effects on creative performance. *Journal of Applied Psychology, 83*(2), 261.

Zhou, J. (2003). When the presence of creative coworkers is related to creativity: Role of supervisor close monitoring, developmental feedback, and creative personality. *Journal of Applied Psychology, 88*(3), 413–422.

Zhou, J. (2008). Promoting creativity through feedback. In J. Zhou & C. E. Shalley (Eds.), *Handbook of organizational creativity* (pp. 125–145). New York: Lawrence Erlbaum Associates.

2

An Inspiration to Study Inspiration

Regina Conti and Brynn April

My (Regina Conti's) first academic publication was a chapter that Teresa Amabile invited me to coauthor to contribute to a festschrift in honor of creativity researcher Frank Barron (Amabile, Conti, & Collins, 1996). After attending the thoroughly inspiring conference in honor of Teresa, I (Regina) was delighted to learn that one of my most promising students this year (Brynn April) was interested in studying the role of inspiration in the creative process. So, I invited her to coauthor this chapter, in which we will consider inspiration as a key element of the intrinsic task motivation that fuels creativity in Amabile's (1983, 1996) model.

Much of Amabile's early work was devoted to studying the detrimental effects of various extrinsic motivators in the social environment, such as contracted for reward, evaluation, time pressure, competition, and surveillance on creativity (Amabile, 1979; Amabile, DeJong, & Lepper,

R. Conti (✉) · B. April
Colgate University, Hamilton, NY, USA
e-mail: rconti@colgate.edu

R. Reiter-Palmon et al. (eds.), *Creativity at Work*,
Palgrave Studies in Creativity and Innovation in Organizations,
https://doi.org/10.1007/978-3-030-61311-2_2

1976; Amabile, Goldberg, & Capotosto, 1982; Amabile, Goldfarb, & Brackfield, 1990). Later, Amabile's work explored the synergistic potential of extrinsic motivators and documented situations in which these pressures in the social environment actually contributed to intrinsic motivation and thus creativity (Amabile, 1993). One question that remains however, is how intrinsic motivation itself operates: what are the elements of the intrinsic task motivation that keeps people excited and engaged in the creative work they do? We propose that people get energizing jolts of intrinsic motivation during moments of inspiration. And, thus, inspiration is a key element of intrinsic task motivation. In this chapter, we integrate the concept of inspiration into Amabile's (1996) model of the creative process. In doing so, we draw on Amabile's writing and research, as well as the broader literature on inspiration. In addition, Amabile's leadership, teaching and mentoring provide a model for how to inspire and thus fuel intrinsic motivation for creative work.

What Is Inspiration?

Inspiration is the spark that ignites intrinsic task motivation, the fuel of creativity (Amabile, 1983, 1996). Inspiration emerges from exciting new ideas and powers a person toward the finish line of the creative process. Intrinsic motivation to begin a creative task emerges from an individual's enduring interests and personality characteristics, and is maintained by a supportive social environment. Then, when the right conditions are present, something influences the individual in such a way as to create a burst of intrinsic energy—a sense of urgency to produce a creative product (Thrash & Elliot, 2003). These are moments of inspiration.

Inspiration has been most thoroughly studied by Thrash and colleagues (Oleynick, Thrash, LeFew, Moldovan, & Kieffaber, 2014; Thrash & Elliot 2003; Thrash, Maruskin, Moldovan, Oleynic, & Belzak, 2017) as a motivational state that compels a person to bring a novel idea to fruition. Thus, in the terms of Amabile's (1996) process model, inspiration is part of intrinsic task motivation—the part prompted by exhilarating experiences and the part that gives the individual a sense of urgency to bring an interesting idea that emerged in the response generation stage to the response validation and communication stage. In Fig. 2.1, we depict inspiration as a starburst within the intrinsic task motivation component. We add three bold arrows to the process model to show that (1) stimulating elements of the environment prompt response generation, (2) response generation produces inspiration, and (3) inspiration fuels the final stage of the creative process.

Defining inspiration in this way gives a sense of inspiration as coming from a growth promoting environment, and leads to vigorous work toward a creative product. In their articulation of the intrinsic motivation principle of creativity, Hennessey and Amabile (2010) define

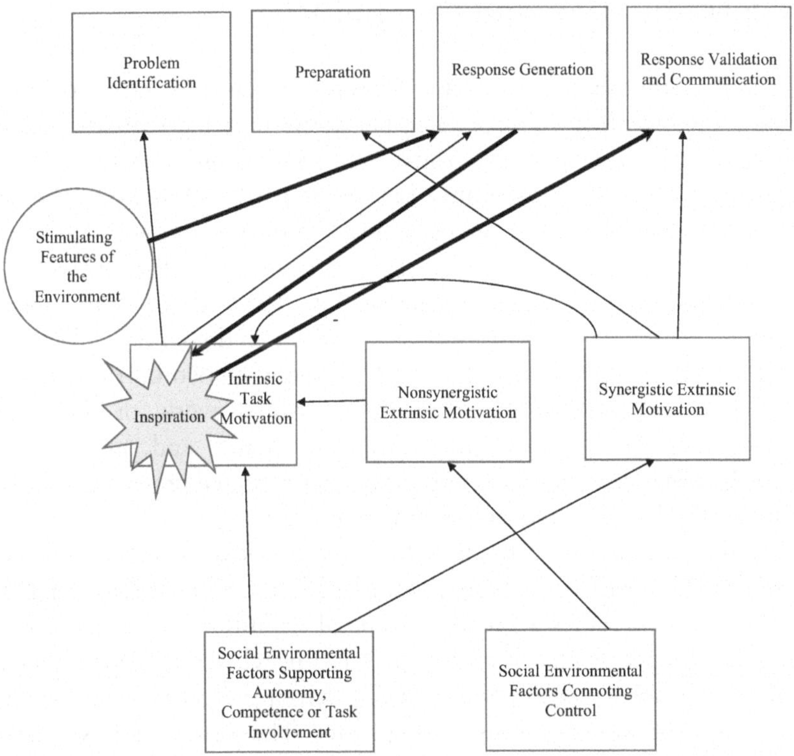

Fig. 2.1 The role of inspiration in Amabile's (1983, 1996) model of the creative process

intrinsic motivation as the drive to do something for the sheer enjoyment, interest, and personal challenge of it, suggesting that intrinsically motivated individuals are having energizing experiences that fuel their creative work. It is those experiences that produce the element of intrinsic task motivation that we call inspiration. One such experience can create a state of intrinsic motivation that inspires a single creative act, while repeated experiences of inspiration in a domain will contribute to the trait intrinsic motivation that is characteristic of highly creative people.

Can We Distinguish Inspiration from Intrinsic Task Motivation and Creativity?

As Edison famously pointed out, "What it boils down to is one per cent inspiration and ninety-nine per cent perspiration," suggesting that inspiration is just a tiny part of creative task motivation (Rosanoff, 1932, September). Intrinsic task motivation, while partly a function of inspiration, emerges also from an individual's enduring interests, attitudes toward the task, perceptions of one's own motivations for undertaking the task, and unique characteristics (Amabile, 1983, 1996). While inspiration is central to intrinsic task motivation, it does not replace the steadfast effort that is necessary for high-quality work, the personality characteristics that bring people to creative work, or the social environment that supports autonomy, competence, and task involvement. It works alongside these important motivational processes to bring short-lived jolts of energy to the creative process.

Another important distinction to make is between inspiration and creativity. The two concepts may seem largely interchangeable. Amabile (1983, 1996) provides a broad conceptual definition of creativity that names a product or idea as creative if it is a novel, yet appropriate solution to a problem, while operationally defining creativity by looking for agreement among experts' judgments. The distinction we make between these related concepts is that creativity is an element of the solution to a problem, while inspiration characterizes the intrinsically motivated experience that is produced by creative idea generation and fuels the validation and communication of that idea. Thrash, Maruskin,

Cassidy, Fryer, and Ryan (2010b) provide evidence for this distinction by documenting a temporal discrepancy between inspiration and creativity, where the formation of creative ideas both precede and predict the experience of inspiration. This process is documented in their partial transmission model which describes inspiration emerging from creative idea generation, along with effort, awe and positive affect, and leading to a highly creative product (Oleynic et al., 2014).

Having explained how inspiration is related to intrinsic task motivation and creativity, we can begin our exploration of the role that inspiration plays in the creative process by examining those experiences that produce inspiration. Then, we can describe the role that inspiration plays in transforming a potentially creative idea into a creative outcome.

What Types of Experiences Are Inspiring?

A review of the literature suggests three features of an experience produce inspiration: (1) the generation of a creative idea; (2) exposure to greatness, originality, beauty or other admirable characteristics either in a person or a stimulus object; (3) an environment that supports or promotes creative idea generation by giving the potential creator the confidence and tools to realize their potential (Thrash et al., 2010b). Each of these three features can play a role in producing inspiration, but the first (creative idea generation) is a more proximal cause of inspiration, while the second and third are more distal causes. The second is a set of environmental variables that contribute to creative idea generation, while the third refers to the social environmental factors that support intrinsic task motivation more generally.

The notion that inspiration emerges from the generation of a creative idea is common among stories of illumination or insight in which an "aha moment" brings both a potential breakthrough idea and enormous excitement. Thrash and Elliot (2004) point out that the idea that produces inspiration can come from within an individual as she or he mulls over possible solutions to a problem or from a stimulus in the environment that presents a possibility to the individual. Thrash et al. (2010b) showed a direct connection between the creativity of the ideas that research participants experienced and the level of inspiration they reported. Further support comes from a study by Conti, Amabile, and Pollack (1995) which showed that creative idea generation boosted the intrinsic task motivation of college students learning new material. From this work we can see that environments that encourage creative thinking produce inspiration. But what is it about the environment that prompts creative ideas?

One set of answers to this question recognizes that the creative idea may come, in part, from a stimulus in the environment. A painter watches a beautiful bird take flight and is inspired to paint it. A poet is moved by the empathy of a small child and is inspired to write about it. Often the stimulus itself does not directly appear in the creative product, but a characteristic of that stimulus produces a desire to reproduce it. For example, Amabile (1996) describes being inspired by the letters and diaries of creative geniuses in fields far from her own such as Einstein and Dostoevsky. She also tells stories of being inspired by her first psychology professors, Harvey Pines, and Dewey Bayer, and later by her graduate advisors Mark Lepper and Lee Ross. That inspiration may have come from admiring the qualities of these accomplished teachers and researchers (Amabile, 2016, 2019). Indeed, exposure to extraordinary competence led to experiences of inspiration in research by Thrash, Elliot, Maruskin, and Cassidy (2010a). This notion that stimuli in the environment, including people, creative products, and awe-producing sights and sounds produce inspiring ideas is the core of the transmission model of inspiration (Thrash & Elliot 2004). Thus, environments that promote inspiration are those that provide opportunities to experience greatness, novelty, and beauty.

The physical environment often includes sights that have these inspiring qualities. Csikszentmihalyi (1996) suggests this idea, discussing how Chinese sages choose to write their poetry on island pavilions or gazebos. Several researchers have examined this in greater depth, looking at the physical environment itself and its impact on the production of creative ideas. McCoy and Evans (2002), for example, asked sixty participants from an undergraduate psychology class to rate pictures of environments for their creative potential. They found that environments with a greater complexity, more furniture, more visual detail, natural surfaces, exposed wood or stone, cool colors, glass, and a natural view were more conducive to creativity. Not only were these environments rated as being more creative, but participants placed within matching variations of the chosen environments also performed higher on the Torrance Test of Creative Thinking. Such ideas begin to introduce how the environment can help drive the processes of creativity.

To expand upon this further, I (Brynn April), worked with Regina Conti to conduct a year-long honor's thesis project. In considering these ideas, we designed an experiment to test the effects of nature and novelty in the environment on inspiration and creativity in the writing process. To do so, my sixty-seven research participants were randomly assigned to one of four conditions. They were placed into one of two rooms set up as either a nature environment with plants, or office-like environment with folders and papers. Before the session began, either a large orange traffic cone, which would be unusual to find in an academic building, or an ordinary office garbage can was also placed in the room to manipulate environmental novelty. For the task, participants were asked to write a story using a Thematic Apperception Test picture. After completion of the task, they were given a questionnaire. The creativity of the stories was assessed by five writing experts using Amabile's (1982) Consensual Assessment Technique. When looking at the effects of nature and novelty on creativity and inspiration, I found a marginally significant positive effect of the traffic cone on creativity, such that those students who wrote in a room with a novel object produced more creative stories. This effect begins to reveal how a novel environment has the potential to positively influence the creative process.

In sum, environments that expose people to interesting and impressive people, sights, and sounds are environments in which inspiration is likely to happen. Thus, to facilitate the creative process, we need to provide stimulating experiences that foster novel idea generation. Once a fresh new idea inspires the person, she is motivated to do the hard work of creating a final product.

What Does Inspiration Produce?

Inspiration produces highly creative work. At this point, that much is clear. One arm of inspiration emerges from the environment to facilitate the production of creative ideas, while the other reaches from the creative idea toward its implementation. Inspiration, thus, provides some of the energy for the labor-intensive stage of response validation and communication. We might term the work of this stage innovation. Amabile (2016) defines creativity as the generation of new and useful ideas (response generation), while she defines innovation as the implementation of creative ideas. Given this way of thinking, creative idea generation produces inspiration, and inspiration produces innovation or an actual creative product. But inspiration may go even further than this. The experience of inspiration may be valuable in itself.

Indeed, people talk of inspiring experiences as enlivening and growth promoting, as transformative and clarifying. Thrash and Elliot (2004) discuss consequences of inspiration that go beyond creativity to include work mastery, absorption, perceived competence, self-esteem, optimism, and self-determination. Thrash et al. (2010a) showed in 4 studies that inspiration causes increases in well-being, even when personality and prior levels of well-being are controlled. Such findings seem to further distinguish these processes and indicate how they work together in creating and producing not only a creative product but a highly rewarding experience. They also found that other desirable elements of performance, including efficiency and total output, were positively related to inspiration and creativity. Thus, inspiration produces more than creativity. Inspiration makes people happier and better at what they do.

What Makes Teresa M. Amabile so Inspiring?

What a fortunate coincidence that we are studying sources of inspiration this year, as our experiences with Teresa and her work serve as perfect examples. Teresa has inspired many students through her distinguished teaching career at Brandeis University and the Harvard Business School.

She has inspired people around the world with her many live presentations, including a TEDx talk, TV appearances, radio, television, and news media interviews, and of course with her many noteworthy articles, chapters, and books. We both have experienced the thrill of reading one of Teresa's articles, or watching one of her talks and leaving with an exciting idea for a new study. Teresa and her impressive body of work embodies those characteristics that others want to reproduce in themselves and in their own work.

At the same time, Teresa is a master at creating environments that nurture people to realize their own creative potential. I (Regina) had the good fortune of having Teresa as a graduate advisor and fondly recall the warm supportive culture of Teresa's research group at Brandeis University. Teresa was full of curiosity about the work we were doing and her energy was contagious, leaving all of us feeling that we were part of something exciting. She not only loved the work, but the people who made it happen. I remember all of the ways that she made me feel as though my ideas were valuable and worth pursuing, and all of the hours she invested in helping me to build the skills I would need for an academic career. As I supervise Brynn's honors thesis, I hope to create a similarly supportive environment for her and all of my students at Colgate University. We are both grateful for the energy we have gained from Teresa's outstanding contributions as a teacher and as a scholar and hope that the inspiration she has given us will carry us through the research on inspiration we are pursuing this year and on to a future where we will play some small part in carrying out her impressive legacy.

References

Amabile, T. M. (1979). Effects of external evaluation on artistic creativity. *Journal of Personality and Social Psychology, 37,* 221–233.

Amabile, T. M. (1982). Social psychology of creativity: A consensual assessment technique. *Journal of Personality and Social Psychology, 43*(5), 997–1013.

Amabile, T. M. (1983). *The social psychology of creativity.* New York: Springer-Verlag.

Amabile, T. M. (1993). Motivational synergy: Toward new conceptualizations of intrinsic and extrinsic motivation in the workplace. *Human Resources Management Review, 3*(3), 185–201.

Amabile, T. M. (1996). *Creativity in context: Update to the social psychology of creativity.* with updates by T. Amabile, M. A. Collins, R. Conti, E. Phillips, M. Picariello, J. Ruscio & D. Whitney. Westview Press.

Amabile, T. M. (2016). The motivation for creativity. In R. Sternberg, S. Fiske, & D. Foss (Eds.), *Scientists making a difference: One hundred eminent behavioral and brain scientists talk about their most important contributions* (pp. 275–278). Cambridge University Press.

Amabile, T. M. (2019). Educating leaders who make a difference in the world. *Perspectives on Psychological Science, 14*(1), 7–11.

Amabile, T. M., Conti, R. & Collins, M. A. (1996). Frank Barron's influence on current and future generations of creativity researchers: Some personal reflections. In A. Montuori (Ed.), *Create to be free: Essays in honor of Frank Barron* (pp. 93–101). Cresskill, NJ: Hampton Press, Inc.

Amabile, T. M., DeJong, W., & Lepper, M. (1976). Effects of externally imposed deadlines on subsequent intrinsic motivation. *Journal of Personality and Social Psychology, 34,* 92–98.

Amabile, T. M., Goldberg, N., & Capotosto, D. (1982). Effects of reward and choice on adults artistic creativity. Unpublished manuscript, Brandeis University.

Amabile, T. M., Goldfarb, P., & Brackfield, S. C. (1990). Social influences on creativity: Evaluation, coaction and surveillance. *Creativity Research Journal, 3,* 6–21.

Conti, R., Amabile, T. M. & Pollack, S. (1995). The positive impact of creative activity: Effects of creative task engagement and motivational focus on college students' learning. *Personality and Social Psychology Bulletin, 21*(10), 1107–1116.

Csikszentmihalyi, M. (1996). *Creativity: Flow and the psychology of discovery and invention.* New York: Harper-Collins.

Edison, T. (1932, September). Genius is one per cent inspiration, ninety-nine per cent perspiration. *Harper's Monthly Magazine.*

Hennessey, B. A., & Amabile, T. M. (2010). Creativity. *Annual Review of Psychology, 61,* 569–598.

McCoy, J. M., & Evans, G. W. (2002). The potential role of the physical environment in fostering creativity. *Creativity Research Journal, 14*(3–4), 409–426.

Oleynick, V. C., Thrash, T. M., LeFew, M. C., Moldovan, M. C. & Kieffaber, P. D. (2014). The scientific study of inspiration in the creative process: Challenges and opportunities. *Frontiers in Human Neuroscience, 8.*

Thrash, T. M., & Elliot, A. J. (2003). Inspiration as a psychological construct. *Journal of Personality and Social Psychology, 84*(4), 871–889.

Thrash, T. M., & Elliot, A. J. (2004). Inspiration: Core characteristics, component processes, antecedents, and function. *Journal of Personality and Social Psychology, 87*(6), 957–973.

Thrash, T. M., Elliot, A. J., Maruskin, L. A., & Cassidy, S. E. (2010a). Inspiration and the promotion of well-being: Tests of causality and mediation. *Journal of Personality and Social Psychology, 98*(3), 488–506.

Thrash, T. M., Maruskin, L. A., Cassidy, S. E., Fryer, J. W., & Ryan, R. M. (2010b). Mediating between the muse and the masses: Inspiration and the actualization of creative ideas. *Journal of Personality Social Psychology, 98*(3), 469–487.

Thrash, T. M., Maruskin, L. A., Moldovan, E. G., Oleynic, V. C., & Belzak, W. C. (2017). Writer-reader contagion of inspiration and related states: Conditional process analyses within a cross-classified writer x reader framework. *Journal of Personality and Social Psychology, 113*(3), 466–491.

3

The Social Psychology of Creativity Skills: A Reconceptualization of the Componential Model

Johnathan Cromwell

"This has the potential to be groundbreaking."
— T. Amabile, June 2015

Presenting your dissertation work to anyone and getting a response like this can be flattering, rewarding, and above all motivating as you plow through the fields of intellectual terrain in search of a valuable idea. But when it comes from a world-renowned scholar whom you hope to recruit as an advisor, it can be downright humbling. Such were the conditions for one of my first meetings with Teresa. I was a doctoral student who had just begun collecting field data for my dissertation, and I was seeking feedback on several ideas that I thought were interesting. To be clear, I should emphasize the word "potential" in the quote above, as the ideas I presented that day have evolved as much as the pigeons of Paris or

J. Cromwell (✉)
School of Management, University of San Francisco, San Francisco, CA, USA
e-mail: jcromwell@usfca.edu

R. Reiter-Palmon et al. (eds.), *Creativity at Work*,
Palgrave Studies in Creativity and Innovation in Organizations,
https://doi.org/10.1007/978-3-030-61311-2_3

lizards of L.A. (for an interesting story on urban evolution, see Koerner, 2019), and they will evolve even more as they go through the trials of the publication process. But regardless of the quality of ideas, Teresa's words had a tremendous impact on me: they helped me transition from a period of aimlessly wandering through ambiguous knowledge frontiers to one of focusing on a clear and important problem with purpose and conviction. In other words, she helped cultivate my intrinsic motivation—or my labor of love—for conducting quality research, completing a dissertation, and joining a community of scholars.

It is poetically fitting that Teresa had such an impact on me. After all, she had been conducting research on how the social environment affects intrinsic motivation for nearly 40 years, representing one of her most important contribution to the study of creativity and innovation. When she began her career in the 1970s, there had already been decades of research dedicated to understanding creativity (Guilford, 1950; Koestler, 1964; Newell, Shaw, & Simon, 1962; Rothenberg & Greenberg, 1976; Wallas, 1926), which examined a broad range of factors such innate abilities, personality traits, and cognitive styles (for more thorough reviews, see Shalley & Zhou, 2008; Shalley, Zhou, & Oldham, 2004). Although this research was highly diverse and covered multiple psychological domains, it all stemmed from the same theoretical paradigm, which assumed creativity was driven primarily by individual characteristics rather than environmental conditions. With this research landscape as a background, Teresa proposed a new conceptualization of creativity that placed the social and environmental factors surrounding individuals at the forefront of analysis, thereby introducing a new theory for the *social* psychology of creativity (Amabile, 1983).

This theory, known as the componential model of creativity, identifies three essential components that are all necessary and sufficient for producing highly creative outcomes: domain-relevant skills, creativity skills, and task motivation. The first two components account for individual characteristics, and the third component—task motivation—is where social and environmental forces surrounding individuals can exert their primary influence on creativity. Building on the work of her advisors and other intellectual predecessors (Bem, 1972; deCharms, 1968; Deci & Ryan, 1985; Lepper, Greene, & Nisbett, 1973), Teresa argued that different types of task motivation can have different effects on creative performance. People can be intrinsically motivated by internal factors such as a deep personal interest in an activity, which has a positive effect; or they can be extrinsically motivated by external factors such as reward, deadlines, or the desire to impress others, which has a negative effect. Much of her early research supported this argument, showing that people working in the intrinsically motivated state become more deeply engaged in an activity and are more likely to explore divergent cognitive pathways, take risks, and search for more novel and useful ideas (Amabile, 1979, 1985; Amabile & Gitomer, 1984; Amabile, Goldfarb, & Brackfleld, 1990; Amabile, Hennessey, & Grossman, 1986). These findings eventually culminated into the *intrinsic motivation principle of creativity* (Amabile, 1996).

Teresa's initial insight and early research had a huge impact on the field. At the time of writing this chapter, the publications advancing her theory (Amabile, 1983, 1988, 1996; Amabile & Pratt, 2016) had amassed nearly 30,000 citations on Google Scholar, and her core argument that the social environment influences creativity primarily through intrinsic motivation had become fully embedded in various theories of creativity and innovation in the literature (Csikszentmihalyi, 1996; Glynn, 1996; Oldham & Cummings, 1996; Staw, 1990; Sternberg & Lubart, 1991; West, 2002; Woodman, Sawyer, & Griffin, 1993). That is not to say she didn't have any detractors along the way, as many have argued that extrinsic motivation can also have a positive effect on creativity (Cameron & Pierce, 1994; Eisenberger & Aselage, 2009; Eisenberger & Cameron, 1996). Her response has been that some extrinsic motivators can indeed improve creativity, but only when they reinforce and support intrinsic motivation (Amabile, 1993). Unsurprisingly, much empirical evidence supports this argument too, showing that external factors such as (a) providing clear goals for creativity, (b) offering feedback that is supportive and encouraging, and (c) giving indirect rewards for performance can all positively influence creative outcomes (Byron & Khazanchi, 2012; Carson & Carson, 1993; Cerasoli, Nicklin, & Ford, 2014; Deci, Koestner, & Ryan, 1999; Hunter, Bedell, & Mumford, 2007; Shalley, 1991; Shalley & Perry-Smith, 2001).

Therefore, when viewing my 2015 meeting with Teresa through the lens of the theoretical paradigm she established, we can clearly understand why her comment had such a positive effect on my motivation: (a) it helped me focus on a clear and important problem that demanded highly creative effort, (b) it provided me with a firm foundation of support as I navigated through the complexities of constructing new knowledge, and (c) it gave me an opportunity to earn her respect and approval that would (hopefully) result in a glowing letter of recommendation (which it did, eventually—I think). Therefore, her comment was not only a perfect example of how to apply her theory, but if I can actually fulfill the potential she saw, it may also be a forecast for the future success of my work (Berg, 2016). So now, my career will be an individual case study putting her theory to the test, and the question becomes, will the theory hold? With Teresa doing everything in her power to create a positive social environment for my research, it's safe to say that my level of success (or failure) will depend primarily upon my domain-relevant knowledge and creativity skills as a scholar.

By now, you might be wondering: what was the actual substance of our conversation that compelled her to give such an arresting comment? In that meeting, I was describing observations from my field site that were puzzling in the context of her research. Several product designers were telling me how they were actively seeking external constraint from others, which seemed to be fundamental to their creative success. As one designer explained, "Once they nail down the rules of design for the product, I can create infinite variety within those rules." Much of Teresa's work argues that external constraint can harm creativity because it reduces autonomy and inhibits intrinsic motivation. But these designers were claiming the opposite, that they actually *needed* those constraints to *enhance* their creativity. This insight planted a seed in my mind that has grown into a burgeoning research program investigating the relationship between creativity and constraint (Cromwell, 2018; Cromwell, Amabile, & Harvey, 2018).

I'm certainly not the first scholar to tread this trail of discovery (see Acar, Tarakci, & van Knippenberg, 2019 for a thorough review of this literature), but I think a new and interesting opportunity arises when viewing this literature through the lens of the componential model. In short, rather than focusing on how the social environment primarily affects the component of task motivation, scholars may be able to make significant contributions by examining how the environment also affects the component of creativity skills, thus developing a theory for the social psychology of creativity *skills*. Doing so may blaze a new trail of discovery that integrates and builds upon prior work.

The Social Psychology of Creativity Skills

In the original formulation of the componential model, Teresa defined creativity skills as consisting of "cognitive style, application of heuristics for the exploration of new cognitive pathways, and working style" (Amabile, 1983, pp. 362–363), which differed from domain-relevant skills such as "factual knowledge, technical skills, and special talents in the domain in question" (p. 362). Therefore, the component of creativity skills refers primarily to the cognitive processes people use to generate more novel and useful ideas. Although most scholars have focused on how the environment affects the component of task motivation (Liu, Jiang, Shalley, Keem, & Zhou, 2016; Steele, McIntosh, & Higgs, 2017), a parallel stream of research with origins in cognitive psychology (Finke, 1990; Finke, Ward, & Smith, 1992; Ward, 1994) suggests the social environment may have an equally strong effect on creativity skills. But interestingly, they find that external constraint may have a positive effect on this component to enhance creativity, contrasting with prior research showing the opposite effect on intrinsic motivation (cf. Amabile, Conti, Coon, Lazenby, & Herron, 1996; Deci & Ryan, 1985; Hunter et al., 2007; Oldham & Cummings, 1996; Shalley et al., 2004; Woodman et al., 1993).

To illustrate these effects, let me compare two experiments that had very similar designs but dramatically different results, leading the experimenters to draw different conclusions on the psychological processes that facilitate creativity. The first experiment was conducted by Amabile and Gitomer (1984), who recruited children to create collages by using materials that were presented in ten closed boxes. To manipulate external constraint, subjects were divided into a "choice" condition, in which they had full autonomy to choose any five boxes to make a collage, and a "no-choice" condition, in which this autonomy was revoked, and the five boxes were chosen for them by the experimenter. Afterward, the other five boxes were removed and subjects were given ten minutes to complete their work. Results showed that subjects in the choice condition produced more creative collages than those in the no-choice condition, despite spending an equal amount of time on the task. These results support the intrinsic motivation principle of creativity, showing that external constraint can indeed harm creativity by undermining autonomy and reducing intrinsic motivation (Amabile, 1983, 1996).

The second experiment was conducted by Finke (1990), which was part of a series of experiments designed to understand the cognitive processes underlying creative thought. In this experiment, students were recruited to use a subset of three out of 15 materials (e.g., hook, sphere, spring, etc.) to create new inventions in one of eight product categories (e.g., furniture, toys, appliances, etc.). In this experiment, external constraint was manipulated by dividing subjects into three conditions: In the first, subjects were allowed to choose their own subset of materials, and the experimenter gave them a product category; in the second, subjects were given the materials, but could choose their own category; and in third, the experimenter gave subjects both the materials and the category. Subjects then had two minutes to visualize an invention and draw it, and their ideas were rated for creativity by an independent panel of judges. Results showed that subjects in the third, most externally constrained condition produced the most creative ideas.

When comparing these results with those of the first experiment, the findings can, at first blush, seem paradoxical. Amabile and Gitomer found that external constraint reduced creativity, while Finke found that it enhanced creativity. However, these findings can potentially be reconciled by more closely examining the differences between the two experiments. One important difference is that in the first experiment, all boxes of materials were similar to each other, such that any one set of five boxes had a nearly identical set of materials to any other five boxes. This eliminated the possibility that cognitive factors related to specific materials could influence the creative process.[1] For example, if some subjects were more skilled in origami and could choose boxes with more paper, they could possibly produce more creative outcomes (Amabile, 1983). By contrast, subjects in the second experiment were allowed to choose specific materials for the task, thereby enabling such cognitive factors to influence their creative thought.

This is consequential because theories of cognition argue that cues inherent in a task—such as materials used or product category—can trigger particular ideas in the minds of individuals who are engaged in the task, which are constructed from prior experience (Walsh, 1995). In the context of the second experiment above, subjects were more likely to choose materials they were more familiar with, making it easier for them to generate ideas that were similar to cognitive templates that already existed based on prior experience. Consequently, their ideas were less creative. Ward (1994) describes this process as "following the path of least resistance" and argues it is more likely to occur when people have more autonomy on a task rather than less. Many studies find similar results (e.g., Goldenberg, Mazursky, & Solomon, 1999; Hoegl, Gibbert, & Mazursky, 2008; Moreau & Dahl, 2005; Stokes, 2001; van Burg, Podoynitsyna, Beck, & Lommelen, 2012), which together support the *creative cognition theory of creativity* (Finke et al., 1992). According to this theory, constraints place limitations on the categories, features, functions, components, or resources used during the creative process, and they can push people off the path of least resistance. As more constraints are added, tasks become more challenging, and people must search for more distant or unique ideas to satisfy all the constraints. In other words, their creativity skills are enhanced.

[1]This logic is explicitly stated in the endnotes of Amabile and Gitomer (1984).

Reconceptualizing the Componential Model: A Career in the Making

Together, the two experiments above represent different theoretical paradigms that propose contradicting arguments for how the social environment can affect creativity skills. The social-psychology theory of creativity argues that external constraint should inhibit creativity skills by reducing intrinsic motivation, thereby limiting the exploration of divergent cognitive pathways to search for novel and useful ideas. By contrast, the creative-cognition theory argues that external constraint should enhance creativity skills by pushing people off the path of least resistance. Identifying this theoretical puzzle represents the latest species of idea to evolve from my 2015 meeting with Teresa, and I suspect that solving it will be the focal point of my career for many years to come. One potential path forward is to reconceptualize the componential model so that it encompasses both theoretical perspectives and can explain both sets of findings.

One of the core insights of the componential model was that there are three distinct components that are all necessary and sufficient to produce highly creative outcomes (Amabile, 1983, 1988). Since then, Teresa and others have investigated how the broader social environment affects the efficacy of these components in producing creativity (Amabile, 1993, 1996; Amabile et al., 1996; Shalley & Zhou, 2008; Shalley et al., 2004; Steele et al., 2017). In other words, the three components have served as a central hub for the theory, and knowledge has been built outward. This has led to a steady progression of insights for nearly 40 years, culminating in a comprehensive revision of the model that includes new psychological factors such as progress, meaningful work, and affect (Amabile & Pratt, 2016). However, scholars may also be able to build valuable knowledge by starting with the three components and looking inward; that is, exploring how they influence each other in complex and counter-intuitive ways throughout the creativity and innovation process. For example, as suggested by the experiments above, there may be times when intrinsic motivation and creativity skills mutually reinforce each other to promote high levels of creativity, and other times when they mutually counteract each other to limit creativity. Better understanding these relationships and how they change in the context of a dynamic social environment may lead to 40 more years of new and insightful research.

As Teresa's intellectual journey enters a new phase, there is little doubt about the impact she's had on the fields of creativity, innovation, organizational behavior, and social psychology more broadly. Thanks to her research, we can definitively say that intrinsic motivation is at least one essential component to the mysterious and enigmatic process of creativity. However, perhaps the more profound impact she's had comes from her influence on fellow colleagues, researchers, and scholars. Through her discerning eye for quality research, comprehensive reviews of works in progress, and generous time dedicated to developing and growing others, she's cultivated a strong environment for the creation of new and valuable knowledge—not just for creativity, but for many other fields as well, as her former students can surely attest. Therefore, the most fitting tribute to Teresa is that her career has not only been the perfect embodiment of her theory at work, but by actively practicing it, she has ignited countless new careers that aspire to reach the heights of her own. If any one of those careers actually succeeds, and their research truly does become groundbreaking, then her influence will become even more profound and her impact more far-reaching.

Now, with all that said, there is much to be done. Time to get back to work!

References

Acar, O. A., Tarakci, M., & van Knippenberg, D. (2019). Creativity and innovation under constraints: A cross-disciplinary integrative review. *Journal of Management, 45*(1), 96–121.

Amabile, T. M. (1979). Effects of external evaluation on artistic creativity. *Journal of Personality and Social Psychology, 37*(2), 221–233.

Amabile, T. M. (1983). The social psychology of creativity: A componential conceptualization. *Journal of Personality and Social Psychology, 45*(2), 357–376.

Amabile, T. M. (1985). Motivation and creativity: Effects of motivational orientation on creative writers. *Journal of Personality and Social Psychology, 48*(2), 393–399.
Amabile, T. M. (1988). A model of creativity and innovation in organizations. In B. M. Staw & L. L. Cummings (Eds.), *Research in organizational behavior* (Vol. 10, pp. 123–167). Greenwich, CT: JAI Press.
Amabile, T. M. (1993). Motivational synergy: Toward new conceptualizations of intrinsic and extrinsic motivation in the workplace. *Human Resource Management Review, 3*(3), 185–201.
Amabile, T. M. (1996). *Creativity in context: Update to the social psychology of creativity*. Boulder, CO: Harper Collins.
Amabile, T. M., Conti, R., Coon, H., Lazenby, J., & Herron, M. (1996). Assessing the work environment for creativity. *Academy of Management Journal, 39*(5), 1154–1184. https://doi.org/10.2307/256995.
Amabile, T. M., & Gitomer, J. (1984). Children's artistic creativity effects of choice in task materials. *Personality and Social Psychology Bulletin, 10*(2), 209–215.
Amabile, T. M., Goldfarb, P., & Brackfleld, S. C. (1990). Social influences on creativity: Evaluation, coaction, and surveillance. *Creativity Research Journal, 3*(1), 6–21.
Amabile, T. M., Hennessey, B. A., & Grossman, B. S. (1986). Social influences on creativity: The effects of contracted-for reward. *Journal of Personality and Social Psychology, 50*(1), 14.
Amabile, T. M., & Pratt, M. G. (2016). The dynamic componential model of creativity and innovation in organizations: Making progress, making meaning. In B. M. Staw & A. P. Brief (Eds.), *Research in Organizational Behavior, 36*, 157–183.
Bem, D. (1972). Self-perception theory. In L. Berkowtiz (Ed.), *Advances in experimental social psychology* (Vol. 6). New York: Academic Press.
Berg, J. M. (2016). Balancing on the creative high-wire: Forecasting the success of novel ideas in organizations. *Administrative Science Quarterly, 61*(3), 433–468.
Byron, K., & Khazanchi, S. (2012). Rewards and creative performance: A meta-analytic test of theoretically derived hypotheses. *Psychological Bulletin, 138*(4), 809–830.
Cameron, J., & Pierce, W. D. (1994). Reinforcement, reward, and intrinsic motivation: A meta-analysis. *Review of Educational Research, 64*(3), 363–423.

Carson, P. P., & Carson, K. D. (1993). Managing creativity enhancement through goal-setting and feedback. *Journal of Creative Behavior, 27*(1), 36–45.

Cerasoli, C. P., Nicklin, J. M., & Ford, M. T. (2014). Intrinsic motivation and extrinsic incentives jointly predict performance: A 40-year meta-analysis. *Psychological Bulletin, 140*(4), 980–1008. https://doi.org/10.1037/a0035661.

Cromwell, J. R. (2018). Further unpacking creativity with a problem-space theory of creativity and constraint. In G. Atinc (Ed.), *Proceedings of the seventy-eight annual meeting of the academy of management*. Online ISSN: 2151–6561.

Cromwell, J. R., Amabile, T. M., & Harvey, J.-F. (2018). An integrated model of dynamic problem solving within organizational constraints. In R. Reiter-Palmon, V. Kennel, & J. C. Kaufman (Eds.), *Individual creativity in the workplace* (pp. 53–81). New York: Academic Press.

Csikszentmihalyi, M. (1996). *Creativity*. New York: HarperCollins.

deCharms, R. (1968). *Personal causation*. New York: Academic Press.

Deci, E. L., Koestner, R., & Ryan, R. M. (1999). A meta-analytic review of experiments examining the effects of extrinsic rewards on intrinsic motivation. *Psychological Bulletin, 125*(6), 627–668.

Deci, E. L., & Ryan, R. M. (1985). The general causality orientations scale: Self-determination in personality. *Journal of Research in Personality, 19*(2), 109–134.

Eisenberger, R., & Aselage, J. (2009). Incremental effects of reward on experienced performance pressure: Positive outcomes for intrinsic interest and creativity. *Journal of Organizational Behavior, 30*(1), 95–117. https://doi.org/10.1002/job.543.

Eisenberger, R., & Cameron, J. (1996). Detrimental effects of reward: Reality or myth? *American Psychologist, 51*(11), 1153.

Finke, R. A. (1990). *Creative imagery: Discoveries and inventions in visualization.* Hoboken, NJ: Erlbaum.

Finke, R. A., Ward, T. B., & Smith, S. M. (1992). *Creative cognition: Theory, research, and applications*. Cambridge, MA: MIT Press.

Glynn, M. A. (1996). Innovative genius: A framework for relating individual and organizational intelligences to innovation. *Academy of Management Review, 21*(4), 1081–1111. https://doi.org/10.2307/259165.

Goldenberg, J., Mazursky, D., & Solomon, S. (1999). Toward identifying the inventive templates of new products: A channeled ideation approach. *Journal of Marketing Research, 36*(2), 200–210.

Guilford, J. P. (1950). Creativity. *American Psychologist, 5*(9), 444–454.
Hoegl, M., Gibbert, M., & Mazursky, D. (2008). Financial constraints in innovation projects: When is less more? *Research Policy, 37*(8), 1382–1391. https://doi.org/10.1016/j.respol.2008.04.018.
Hunter, S. T., Bedell, K. E., & Mumford, M. D. (2007). Climate for creativity: A quantitative review. *Creativity Research Journal, 19*(1), 69–90.
Koerner, B. I. (2019). Street life. *Wired, 27*(10), 72–85.
Koestler, A. (1964). *The act of creation.* New York: Dell.
Lepper, M. R., Greene, D., & Nisbett, R. E. (1973). Undermining children's intrinsic interest with extrinsic reward: A test of the "overjustification" hypothesis. *Journal of Personality and Social Psychology, 28*(1), 129–137.
Liu, D., Jiang, K., Shalley, C. E., Keem, S., & Zhou, J. (2016). Motivational mechanisms of employee creativity: A meta-analytic examination and theoretical extension of the creativity literature. *Organizational Behavior and Human Decision Processes, 137*, 236–263. https://doi.org/10.1016/j.obhdp.2016.08.001.
Moreau, C. P., & Dahl, D. W. (2005). Designing the solution: The impact of constraints on consumers' creativity. *Journal of Consumer Research, 32*(1), 13–22.
Newell, A., Shaw, J. C., & Simon, H. A. (1962). The processes of creative thinking. In H. Gruber, G. Terrell, & M. Wertheimer (Eds.), *Contemporary approaches to creative thinking* (pp. 63–119). New York: Atherton Press.
Oldham, G. R., & Cummings, A. (1996). Employee creativity: Personal and contextual factors at work. *Academy of Management Journal, 39*(3), 607–634.
Rothenberg, A., & Greenberg, B. (1976). *The index of scientific writings on creativity: General, 1566–1974*. Hamden, CT: Archon Books.
Shalley, C. E. (1991). Effects of productivity goals, creativity goals, and personal discretion on individual creativity. *Journal of Applied Psychology, 76*(2), 179–185.
Shalley, C. E., & Perry-Smith, J. E. (2001). Effects of social-psychological factors on creative performance: The role of informational and controlling expected evaluation and modeling experience. *Organizational Behavior and Human Decision Processes, 84*(1), 1–22. https://doi.org/10.1006/obhd.2000.2918.
Shalley, C. E., & Zhou, J. (2008). Organizational creativity research: A historical overview. In J. Zhou & C. E. Shalley (Eds.), *Handbook of organizational creativity* (pp. 3–31). Abingdon, UK: Taylor & Francis.

Shalley, C. E., Zhou, J., & Oldham, G. R. (2004). The effects of personal and contextual characteristics on creativity: Where should we go from here? *Journal of Management, 30*(6), 933–958. https://doi.org/10.1016/j.jm.2004.06.007.

Staw, B. M. (1990). An evolutionary approach to creativity and innovation. In M. A. West & J. L. Farr (Eds.), *Innovation and creativity at work* (pp. 287–308). New York: Wiley.

Steele, L. M., McIntosh, T., & Higgs, C. (2017). Intrinsic motivation and creativity: Opening up a black box. In M. D. Mumford & S. Hemlin (Eds.), *Handbook of research on creativity and leadership* (pp. 100–130). Cheltanham, UK and Northampton, MA: Edward Elgar.

Sternberg, R. J., & Lubart, T. I. (1991). An investment theory of creativity and its development. *Human Development, 34*(1), 1–31.

Stokes, P. D. (2001). Variability, constraints, and creativity: Shedding light on Claude Monet. *American Psychologist, 56*(4), 355–359. http://dx.doi.org/10.1037/0003-066X.56.4.355.

van Burg, E., Podoynitsyna, K., Beck, L., & Lommelen, T. (2012). Directive deficiencies: How resource constraints direct opportunity identification in SMEs. *Journal of Product Innovation Management, 29*(6), 1000–1011. https://doi.org/10.1111/j.1540-5885.2012.00976.x.

Wallas, G. (1926). *The art of thought*. New York: Harcourt Brace.

Walsh, J. P. (1995). Managerial and organizational cognition: Notes from a trip down memory lane. *Organization Science, 6*(3), 280–321.

Ward, T. B. (1994). Structured imagination: The role of category structure in exemplar generation. *Cognitive Psychology, 27*(1), 1–40.

West, M. A. (2002). Sparkling fountains or stagnant ponds: An integrative model of creativity and innovation implementation in work groups. *Applied Psychology, 51*(3), 355–387.

Woodman, R. W., Sawyer, J. E., & Griffin, R. W. (1993). Toward a theory of organizational creativity. *Academy of Management Review, 18*(2), 293–321.

4

A Winding Road: Teresa Amabile and Creative Process Research

Colin M. Fisher, Poornika Ananth, and Ozumcan Demir Caliskan

As noted throughout this volume, Teresa Amabile's work is best known for her model of and method for studying creative outcomes—the extent to which a product or service is novel and useful. In this chapter, we focus on a less recognized, but equally important aspect of her work: her models of the creative process. Creative process describes *how* creative work is produced over time, rather than the characteristics of outcomes or creators (Drazin, Glynn, & Kazanjian, 1999; Mainemelis, 2010). If creativity had a "recipe," personal characteristics, resources, and other contextual antecedents would be the ingredients, while the process model is the description of the sequence and manner of combining ingredients over time. Below, we discuss the history of Amabile's process models of creativity (e.g., Amabile, 1983, 1996; Amabile & Pratt, 2016; Fisher & Amabile, 2009), how they have informed subsequent research on creative

C. M. Fisher (✉) · P. Ananth · O. D. Caliskan
UCL School of Management, London, UK
e-mail: colin.fisher@ucl.ac.uk

R. Reiter-Palmon et al. (eds.), *Creativity at Work*,
Palgrave Studies in Creativity and Innovation in Organizations,
https://doi.org/10.1007/978-3-030-61311-2_4

processes (especially in organizations), and new directions for creative process research, as well as the first author's reflections on the process of creating with Teresa Amabile.

A Brief History of Amabile's Process Models of Creativity

Amabile's texts *The Social Psychology of Creativity* (1983) and the updated version *Creativity in Context* (1996) were some of the first to propose models of the creative process grounded in the social psychology of creativity. The models were further updated in a recent publication (Amabile & Pratt, 2016). Table 4.1 details the key contributions and the changes made in each of these models.

These process models advanced creativity research in three ways. The first is by introducing the different activities or steps in the creative process; the second is by emphasizing social nature of creativity; the third is by conceptualizing dynamism within the creative process. We describe each of these contributions below.

Stages of Activity in the Creative Process

One of the main contributions of Amabile's creative process models is the identification of different stages of activity in the creative process. In all iterations, the process model contains five stages: (1) Task identification (2) Preparation; (3) Response Generation; (4) Response Validation and Communication; (5) Outcomes. Two basic arguments underlie this model. First, each stage is necessary for ideas to move from conception to completion. In other words, creativity does not happen all at once in a sudden flash of insight, but emerges through a predictable combination of activities over time. Second, each of these activities is catalyzed by specific combinations of motivation, domain-relevant skills, and creative thinking skills. For instance, motivation is particularly important in task identification (Stage 1), in that people who enjoy doing a kind of work will be more likely to identify novel tasks and problems to work

Table 4.1 Major contributions of and changes to Amabile's models of the creative process

	The Social psychology of creativity: A componential conceptualization (Amabile, 1983)	Creativity in context: Update to "The social psychology of creativity" (Amabile, 1996)	The dynamic componential model of creativity and innovation in organizations: Making progress, making meaning (Amabile & Pratt, 2016)
Stages of activity in the creative process	Introducing a new phase: "Task presentation"	Changing the name of Stage 1 from "Task Presentation" to "Problem or Task Identification"	Recognizing the role of meaningful work
	Introducing a new phase: "Outcome"	Changing the definition of intrinsic and extrinsic motivation. Including synergistic and non-synergic extrinsic motivators which significantly revises the original intrinsic motivation principle	
	Introducing the components of creative production: "Domain-Relevant Skills—Creativity-Relevant Skills—Task Motivation"		

(continued)

Table 4.1 (continued)

	The Social psychology of creativity: A componential conceptualization (Amabile, 1983)	Creativity in context: Update to "The social psychology of creativity" (Amabile, 1996)	The dynamic componential model of creativity and innovation in organizations: Making progress, making meaning (Amabile & Pratt, 2016)
The social nature of the creative process	Theorizing how social factors contribute to different stages of the creative process	Including "Social environment" in the figure	Depicting work environment is an open system susceptible to broader socio-cultural forces
		Changing the label "Creativity Relevant Skills" to "Creativity Relevant Processes"	Acknowledging that team creativity is not a simple aggregation of the creativity of individuals
		Changing the label "Response Validation" to "Response Validation & Communication"	
Dynamism within the creative process	Introducing the feedback cycle: The process outcome can influence task motivation	Noting that it is not strictly sequential process	Introducing the progress principle, i.e., process does not terminate in the face of success of failure
			Discussing the relationship between innovation and creativity

on. In contrast, domain-relevant skills are more important in efficient preparation for the task (Stage 2), such that using and developing expertise equips creators with the raw materials for the subsequent stages. These basic insights paved the way for research that focused on the unique dynamics of specific phases of the creative process beyond idea generation, such as idea elaboration (e.g., Berg, 2014; Perry-Smith & Mannucci, 2017), evaluation and validation (e.g., Berg, 2016, 2019; Lowenstein & Mueller, 2016; Mueller, Melwani, & Goncalo, 2012), and implementation (e.g. Baer, 2012; Lu, Bartol, Venkatramani, Zheng, & Liu, 2019).

The Social Nature of the Creative Process

Building an understanding of the social side of creativity is a second important contribution of Amabile's research on creative processes. Beyond prior research on the personal characteristics of creative individuals, Amabile (1983) broke new ground by theorizing how social factors contribute to different stages of the creative process. Specifically, the creative process becomes increasingly social as the creator moves from task identification toward implementation, extending the process from the individual's mind to a point where the idea is shared with others. This implies that social interaction and support are crucial for the success of a creative process. However, social support may be required at the earlier stages to promote divergence and shift perspectives. The dual propositions in the social model of the creative process laid the foundation for subsequent research on the specific ways in which social interaction influences the creative process at different times (e.g., Hargadon & Bechky, 2006; Harrison & Rouse, 2015; Perry-Smith & Mannucci, 2017).

Dynamism Within the Creative Process

Although Amabile (1983) depicted the creative process as a linear progression through these phases, she seeded the notion of dynamism in the creative process, arguing that, the creative process is iterative. Depending on the success or failure of individual stages within the process, people might return to earlier stages of the process again. Updates to the model in 1996 and 2016 further advanced the notion of dynamism in the creative process, arguing that success, failure, and progress can have different influences for subsequent engagement in creative processes and can reciprocally influence intrinsic motivation and domain-relevant skills. For example, progress toward developing an outcome increases intrinsic motivation, which in turn increases the possibility of re-engaging with the creative process and continuing the search for a novel outcome. Furthermore, the increased intrinsic motivation could also influence domain-relevant skills and creativity relevant processes by encouraging learning and spending more effort on breaking free of habitual mindsets. In other words, the creative process proposed is truly dynamic; the experiences and outcomes of each iteration shape subsequent iterations by influencing different components relevant to creativity. Recent research has further elaborated the specific ways in which creative experiences and interactions involve dynamic and reciprocal influences (e.g., Harrison & Rouse, 2014, 2015; Harvey & Kou, 2013).

New Directions for Creative Process Research

Amabile's work on creative processes is not merely an influence but a dialogue that has paved a path for new research. Amabile and Pratt (2016) exemplify this approach by synthesizing recent research to update and develop a dynamic componential model of creativity and innovation. Keeping in line with this tradition, we identify three areas for future research on creative processes based on recent developments in the field.

Understanding Nonlinear Processes

Amabile and Pratt (2016) introduce feedback loops that explain how psychological factors such as motivation and emotion undergird iterations within the creative process and connect creativity and organizational innovation. However, the authors also state that even though they have "added new dynamic elements to the model, much is unknown about them." (p. 179). We believe that this provocation provides the foundation for more systematic inquiry into the nonlinear dynamics of creation. Research has already started to consider the temporal dynamics of nonlinear processes (e.g., Fisher & Amabile, 2009; Harrison & Rouse, 2014), and the psychological experiences associated with nonlinear creative processes (e.g., Fisher & Barrett, 2019; Harvey, 2014). We see room for further research that explicitly considers when creative processes may be linear versus nonlinear, what nonlinearity might entail (i.e., are stages skipped, combined, repeated), how ideas that are developed through nonlinear processes may differ from ideas that are developed through linear creative processes, and how creators may cope with some of the challenges of nonlinearity.

Investigating Multiple Creative Processes

A crucial contribution of Amabile's research on creativity is the introduction of the final stage of the process model: outcome assessment. It is here that she introduces the idea that a creative process can have three possible outcomes: success, failure, and progress. Whereas success or failure would result in the conclusion of the creative process, the experience of progress can lead creators to return to earlier phases of the idea journey. The most recent update to the model (Amabile & Pratt, 2016) considers the influence of success or failure on future creative work. In this idea we see the sparks for a fruitful new area of enquiry—an investigation of multiple creative processes (Fisher & Amabile, 2009). Whereas research on creativity and creative processes have primarily focused on individual idea journeys, we see potential for the emergence of a new body of research that focuses on (a) the process of developing multiple creative ideas (b) starts, stops, and overlaps between different ideas, and (c) the practices associated with managing several simultaneous creative processes (e.g., Ananth & Harvey, 2019).

Considering New Technologies and New Work Practices

The role of the social environment on individual and team creativity has been prominent even in early versions of Amabile's process models. In the most recent update, Amabile and Pratt (2016) depicted the work environment as "an open system, susceptible to broader socio-cultural forces." Indeed, emergence of new work practices, such as remote work, co-working, and on-demand work, and technologies, such as artificial intelligence, rapid prototyping, and robotics, are changing the landscape of creative work. More and more people have autonomy over what to work on, as well as where, when and with whom to work. Considering these changes, we expect future investigations of whether and how new work environments influence the experiences of creative workers and the creative process; whether individuals and the creative activity itself influence, in turn, work environments (e.g., Demir Caliskan & Fisher, 2020) and how people create, use, and collaborate with new technologies for creative work (Amabile, 2020).

The Process of Creating with Teresa Amabile

[The following was written by the first author about his work with Teresa Amabile as her student and collaborator]

My experience studying the creative process with Teresa Amabile illustrates both her embrace of amending her own work, and the nonlinear and unpredictable path of the creative process itself. I discovered Teresa's research on creativity when reviewing literature for my Master's thesis about improvisation in different art forms. At the time, I knew nothing about social psychology or organizational behavior—I was working as a jazz trumpet player in New York City and considering different options for studying improvisation as part of a Ph.D. Up until finding her work, I had been applying to musicology programs, but was taken with her work on the social psychology of creativity. I applied to the Ph.D. program at Harvard specifically to work with her and, in my application, noted that I thought improvisation was an important creative avenue that didn't quite fit her description of the creative process. To my lasting surprise, she agreed to work with me.

Despite my total lack of experience in OB or psychology, Teresa always treated me as a valued colleague who had an important perspective—not as an acolyte needing to receive her wisdom. We spent many months in my first year of grad school debating what improvisation was and how it related to creativity, culminating in our paper on improvisational creativity (Fisher & Amabile, 2009). In this paper, we argued why improvisation is inherently a creative process, in that it is intended to generate useful novelty. However, in contrast to the traditional "compositional" creative process described above, preparation is the first step in improvisation, preceding task identification. Task identification, response generation, and response execution then emerge simultaneously. These process-based differences impact the kinds of expertise, creativity relevant processes, and work environments that promote improvisational creativity. Importantly, we suggest that the sequence of traditional stages of the creative process affect its antecedents and consequences, such that trying to explain all creativity with a single sequence of stages may be misguided.

From both our work together and the research reviewed above, I am more convinced than ever that creativity researchers need to focus more on studying the creative process. The ways in which creative processes are nonlinear have implications for both the individual skills, contextual antecedents, and kinds of collaborations that are important in creative work (Fisher & Barrett, 2019; Perry-Smith & Mannucci, 2017). For instance, together with our amazing coauthor Julianna Pillemer, we have found the importance of helping in creative work (Fisher, Amabile, & Pillemer, 2020; Amabile, Fisher, & Pillemer, 2014), including how leaders use "deep help" to catalyze creative progress in multiple ways (Fisher, Pillemer, & Amabile, 2018).

During this research, there was always an implicit meta-commentary on the creative process because research IS a creative process—or, at least it is with Teresa. And, Teresa was constantly putting into practice the results of her research and what we were finding. In her work with me, she embodied the "supervisor support" and providing "catalysts" and "nourishers" for work progress that she had discovered in her earlier work (Amabile, Conti, Coon, Lazenby, & Herron, 1996; Amabile & Kramer, 2011). And, she was constantly open to new ways of thinking and working.

What I still find amazing is how willing Teresa was to listen to the ramblings of a novice researcher trying to find his way toward amending a key aspect of her work. Moreover, she patiently tolerated my more freewheeling (re: disorganized, unreliable) creative process that I know clashed with her conscientious and disciplined proclivities. And, over the years, I have realized how much I owe to Teresa's patient nurturing of me and our work together. Working with her has been an amazing journey toward understanding the winding roads of the creative process. I've tried to carry on these same ideas in my work with doctoral students and collaborators as we continue to try to understand the secrets of the creative process (e.g., Hua & Fisher, 2020; Demir Caliskan, & Fisher, 2020; Fisher, Harvey, Ananth, & Xie, 2019; Fisher, Demir Caliskan, Hua, & Cronin, 2020) and continue the journey Teresa started us on.

References

Amabile, T. M. (1983). *The social psychology of creativity*. New York: Springer.

Amabile, T. M. (1996). *Creativity in context*. Boulder, CO: Westview Press.

Amabile, T. (2020). Guidepost: Creativity, artificial intelligence, and a world of surprises guidepost letter for Academy of Management Discoveries. *Academy of Management Discoveries*, forthcoming.

Amabile, T. M., Conti, R., Coon, H., Lazenby, J., & Herron, M. (1996). Assessing the work environment for creativity. *Academy of Management Journal, 39*(5), 1154–1184.

Amabile, T. M., Fisher, C. M., & Pillemer, J. (2014). IDEO's culture of helping. *Harvard Business Review, 92,* 54–61.

Amabile, T., & Kramer, S. (2011). *The progress principle: Using small wins to ignite joy, engagement, and creativity at work*. Cambridge, MA: Harvard Business Press.

Amabile, T. M., & Pratt, M. G. (2016). The dynamic componential model of creativity and innovation in organizations: Making progress, making meaning. *Research in Organizational Behavior, 36,* 157–183.

Ananth, P., & Harvey, S. (2019). *Ideas in the space between selection and rejection: Towards a theory of stockpiling creative ideas*. Paper presented at the meeting of the Academy of Management, Boston, MA.

Baer, M. (2012). Putting creativity to work: The implementation of creative ideas in organizations. *Academy of Management Journal, 55*(5), 1102–1119.

Berg, J. M. (2014). The primal mark: How the beginning shapes the end in the development of creative ideas. *Organizational Behavior and Human Decision Processes, 125*(1), 1–17.

Berg, J. M. (2016). Balancing on the creative highwire: Forecasting the success of novel ideas in organizations. *Administrative Science Quarterly, 61*(3), 433–468.

Berg, J. M. (2019). When silver is gold: Forecasting the potential creativity of initial ideas. *Organizational Behavior and Human Decision Processes, 154*, 96–117.

Demir Caliskan, O. & Fisher, C. M. (2020). Project switches in collective creative spaces: An inductive study of makerspaces. In O. Demir Caliskan & M. Hua (Chairs), *New perspectives on developmental sequences and cycles in creative work.* Symposium presented at the meeting of the Academy of Management, Vancouver, B.C.

Drazin, R., Glynn, M. A., & Kazanjian, R. K. (1999). Multilevel theorizing about creativity in organizations: A sensemaking perspective. *Academy of Management Review, 24*(2), 286–307.

Fisher, C. M., & Amabile, T. M. (2009). Creativity, improvisation and organizations. In T. Rickards, M. A. Runco, & S. Moger (Eds.), *The Routledge companion to creativity* (pp. 13–24). New York: Routledge.

Fisher, C. M., Amabile, T. M., & Pillemer, J. (2020). Rolling up your sleeves: How and when managers should provide hands-on help to employees. *Harvard Business Review,* forthcoming.

Fisher, C. M., & Barrett, F. J. (2019). The experience of improvising in organizations: A creative process perspective. *Academy of Management Perspectives, 33*(2), 148–162.

Fisher, C. M., Demir Caliskan, O., Hua, M. Y., & Cronin, M. A. (2020b). Trying not to try: The paradox of intentionality in jazz improvisation and its implications for organizational scholarship. In R. Bednarek, M. P. Cunha, J. Schad, & W. Smith (Eds.), *Research in the sociology of organizations: Interdisciplinary dialogues and paradox theory* (Vol. 66). Melbourne: Emerald Publishing.

Fisher, C. M., Harvey, S., Ananth, P., & Xie, W. X. (2019). Bridging, balancing, and blending: The role of liminal practices in creative work. In

P. Ananth & W. X. Xie (Chairs), *New perspectives on processes and practices in creative work.* Symposium presented at the meeting of the Academy of Management, Boston, MA.

Fisher, C. M., Pillemer, J., & Amabile, T. M. (2018). Deep help in complex project work: Guiding and path-clearing across difficult terrain. *Academy of Management Journal, 61*(4), 1524–1553.

Hargadon, A. B., & Bechky, B. A. (2006). When collections of creatives become creative collectives: A field study of problem solving at work. *Organization Science, 17*(4), 484–500.

Harrison, S. H., & Rouse, E. D. (2014). Let's dance! Elastic coordination in creative group work: A qualitative study of modern dancers. *Academy of Management Journal, 57*(5), 1256–1283.

Harrison, S. H., & Rouse, E. D. (2015). An inductive study of feedback interactions over the course of creative projects. *Academy of Management Journal, 58*(2), 375–404.

Harvey, S. (2014). Creative synthesis: Exploring the process of extraordinary group creativity. *Academy of Management Review, 39*(3), 324–343.

Harvey, S., & Kou, C. Y. (2013). Collective engagement in creative tasks: The role of evaluation in the creative process in groups. *Administrative Science Quarterly, 58*(3), 346–386.

Hua, M., & Fisher, C. M. (2020). Re-defining problems and developing ideas through elaborative play: An inductive study of circus R&D. In S. Harrison, A. Carlsen & M. Skerlavaj (Chairs), *Broadening our insight: Bridging and blurring boundaries between creativity and innovation.* Symposium presented at the meeting of the Academy of Management, Vancouver, B.C.

Loewenstein, J., & Mueller, J. (2016). Implicit theories of creative ideas: How culture guides creativity assessments. *Academy of Management Discoveries, 2*(4), 320–348.

Lu, S., Bartol, K. M., Venkataramani, V., Zheng, X., & Liu, X. (2019). Pitching novel ideas to the boss: The interactive effects of employees' idea enactment and influence tactics on creativity assessment and implementation. *Academy of Management Journal, 62*(2), 579–606.

Mainemelis, C. (2010). Stealing fire: Creative deviance in the evolution of new ideas. *Academy of Management Review, 35*(4), 558–578.

Mueller, J. S., Melwani, S., & Goncalo, J. A. (2012). The bias against creativity: Why people desire but reject creative ideas. *Psychological Science, 23,* 13–17.

Perry-Smith, J. E., & Mannucci, P. V. (2017). From creativity to innovation: The social network drivers of the four phases of the idea journey. *Academy of Management Review, 42*(1), 53–79.

5

Teresa M. Amabile: Thought Leadership in Organizational Creativity Research

Lucy L. Gilson

Trying to decide which of Teresa Amabile's work has made the greatest impact on my research, let alone the field, is really difficult. Almost everything that is currently being studied or has been studied within the domain of organizational creativity, is in part based upon one of her seminal works. In fact, the most commonly used definition of creativity; the production of ideas, products, or procedures that are novel and potentially useful can be attributed to Teresa Amabile (1996). This definition is pivotal to how we think about creativity in organizations today in that it stresses the role of both novelty and usefulness. Prior to this definition, novelty had been considered as the foundation of creativity and thus, the focal point for most theory and research (e.g., Campbell,

---

To appear in R. Reiter-Palmon (Ed.). *Studies in Creativity and Innovation in Organizations.* London: Palgrave MacMillan

---

L. L. Gilson (✉)
University of Connecticut, Storrs, CT, USA
e-mail: Lucy.gilson@uconn.edu

R. Reiter-Palmon et al. (eds.), *Creativity at Work*,
Palgrave Studies in Creativity and Innovation in Organizations,
https://doi.org/10.1007/978-3-030-61311-2_5

1960; Ford, 1996; Guilford, 1957). By introducing usefulness, Amabile shifted the emphasis of creativity away from simply the new, and asked us to consider creativity in context, suggesting that what is creative varies based on job, field of work, or organization because what is appropriate or useful is domain-specific. This subtle, but important, reframing of creativity opened the door for the consideration of usefulness as value and from an organizational perspective, has served to differentiated creativity from foolishness (Goldenberg, Lehmann, & Mazursky, 2001).

Defining creativity as a combination of both novley and usefulness set the stage for future work to examine degrees of creativity relative to noncreative or routine work, and has spurned an extensive body of work examining the differences between incremental (minor adaptations that focus on more useful rather than novel ideas) and more radical (major breakthroughs where the focus is on highly novel rather than more useful creative ideas (e.g., Gilson & Madjar, 2011; Mumford & Gustafson, 1988). Work that I conducted with my colleague Rob Litchfield (Litchfield, Gilson, & Gilson, 2015) unpacked what variation in the types of creative ideas might look like. In this work, we start from the premise that creativity exists along a continuum, but propose unpacking variation in the mix of novelty and disentangling usefulness into its two most common conceptions; feasibility and value. One of our arguments here is that usefulness, while important is too all-encompassing of a construct. For example, an idea might score highly on usefulness because it is doable (feasible), but just because you can do it might not mean it is the right idea to pursue because it might not add value. In unpacking novelty and usefulness, a more nuance understanding of creative ideas emerges. Given that ideas are the starting point in the creative process, and that idea collections (Litchfield & Gilson, 2013) can facilitate subsequent idea selection and development, acknowledging that the mix of novelty along with the feasibility and value embodied in the creative idea can vary, allows us to better understand the relationships between idea generation, selection, and subsequently bridge the divide between creativity and innovation.

Another example of how Teresa Amabile's work has set the stage for research in the field of creativity can be traced back to the Componential Model (Amabile, 1983). This groundbreaking work cited over

10,000 times, takes a social-psychological approach proposing that in order for an individual to engage in the creative process they must first poses domain-relevant skills which include, but are not limited to expertise, technical skills, scripts, and factual knowledge about a particular paradigm. The crux here is that individuals need to know something about a domain before they can begin to be creative. However, while domain-relevant skills are often considered as a necessary baseline, without the addition of creativity-relevant skills, they are not sufficient. Creativity-relevant skills refer to an individual's ability to link disparate information, understand complexities, keep options open, suspend judgment, and break out of performance scrips (Amabile, 1996). Lastly, while the first two skills are crucial, what activates them is motivation. Thus, the final, component of the componential model is task motivation. Task motivation encompasses an individual's interest in a task, their desire to engage with it, and ability to persist through challenges. Most frequently operationalized as intrinsic motivation, this component of her framework has been the most controversial, see meta-analysis by Byron and Khazanchi (2012) and discussion in the review of the creativity literature by Shalley, Zhou and Oldham (2004).

A fascination with the role of rewards, and the distinction between radical and incremental creativity led Nora Madjar and I (2011) to design a study to test these relationships using a sample of students engaged in organizational consulting projects. In this study, we found that intrinsic motivation was related to radically creative ideas, whereas extrinsic motivation was a driver of incremental creativity. Our results allowed us to conclude that radical and incremental creativity were distinct constructs and that the motivation to engage in each differed. Specifically, incremental creativity was more strongly associated with necessity and rewards, whereas radical creativity was driven by enjoying the challenge and a drive toward originality.

In addition to research on its individual components, the componential model also has set the stage for the interactionist perspective of creativity (Woodman, Sawyer, & Griffin, 1993). Here, Amibile's 1988 work examining factors in the work environment that can enhance or constrain creativity paved the way for a plethora of work that has sought to understand how individual and contextual factors can best work together to affect engagement in creative processes and creative outcomes. Motivated by the importance of these interactions in organizational settings, my first publication with Christina Shalley and Terry Blum (2000) examined how employee satisfaction and intentions to leave were affected by the degree to which there was complementarity between job required creativity and characteristics of the work environment. Finally, coming full circle, Amabile and Pratt (2016) revisited the componential model to understand how it had held up over the 28 years since it was first introduced, and to revise it based on what had been found in the literature during that period. While the overall framework held up well, they introduced the notion of individual psychological processes and discussed the work environment influences on those process. Of note to me, is the focus on meaningful work and more specifically the notion that creativity is more intrinsically motivating if it is at the heart of something that is worth doing. To expound on this point, Amabile and Pratt delineate between types of work orientation and as an example of craftsmanship they point to the importance of individuals wanting to grow and valuing personal development—growth needs strength, a construct introduced into the creativity literature by Shalley, Gilson, and Blum (2009).

Lastly, one of the lesser acknowledged elements of Amabile's 1988 work was her careful positioning of the relationship between creativity and innovation. Her simple statement that "creativity is the most crucial element of organizational innovation, but it is not, by itself, sufficient" (page 125) clearly tells the reader that creativity and innovation are not one and the same, and thus they can be studied together without the admonition that the work is tautological. This sentence has inspired and guided a great deal of my work on team creativity, standardization, and effectiveness (Gilson, Mathieu, Shalley, & Ruddy, 2005). More specifically, the role of creativity and performance was for many years an enigma even though the opening sentence of most journal articles and book chapters lauded the importance of creativity for some positive outcome. At the team level, using a sample of customer service technicians, we proposed and found that teams who engaged in creative processes had higher levels of objective performance. However, given that teams are often called upon to adhere to strict quality control metrics, we juxtaposed standardized practices with engagement in creative processes finding that standardization weakened the positive effects of creativity on performance, but for customer satisfaction, results were highest when both creativity and standardization were high.

In summary, it is hard to pick the most influential Amabile contribution and I'm guessing every researcher doing work in the creativity domain today will have his or her own favorite. To some degree this is because we can all find something novel and useful in her work. While there is still much work to be done in understating what drives creativity, the interplay between novelty and usefulness, how individual and contextual factors interact to drive creativity, and how creativity drives innovation and performance—we can be assured that our field has a strong foundation upon which to grow. In effect, we have the domain-relevant skills, many of us have the task motivation, what we now have to continue to work on is developing our creativity-relevant skills to ensure we keep our options open, remember accurately, and use wide categories and diverse pieces of information to grow our field of inquiry.

References

Amabile, T. M. (1983). The social psychology of creativity: A componential conceptualization. *Journal of Personality and Social Psychology, 45*(2), 357–376.

Amabile, T. M. (1988). A model of creativity and innovation in organizations. In B. M. Staw & L.L. Cummings (Eds.), *Research in organizational behavior*. JAI Press, Greenwich, CT.

Amabile, T. M. (1996). *Creativity in context*. Boulder, CO: Westview.

Amabile, T. M., & Pratt, M. G. (2016). The dynamic componential model of creativity and innovation in organizations: Making progress, making meaning. *Research in Organizational Behavior, 36*, 157–183.

Byron, K., & Khazanchi, S. (2012). Rewards and creative performance: A meta-analytic test of a theoretically derived hypotheses. *Psychological Bulletin, 138*(2012), 809–830.

Campbell, D. T. (1960). Blind variation and selective retention in creative thought as in other knowledge processes. *Psychological Review, 67,* 380–400.
Ford, C. M. (1996). A theory of individual creative action in multiple social domains. *Academy of Management Review, 21,* 1112–1142. https://doi.org/10.5465/AMR.1996.9704071865.
Gilson, L. L., & Madjar, N. (2011). Radical and incremental creativity: Antecedents and processes. *The Psychology of Aesthetics, Creativity, and the Arts, 5,* 21–28.
Gilson, L. L., Mathieu, J. E., Shalley, C. E., & Ruddy, T. M. (2005). Creativity and standardization: Complementary or conflicting drivers of team effectiveness. *Academy of Management Journal, 48,* 521–531.
Goldenberg, J., Lehmann, D. R., & Mazursky, D. (2001). The idea itself and the circumstances of its emergence as predictors of new product success. *Management Science,* 47, 69–84.
Guilford, J. P. (1957). Creative abilities in the arts. *Psychological Review, 64,* 110–118.
Litchfield, R. C., & Gilson, L. L. (2013). Curating collections of ideas: Museum as metaphor in the management of creativity. *Industrial Marketing Management, 42,* 106–112.
Litchfield, R., Gilson, L. L., & Gilson, P. W. (2015). Creative contributions: Toward a more nuanced approach. *Group and Organization Management, 40*(2), 238–265.
Mumford, M. D., & Gustafson, S. B. (1988). Creativity syndrome: Integration, application, and innovation. *Psychological Bulletin, 103,* 27–43. https://doi.org/10.1037/0033-2909.103.1.27.
Shalley, C. E., Gilson, L. L., & Blum, T. C. (2000). Matching creativity requirements and the work environment: Effects on satisfaction and intentions to leave. *Academy of Management Journal, 43,* 215–223.
Shalley, C. E., Gilson, L. L., & Blum, T. C. (2009). Interactive effects of growth need strength, work context, and job complexity on self-reported creative performance. *Academy of Management Journal, 52,* 489–505.
Shalley, C. E., Zhou, J., & Oldham, G. R. (2004). The effects of personal and contextual characteristics on creativity: Where should we go from here? *Journal of Management*, 30, 933–958.
Woodman, R. W., Sawyer, J. E., & Griffin, R. W. (1993). Toward a theory of organizational creativity. *Academy of Management Review, 18,* 293–321.

6

Memes, Meaning, and Creativity: A "Found" Interpretation of 5 Decades of Teresa Amabile's Research

Spencer Harrison

Memes are central to creativity. Memes are juxtapositions of ideas that seemingly exist as independent building blocks. A collection of cultural LEGOS: A refrain from a popular song, sampled and repeated, so that Queen's "Under Pressure" somehow echoes in Vanilla Ice's "Ice Ice Baby" or DaVinci's "Last Supper" recreated in endless permutations until it appears as the cover for a season of Battlestar Galactica with Christ replaced by Tricia Helfer in a red dress. While creativity is the generation of something novel and useful, novelty and usefulness are relative. It is rare that anything is truly new. This might be why the Greeks were reverential in their use of the verb "create." Creation was the work of gods. Humans simply made do with the raw materials left to them. Perhaps they could harness color in art, sound in music, word in poetry, or natural forces with science, but humans were more Tantalus than Zeus.

S. Harrison (✉)
INSEAD, Fontainebleau, France
e-mail: spencer.harrison@insead.edu

R. Reiter-Palmon et al. (eds.), *Creativity at Work*,
Palgrave Studies in Creativity and Innovation in Organizations,
https://doi.org/10.1007/978-3-030-61311-2_6

Playing with His elements. Approximating discovery and creation. Never fully tasting the water of invention. Which begs the question: when we are creative, are we actually creative?

If this is a useful question, it seemingly dims the light bulb of creativity. Indeed, take the above paragraph as evidence. I make references to toys (LEGOs), music (Queen, Vanilla Ice), art (DaVinci), television (Battlestar Gallactica), and literature (Greek mythology). Each reference on its own is mundane. It is the co-location of the references within a paragraph that creates novelty. What happens if the references are removed?

Memes are central to creativity. Memes are juxtapositions of ideas that seemingly exist as independent building blocks: a collection of a culture's ideas~~Legos. A refrain from a popular song, sampled and repeated, so that Queen's "We Will Rock You" somehow echoes in Vanilla Ice's "Ice Ice Baby." DaVinci's "Last Supper" recreated in endless permutations until it appears as the cover for a season of Battlestar Galactica with Christ replaced by Tricia Helfer in a red dress.~~ While creativity is the generation of something novel and useful, novelty and usefulness are relative. It is rare that anything is truly new. ~~This might be why the Greeks were reverential in their use of the verb "create." Creation was the work of gods. Humans simply made do with the raw materials left to them. Perhaps they could harness color in art, sound in music, word in poetry, or natural forces with science, but humans were more Tantalus than Zeus. Playing with His elements. Approximating discovery and creation. Never fully tasting the water of invention.~~ Which begs the question: when we are creative, are we actually creative?

Perhaps this edited paragraph scores more highly on the usefulness side of creativity. It also might be true that by removing the memes, the paragraph is less creative overall. Or it could be, by blacking out what has been removed, I have preserved the effort that it took to change the first idea and thereby preserving the new paragraph as a conversation with the old paragraph. For example, the insight I am trying to achieve above is perhaps better described in a paper from Milner (lightly edited):

> [M]emes' – discursive artifacts spread by cultural participants who remix them along the way – balance the familiar and the foreign. They're at once

> universal and particular. Memes intertwine what Tannen ([1989]2007) calls 'fixity' and 'novelty'. In this way, memes are a multimodal dialogue between individual creator and popular imagination. They're a form of populist 'vernacular creativity' (Burgess, 2007) that depends on a balance between the new and the expected. (2013: 1–2)

Or consider this description by Csikszentmihalyi:

> It is useful to think about creativity as involving a change in memes – the units of imitation that Dawkins (1976) suggested were the building blocks of culture. Memes are similar to genes in that they carry instructions for action. The notes of a song tell us what to sing; the recipe for a cake tells us what ingredients to mis and how long to bake it. But whereas genetic instructions are transmitted in chemical codes that we inherit on our chromosomes, the instructions contained in memes are transmitted through learning. By and large we learn memes and reproduce them without change; when a new song or a new recipe is invented, then we have creativity. (1999: 316)

The dividing line between redundancy and recombination can be thin. But for as much as there are arguments for the need for "space" for creativity—time (cite), social distance (cite), resources (cite), even physical space (cite), perhaps especially green space (cite)—creativity seems to thrive in these thin spaces between the old and new. The ability to carve new meaning from old. Creators cannot disassociate from those that created before. Indeed creative work—effortful attempts at generating novel and useful ideas, whether successful or not—is inherently a conversation with history, context, and identity. More succinctly, creative work is a conversation with constraints, not the removal of them.

Taking this notion seriously, creativity researchers, could do more to understand how the new idea emerged from the old and what it means for the group interpreting it.

Science and Creativity

Let me try that again, but, as I did before, I will edit a prior paragraph to create new meaning:

Science seems to thrive in these thin spaces between the old and new. The ability to carve new meaning from old. Scientists cannot disassociate from those that created before. Indeed scientific work—effortful attempts at generating novel and useful ideas, whether successful or not—is inherently a conversation with history, context, and identity. More succinctly, scientific work is a conversation with constraints, not the removal of them.

I have highlighted the links between memes and creativity and the links between science and creativity to heighten the meaning of both. Doing so suggests the need for more tools for understanding creative work and for seeing science as a special case of creative work. It also suggests that future scientific work exists in conversation with past work, and scientists in conversation with each other.

Teresa Amabile's work is precious in this regard. Over five decades and counting, she has amassed an amazing collection of LEGOs. For example, consider 5 of Amabile's papers, one selected from each decade of here career. Although a small sample, this approach provides an overview of how her work evolved in conversation with other work over time.

The first paper establishes the importance of motivation, a long running theme in Amabile's work that helped re-orient the literature to deeply understand the relationship between intrinsic and extrinsic motivation. Amabile's focus on intrinsic motivation helped shift researchers away from a focus on biography, individual differences, and, deviance or mental disorder as the primary independent variables predicting creativity. In perhaps more lay terms, Amabile recaptured the childlike joy of creativity.

The second paper further pushed the field toward a true social psychology of creativity by theorizing a fully contextualized process model of creativity. Once again, this paper fundamentally altered the way we thought of creativity in at least two ways. First, by highlighting that creativity was not simply a result of expertise, or just the right amount of motivation. Instead, she convincingly showed that creativity required an eclectic mixture of "components." But she didn't stop there. She situated these components within the context of an organization *and* suggested how they played out over the course of a process *AND* described how this fits into a multilevel process that connected creativity to innovation (while at the same time weaving in the results of a cool qualitative study). This paper is the theoretical version of Christopher Nolan's Inception, a dream built within a dream to house another dream. Very few papers tackle this much tricky theoretical terrain so rigorously.

The third paper extended these themes by empirically showing the importance of context in creative work, using data from over 20 organizations gathered over an 8-year time frame. This paper was "big data" before the term had been coined. Notably, the paper pushed researchers to further disconnect creativity from myths of genius creators to understand a more common, perhaps even more powerful form of creativity: creativity emerging from organizations able to cultivate well-tended gardens of freedom, resources, and encouragement.

The fourth paper focuses on the relationship between creativity and emotion and uses a mixed method, daily data approach to reveal that emotion and creativity share a cyclical self-constituting cycle. A sort of mini, daily ecosystem, like a coral reef building itself each day. And like a coral reef, this paper is rich with color—intricate data, rich quotes, and daily descriptions.

The final paper is a "retrospective," a return to paper number two, described above. This time the model, already complex, is further enriched. Enriched is probably the wrong word. Festooned. Festooned with feedback loops and recursive patterns and overlaid with the notion that creativity is also endowed with meaning and emerges from meaning.

As a gestalt the papers are a like composing a photo album of a life, but taking only one photograph per decade. This is, admittedly, a thin slice. Even so, it reveals both a deep sense of focus on the world of creativity and a diverse way of exploring and filling out this world to make open to others to investigate. There are a variety of ways of trying to understand her impact on science and many of these offer the sort of dialogue I've suggested: a conversation with history (how are her ideas being used over time?), context (where and in what disciplines are her ideas having the most impact?), and identity (who has she impacted and what does her impact mean to them?). The genre of the scientific review is well designed to handle the first two. Indeed, the brief descriptions above hint at the former two. But scientific reviews, as a genre, might struggle more with the third: how can we discuss how one person's identity has impacted our own?

As I have throughout this essay, I will repeat myself with edits. That is, I would like to rereview the five papers by Amabile summarized above, but in a different, even more distilled way. I will simply provide a page from each article. And then, what happens, if we remove letters, words, and sentences, and focus on meaning in a different way. What is the beauty underneath the science, the novelty woven into the usefulness?

I found a poem, written across 5 decades.

----

no desire to exit

Perhaps
The use of
contradictory results
might show
traditions within
creativity

Teresa
said, "I'm always looking for the
elegant
exits from the maze
not
the well-worn pathway."
and
Since
There is no desire to exit,

Her work
is fashioned
by the design
of
wide elements
uncovered
within units of fact

intertwined with
strong
chemicals
:
enjoyment
speed
excitement
,
collected over long periods of time

This is progress
"getting warmer"
finding
we believe
we believe
we believe

A poem that arches into a question mark.

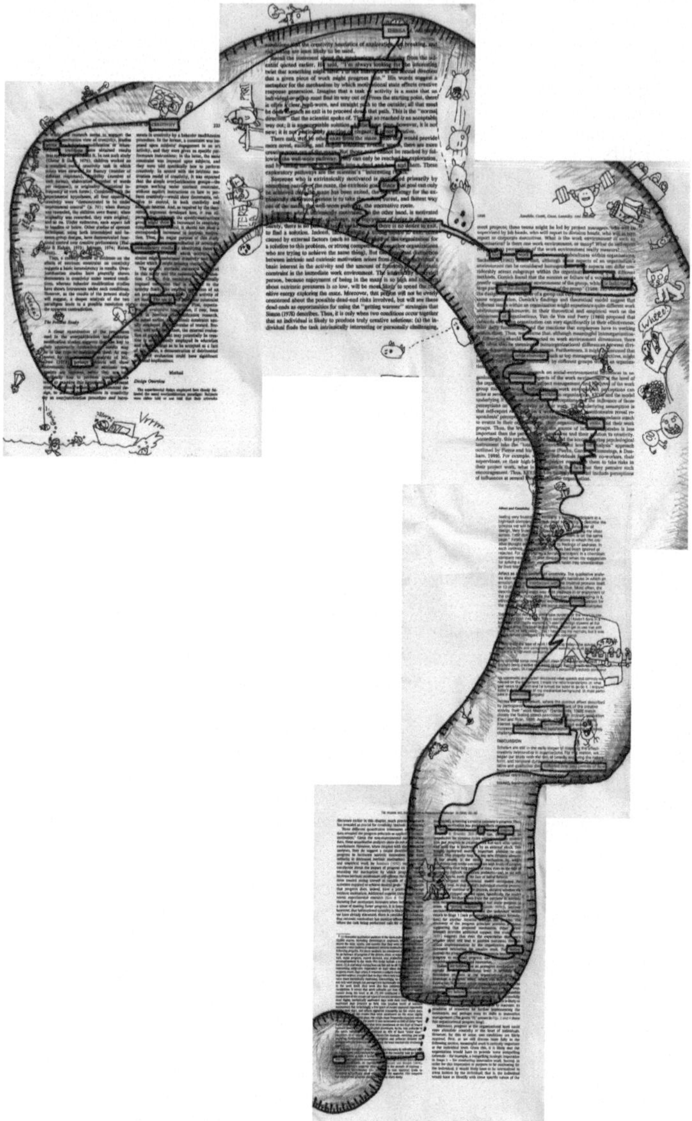

It is a different summary of her work.

Repeating myself again: creativity researchers, could do more to understand how the new idea emerged from the old and what it *means* for the group interpreting it. I find it prescient that Amabile emphasized the importance of meaning in her later work. That, in itself is a gift. I hope all who are interested in creativity, continue to find new meanings in her work as we interpret it. In some cases that will require focusing on details. In others it will require deleting what was there to create space for other ideas. It may require connections across decades. In the end, "perhaps the use of contradictory results might show traditions within creativity." I believe. I believe. I believe.

References

Csikszentmihalyi, M. 1999. Implications of a System Perspective for the Study of Creativity. In *Handbook of Creativity*, ed. R. Sternberg, 313–328. New York: Cambridge University Press.

Milner, R.M. 2013. Media Lingua Franca: Fixity, Novelty, and Vernacular Creativity in Internet Memes. Selected Papers of Internet Research, 3.

7

So Much More Than a Graduate School Mentor!

Beth A. Hennessey

I have known Teresa for a LONG time. Long before she became a hot shot researcher or made her way to Harvard Business School. The Teresa Amabile I first met in 1981 was a young assistant professor and mother with hair down to her waist. I was a 26-year-old with three years' experience teaching kindergarten, first, and second graders. I'd made the difficult decision to leave teaching to pursue graduate school because I was driven by the question of how to set up classrooms so that they would be more conducive to children's intrinsic motivation and creativity. My experience as an educator had prompted me to make an intuitive connection between motivational orientation and creativity—exactly the same connection Teresa was investigating as a researcher.

B. A. Hennessey (✉)
Wellesley College, Wellesley, MA, USA
e-mail: bhenness@wellesley.edu

R. Reiter-Palmon et al. (eds.), *Creativity at Work*,
Palgrave Studies in Creativity and Innovation in Organizations,
https://doi.org/10.1007/978-3-030-61311-2_7

I began my PhD program at Brandeis knowing next to nothing about academe. In fact, I'd never even taken a course in Psychology or read an empirical journal article! Starting from scratch, Teresa slowly acquainted me with notions such as random assignment to condition, repeated measures and mixed experimental designs, and inter-rater reliability. She watched patiently as I slowly wrapped my head around the statistical analysis and the intricacies of SPSS. She taught me to think like a scientist and she taught me to WRITE! Never once did Teresa question my ability, and our research collaborations began almost immediately. Right from the start, I realized that I'd hit the jackpot. Not only had I been paired with a whip-smart mentor who generously spent hours of her time helping me to get my bearings, but I'd also found a true and dedicated friend. Across four decades, we have supported one another through more than our share of both professional and personal triumphs and trials. Recently, I was diagnosed with a life-threatening illness, and outside of my immediate family, Teresa has been my rock. It is not at all hyperbole to say that I don't know what I'd do without her!

My first empirical paper was co-authored with Teresa and another student, research assistant, Barbara Grossman, and was published in 1986 (Amabile, Hennessey, & Grossman, 1986), while I was still a student. We submitted that paper describing three separate studies of the effects of contracted-for reward on creativity to the *Journal of Personality and Social Psychology* and were soon notified that it was accepted for publication without any required edits or modifications. I remember well Teresa explaining that I'd most likely never again receive such an acceptance letter. Sadly, she was all too right!

The primary finding reported in this paper was that, for children and adults alike, contracting to do an activity in order to receive a reward will have negative effects on creativity, but receiving no reward or only a noncontracted-for reward will have no such negative effects. This proposition laid the foundation for the intellectual journey that both Teresa and I were to take, sometimes working together and sometimes separately, for decades to come. It is one thing to demonstrate the deleterious effects of expected reward but quite another to uncover the mechanisms underlying those effects.

The Intrinsic Motivation Principle of Creativity

While I was still in graduate school, Teresa formulated her Intrinsic Motivation Principle of Creativity. This proposition that intrinsic motivation is conducive to creativity whereas extrinsic motivation is usually detrimental (Amabile, 1983, 1996) was to become the bedrock of our own research as well as the work of many others focused on the social psychology of creativity. Yet, over time, the work of some behaviorally trained psychologists (e.g., Eisenberger, Pierce, and Cameron) appeared to demonstrate that an extrinsic motivational orientation prompted by the promise of a reward can, under very specific conditions, have either no impact or even a positive impact on task interest and qualitative aspects of performance.

Intellectual debate is important and oftentimes incredibly stimulating for the researchers and theorists involved. Without debate, our scientific understanding would remain stagnant. But for Teresa and myself, this was far more than just a cerebral argument. Our firm belief in the link between intrinsic motivation and creativity, grounded in the results of hundreds of empirical studies carried out by ourselves and others, lies at the core of who we are. Since my days as a fledgling elementary school teacher, I have viewed this connection between intrinsic motivation and creativity as fundamental; and, despite my better efforts to remain impartial and unemotional, critiques of our work have sometimes felt like a punch in the gut. In 1997, I dodged a bullet when a working trip to China made it impossible for me to join Teresa in a symposium centered on this controversy. But the next year, I remember all too well juggling the care of a toddler with our hurried attempt to compose a written rebuttal to a lead paper that had unexpectedly appeared in *American Psychologist.* No one from our "camp" had been asked to review this submission, and it took some real effort before Teresa and I and a few of our colleagues could make our voices heard via written rebuttal.

Over time, Teresa and I have come to understand that, among other problems, the experimental paradigms utilized in the contradictory behaviorist literature frequently fail to incorporate truly intrinsically motivated tasks. Differences in the definitions of creativity driving investigations, the algorithmic or heuristic nature of the experimental tasks employed, and the instructions given to study participants have also contributed to contradictory experimental findings (see Hennessey & Amabile, 2010). Importantly, it has also been shown that under some circumstances, certain forms of reward may "crowd in" (Frey, 1997) and enhance intrinsic motivation through a process of motivational synergy (Amabile, 1996, 1997a; Hennessey & Zbikowski, 1993). This process is most likely to occur when intrinsic task motivation is both strong and salient, and when the rewards delivered confirm competence and the value of an individual's work, or enable an individual to become more deeply engaged in work that was already intrinsically interesting. While these and other related research insights have served to temper the original virtually exclusive emphasis on intrinsic motivation and its facilitation of creativity, the fact remains that for the majority of persons in the majority of circumstances, intrinsic motivation and creativity are bound to suffer in the face of an expected reward and other extrinsic constraints (see Amabile, 1998; Hennessey, 2003; Hennessey & Amabile, 1998).

The Creative Intersection

The Intrinsic Motivation Principle of Creativity focuses on the individual's motivational orientation and its impact on creative performance. But intrinsic motivation is not the only essential ingredient for creative behavior. Amabile and colleagues, myself included, have long argued that it is a mistake to stop at the individual level of analysis—the person doing the creating (see Amabile, 1996; Hennessey, 2003, 2015). And, in fact, even the additional attention paid by social psychologists to aspects of the environment that may impact motivational orientation does not tell the whole story. A whole confluence of environmental and person variables has been shown to be necessary for creativity. For a creative solution to be found or a creative idea or product to be generated, an individual must approach a problem with the appropriate *domain skills* (background knowledge and expertise in a given discipline or area), *creativity skills* (willingness to take risks, experiment, play with ideas), and *task motivation*. Under ideal circumstances, the coming together of these three factors forms what Amabile (1997b) terms the "creative intersection" (see Fig. 7.1).

The bulk of my own scholarly theorizing and experimentation over the last 30 or more years has been directed at potential killers of children's motivation (and creativity) in the classroom, with the promise of a reward, the threat of an evaluation, and the imposition of time limits and/or situations of competition consistently emerging as especially damaging (see, for example, Amabile, 1998; Amabile, Hennessey and Grossman, 1986; Hennessey, 1989, 2003, 2010, 2019). This empirical work parallels nicely Teresa's own research centered on adults in the workplace. Regardless of a creator's age, if the overall atmosphere of a school or corporation is not conducive to intrinsic motivation, then all the domain knowledge and creativity skills in the world are not likely to make up for this detriment.

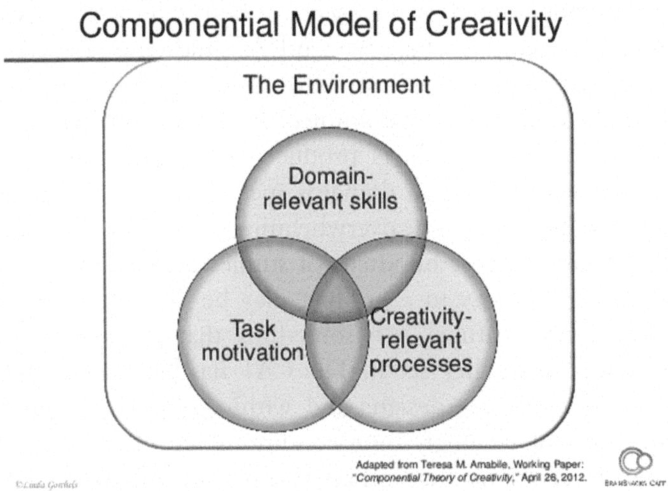

Fig. 7.1 Componential model

How Can We Measure Creativity?

Fundamental to any study of creativity, experimental or otherwise, is a reliable method for assessing creativity, either within or across individuals. Teresa's Consensual Assessment Technique (CAT) meets these criteria and has, in fact, been termed by some practitioners as the gold standard of creativity measurement procedures (Baer & McKool, 2014). Over the years, Teresa and I have collaborated on a number of updates to her original consensual assessment technique. When it was first introduced into the literature, this procedure allowed for the move away from a reliance on the study of Big-C, highly eminent creative individuals toward an examination of the relative creativity of products produced by "everyday" artists, employees, and children in classrooms.

The CAT is based on the assumption that a panel of independent raters generally familiar with the genre in which products have been produced but not trained in any way are best able to make creativity assessments. In situations where the work of children or everyday adults is to be assessed, judges need not have acquired advanced degrees or notoriety in the domain being examined. In situations where judgments are to be made about products produced by highly trained individuals, e.g., persons working in domains such as physics or engineering, expert raters are necessary. The overwhelming consensus reached by both categories of judges across hundreds of studies demonstrates unequivocally that while creativity in a product may be difficult to characterize in terms of specific features, it is something that people can recognize and agree upon when they see it. The CAT has been successfully used in both between-subjects designs and within-subjects designs focused on the question of whether some conditions are more conducive (or detrimental) to creativity than others (Hennessey, Amabile, & Mueller, 2011).

In my own research, the consensual assessment approach has served me especially well. Teachers consistently yield highly reliable judgments of students' product creativity, most often reaching levels of agreement of 90% or better. Over time, this phenomenon became so intriguing to me that I set out to explore specifically the phenomenon of consensual assessment. My experimental investigations in this area have examined a number of features of the consensual assessment process including the relation between judges' ratings of finished products and their ratings of the process that went into producing those products (Hennessey, 1994) and an exploration of the application of assessment procedures both within and across cultures (Hennessey, Kim, Guomin, & Sun, 2008). Teresa has also explored the underpinnings of consensual assessment—expanding the research lens to include assessments of team projects in the workplace (e.g., Moneta, Amabile, Schatzel, & Kramer, 2010).

A Confluence of Approaches

My research on the underpinnings of consensual assessment is just one of many examples of how over the years, my own scholarship and theorizing have been influenced and buoyed by Teresa's work and encouragement. In the 35 years since I earned my PhD, Teresa and I have collaborated on 13 separate publications. We go our own separate ways for a while and then double back to share ideas and insights. Understandably, the frequency of our "formal" collaborations has ebbed and flowed—with more joint publications at the start of my career and fewer in more recent years. But now that both of us are nearing the end of our journey as researchers and theorists, I am struck by the fact that our newest projects and ways of thinking are coming together in a variety of interesting and important ways—most especially with regard to our now shared, and somewhat newfound, appreciation for the importance of each individual's unique psychological state as they approach and engage in a task or project necessitating creativity. In other words, the construction of a workplace or classroom situation that will promote creativity is not a one-size-fits-all (or even a one-size-fits most) proposition. At issue is the unique constellation of attributes brought by each individual, their unique interpretation of the situation they find themselves in.

Looking back, the seeds of this realization may have their origins in the 1986 paper co-authored by Teresa, myself, and Barbara Grossman. In one of the three studies described in that publication, we contrasted the motivation and creative performance of two groups of children. One group was told that if they promised to later complete a variety of creativity tasks, they would first be rewarded with the opportunity to use an instant camera. By contrast, the second group of children were not led to view the picture-taking as a task-contingent reward. Instead, they were simply introduced to a series of tasks to complete—picture-taking and a group of creativity exercises. No reward contingency was established between the picture-taking and the tasks to follow. Everyone took pictures with the instant camera and went on to complete a variety of creativity tasks. For children who perceived that they were contracting to complete the creativity tasks in order to first have the chance to use the instant camera, levels of intrinsic task motivation and creativity were relatively low. For children who were not led to view the picture-taking as a task-contingent reward and who did not perceive that their participation had been coerced, levels of motivation and creativity were significantly higher.

This early study prompted both Teresa and me to revisit this question of individual differences in how extrinsic constraints are perceived. After a few years of unsuccessfully trying to conduct research that might lead to a change in the culture of schools (downplaying rewards, competition, and the anticipation of evaluation), I asked myself whether we might instead change students' perceptions of and reactions to these constraints. In our first series of "immunization" studies (Hennessey, Amabile, & Martinage, 1989), we demonstrated that the undermining of school children's intrinsic motivation and creativity may be counteracted by means of videotaped modeling and directed discussion sessions that explicitly (a) deal with ways to cognitively distance oneself from reward contingencies and (b) focus on intrinsic reasons for working in school. Later, another study incorporated important refinements of our earlier immunization attempts and provided particularly strong evidence for the hypothesis that children participating in sessions designed to focus on intrinsic reasons for doing things in school will later treat reward as an actual augmentation of intrinsic motivation (Hennessey & Zbikowsky, 1993). Again, it was the children's *perception* of the reward and not the offer of reward itself that impacted their task motivation and creativity of performance.

This series of immunization studies parallels nicely Teresa's recent important work on what she and her husband and coauthor term "The

Progress Principle" (Amabile & Kramer, 2011). Years of research into the innovative successes and failures of seven corporations reveals that if managers are to promote the creativity of their workforce, they must pay attention to the "inner work lives" of employees. In other words, as was the case with the students in the immunization studies, the creativity, productivity, and happiness of the adult workers profiled in this book was found to be largely dependent on their individual perceptions of their managers, colleagues, and organization. Perception matters!

Decades of Fruitful Collaboration

Without a doubt, for both Teresa and myself, our most taxing collaboration of all was our 2010 contribution to *Annual Review of Psychology*. Putting together a comprehensive review of the extensive creativity literature almost killed us, but we believed that it was important work and we were anxious to influence the future direction of creativity research, arguing that contemporary scholarship on creativity reflected a growing fragmentation in the field. Few, if any, "big" questions were being pursued. Instead, investigators in one subfield seemed entirely unaware of advances in another. We saw a crucial need for a systems view of creativity and we encouraged investigators to recognize that creativity arises from a complex web of interrelated forces operating at multiple levels (Hennessey & Amabile, 2010).

Ten years have passed since the publication of that review, and an examination of the most current research suggests that a growing number of papers are now reflecting a systems approach as well as a multidisciplinary perspective. Teresa has long argued for a systems approach to the study of creativity. In fact, her 1988 "componential model" may well be the oldest theory of creativity and innovation to attempt a comprehensive exploration of both individual and environmental factors impacting creative behavior and the many ways these two forces are intertwined. More recently, Teresa and colleagues (Amabile, 2012; Amabile & Pratt, 2017) presented significant revisions to this model focusing especially on individual-level psychological processes that work in a sort of "progress loop" exerting powerful influences.

For my own part, I am now focusing on the impact of culture. Having gathered data in schools around the globe, my own current research goal is to "fit" my experimental findings to a multifaceted systems model that can be applied to both workplace and classroom settings. At its core, this model argues that creativity must be explored at the "little-c" cultural level (e.g., the culture of the classroom or workplace), at the societal level, and at the "Big-C" cultural level (i.e., culture writ large) (Hennessey, 2015, 2017). In the years to come, I hope to again collaborate with Teresa on studies of culture and other possible influences on creativity. As a graduate student, I used to worry that I would one day run out of questions to investigate or lose passion for my work. But, over time, I came to realize that the intrinsic motivation, curiosity, and creativity that drive my scholarship know no bounds. Words cannot possibly express how deeply grateful I am to Teresa for setting me on this path.

References

Amabile, T. M. (1983). *The social psychology of creativity*. New York: Springer-Verlag.

Amabile, T. M. (1996). *Creativity in context*. Boulder, CO: Westview.

Amabile, T. M. (1997a). Entrepreneurial creativity through motivational synergy. *Journal of Creative Behavior, 31,* 18–26.

Amabile, T. M. (1997b). Motivating creativity in organizations: On doing what you love and loving what you do. *California Management Review, 40,* 39–58.

Amabile, T. M. (1998). How to kill creativity. *Harvard Business Review, 76,* 76–87.

Amabile, T. M. (2012). *Componential theory of creativity*. Retrieved from https://www.hbs.edu/faculty/Publication%20Files/12-096.pdf.

Amabile, T. M., Hennessey, B. A., & Grossman, B. (1986). Social influences on creativity: The effects of contracted-for reward. *Journal of Personality and Social Psychology, 50,* 14–23.

Amabile, T. M., & Kramer, S. J. (2011). *The progress principle: Using small wins to ignite joy, engagement, and creativity at work*. Boston: Harvard Business Review Press.

Amabile, T. M., & Pratt, M. G. (2017). The dynamic componential model of creativity and innovation in organizations: Making progress, making meaning. *Research in Organizational Behavior, 37,* 157–183.

Baer, J., & McKool, S. S. (2014). The gold standard for assessing creativity. *International Journal of Quality Assurance in Engineering and Technology Education, 3,* 81–93.

Frey, B. S. (1997). *Not just for the money: An economic theory of personal motivation.* Cheltenham, UK and Brookfield, USA: Edward Elgar.

Hennessey, B. A. (1989). The effect of extrinsic constraints on children's creativity while using a computer. *Creativity Research Journal, 2,* 151–168.

Hennessey, B. A. (1994). The consensual assessment technique: An examination of the relationship between ratings of process and product creativity. *Creativity Research Journal, 7,* 193–208.

Hennessey, B. A. (2003). The social psychology of creativity. *Scandinavian Journal of Educational Psychology, 47,* 253–271.

Hennessey, B. A. (2010). Intrinsic motivation and creativity in the classroom: Have we come full circle? In R. A. Beghetto & J. C. Kaufman (Eds.), *Nurturing creativity in the classroom* (pp. 329–361). New York: Cambridge University Press.

Hennessey, B. A. (2015). Creative behavior, motivation, environment and culture: The building of a systems model. *The Journal of Creative Behavior, 49,* 194–210.

Hennessey, B. A. (2017). Taking a systems view of creativity: On the right path toward understanding. *The Journal of Creative Behavior, 51,* 341–344.

Hennessey, B. A. (2019). Motivation and creativity. In J. C. Kaufman & R. J. Sternberg (Eds.), *Cambridge handbook of creativity* (2nd ed., pp. 374–395). New York: Cambridge University Press.

Hennessey, B. A., & Amabile, T. M. (1998). Reward, intrinsic motivation, and creativity. *American Psychologist, 53,* 674–675.

Hennessey, B. A., & Amabile, T. M. (2010). Creativity. *Annual Review of Psychology, 61,* 569–598.

Hennessey, B. A., Amabile, T. M., & Martinage, M. (1989). Immunizing children against the negative effects of reward. *Contemporary Educational Psychology, 14,* 212–227.

Hennessey, B. A., Amabile, T. M., & Mueller J. S. (2011). Consensual assessment. In M.A. Runco, & S.R. Pritzker (Eds.), *Encyclopedia of creativity* (2nd ed., Vol. 1, pp. 253–260). San Diego: Academic Press.

Hennessey, B. A., Kim, G., Guomin, Z., & Sun, W. (2008). A multi-cultural application of the consensual assessment technique. *International Journal of Creativity and Problem Solving, 18*, 87–100.

Hennessey, B. A., & Zbikowski, S. M. (1993). Immunizing children against the negative effects of reward: A further examination of intrinsic motivation training techniques. *Creativity Research Journal, 6*, 297–307.

Moneta, G. B., Amabile, T. M., Schatzel, E., & Kramer, S. J. (2010). Multi-rater assessment of creative contributions to team projects in organizations. *European Journal of Work and Organizational Psychology, 19*, 150–176.

8

Going Back to the Drawing Board Until the Foundation of Creative Work Is Sound

Giovanni B. Moneta

Introduction

The componential model of creativity (Amabile, 1983, 1988, 1996) details the alternation of divergent and convergent thinking processes from beginning to completion of a creative task through a five-stage loop: task representation, preparation, response generation, response validation, and outcome evaluation. The creative problem solver will typically engage in a chain of five-stage loops in order to have a realistic chance of success. Working with Teresa Amabile offered me the opportunity to conduct leading edge research under her expert guidance. This, I learned, implies a unique combination of determination, insight, and ability to recognize those critical failures that require going back to the drawing board until the foundation of creative work is sound.

G. B. Moneta (✉)
School of Social Sciences—Psychology,
London Metropolitan University, London, UK
e-mail: g.moneta@londonmet.ac.uk

R. Reiter-Palmon et al. (eds.), *Creativity at Work*,
Palgrave Studies in Creativity and Innovation in Organizations,
https://doi.org/10.1007/978-3-030-61311-2_8

Years later, I realized that what I had learned in practice by working with Teresa and the other members of her team could be better understood by importing and modifying models of *flow*, which can be briefly defined as a predominantly cognitive state of deep concentration and task-absorption that makes a person feel one with the activity (Csikszentmihalyi, 1975/2000) and is often associated with enhanced task performance. This essay applies recent developments of the flow model that will hopefully be developed even further to model the process through which knowledge managers, such as Teresa, lead teams to creative achievement through a radical and adaptive problem restructuring.

The most recent development of the componential model (Amabile & Pratt, 2017) focuses on the dynamic nature of the creative process, and highlights the importance of recursive loops in real-life, complex problem solving. The updated model also identifies subjective experience and affect as key contributors to each stage of the creative process and, most important, to the transitions from one stage to the next and to the decisions to re-engage in new loops by seeking a radically new task representation. The present essay proposes three possible links between flow theory (Csikszentmihalyi, 1975/2000) and the componential model. First, because if its nonlinear dynamic nature, the experience of flow may be a catalyst for recursion through the five stages of the creative process noted in the componential model. Second, the turbulent nature of the process leading to flow may work as a signal to the problem solver that a radical restructuring of the problem is needed. Finally, the creative process resulting from a turbulent path toward flow is not a linear progression through stages.

A Brief History of Linear and Symmetric Flow Models

The first model of the flow state (Csikszentmihalyi, 1975/2000, p. 17), which is reproduced with some additions in Fig. 8.1, partitions the world of subjective experience in three main states—flow, anxiety, and boredom—that are represented as non-overlapping areas of a Challenge

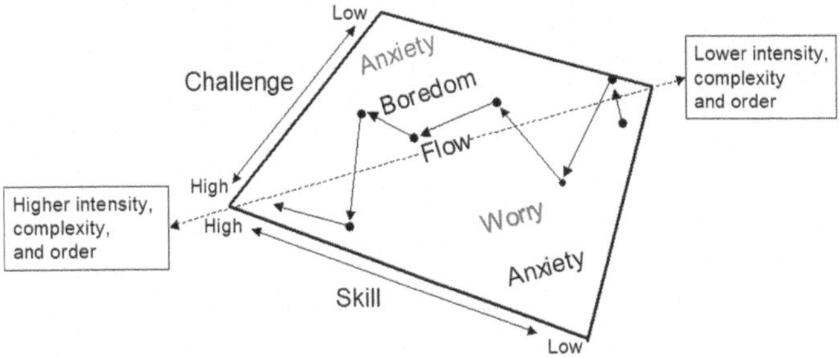

Fig. 8.1 The first model of the flow state (adapted from Csikszentmihalyi, 1975)

by Skill Cartesian space. The flow state is posited to occur when there is an equivalent ratio of perceived challenges from the activity to perceived skills in carrying out the activity. This can occur when both challenges and skills are low, when both are medium, and when both are high: in all these cases there is a balance of challenges and skills and hence a person should be in flow. Yet, not all flow states are the same: when achieved in high-challenge/high-skill situations flow will be more intense, ordered, and complex than when it is achieved in low-challenge/low-skill situations (Csikszentmihalyi, personal communication, 1987). The anxiety state is posited to occur when the perceived challenges from the activity exceed the perceived skills in carrying out the activity, whereas the boredom state is posited to occur when the perceived skills in carrying out the activity exceed the perceived challenges from the activity. Csikszentmihalyi (1975/2000) viewed the model as the experiential map through which a person "walks" in the quest of flow of ever growing complexity: the shown trajectories represent the hypothetical walk of a person who starts an endeavor in a state of low-complexity flow, crosses into the anxiety and boredom states, and eventually reaches a state of high-complexity flow.

Csikszentmihalyi and LeFevre (1989) proposed a new model and operationalization of the flow state, the quadrant model, which is shown in Fig. 8.2. The model partitions the world of subjective experience in four main states—flow, anxiety, boredom, and apathy—that are represented as quadrants of a Challenge by Skill Cartesian space in which both axis variables are standardized with the 0-value representing the mean

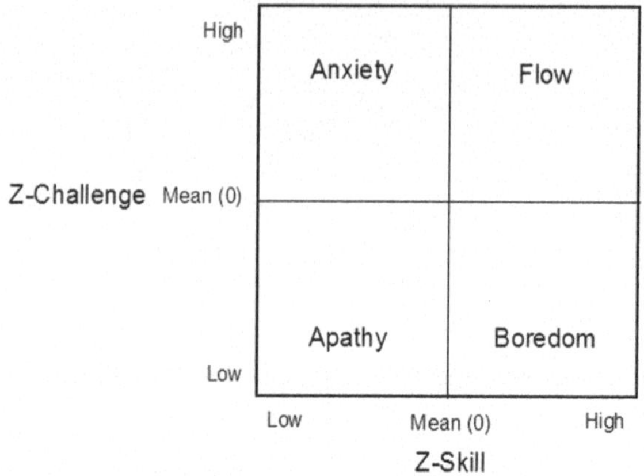

Fig. 8.2 The quadrant model of the flow state (adapted from Csikszentmihalyi and LeFevre, 1989)

for an individual. The model represents flow as a state in which an individual perceives challenges and skills greater than his or her average and in relative balance with each other.

In order to understand whether the balance of challenges and skills has a unique effect on the level of flow experienced, researchers then developed regression models in which subjective experience is the criterion variable, and challenges, skills and the interaction of the two are the predictors (Moneta & Csikszentmihalyi, 1996, 1999; Pfister, 2002). Figure 8.3 shows one such model in which the interaction of challenges and skills is operationalized as the absolute difference between challenge and skill, which can be equal to 0 (if challenge equals skill) or greater than 0 (if challenge and skill differ in any way). The regression coefficient of the absolute difference between challenge and skill represents the effect of the imbalance of challenge and skill on experience. The figure shows that experience (e.g., concentration, absorption, and merging of action and awareness) varies from low to high levels as a function of challenges and skills. The model is fully consistent with the theory: challenge and skill have positive effects on experience, and their absolute difference (representing imbalance of challenge and skill) has a negative effect. The experience surface looks like a roof. The edge of the roof (i.e., the line where the two sloped planes of the roof intersect each other) represents

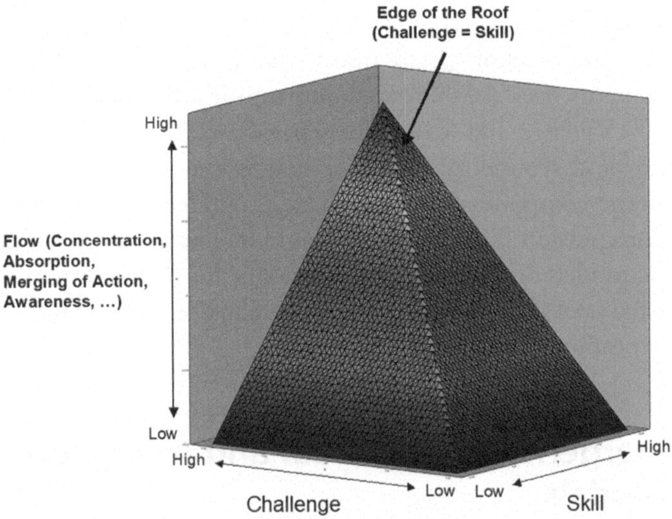

Fig. 8.3 The three-dimensional representation of the absolute difference regression models of the flow state (adapted from Moneta & Csikszentmihalyi, 1996, 1999)

the optimal challenge/skill ratio. In this ideal case, the edge of the roof is perpendicular to the diagonal line of balance of the Challenge by Skill Cartesian plane (i.e., each point of the edge corresponds to an observation in which challenge equals skill). The effect of the imbalance on experience is represented by the slope of the roof: the steeper the slope, the greater the negative effect of the imbalance of challenge and skill. If the slope of the roof is null, then the roof will just be an inclined plane with no edge, and hence there would be no optimal challenge/skill ratio. The ideal flow state can be operationalized in this model as the absolute maximum of the surface, which in this case is on the edge of the roof, perpendicular to the observation for which both challenge and skill achieve their maximum.

Although these three models differ somewhat in the identification and operationalization of the flow state, they share one fundamental property: symmetry of the experience surface relative to the main diagonal of the Challenge by Skill Cartesian plane. All models state that there are two main deficit states, one characterized by challenges greater than skills, and the other characterized by skills greater than challenges, and the two deficit states are psychologically undifferentiated in terms of their experiential consequences and barriers/opportunities they offer for achieving balance of challenge and skill, and hence flow. The key implication of these linear and symmetric models is that, if the creative process represented by the componential model were grounded in the state of flow, then the progression through stages would be linear. As such, linear and symmetric models of flow can hardly account for the recursions through the five stages of the creative process emphasized in the most recent, dynamic componential model.

The Emergence of Nonlinear and Asymmetric Flow Models

Given that a linear and symmetric modeling of the flow state is useless in order to explain the dynamic nature of the creative process, a key question arises: is flow truly achieved through a linear, step-by-step and continuous process? Or, is it possible that at least in some domains and when tackling complex problems, the flow state is achieved through a turbulent path characterized by those sudden discontinuities that problem solvers often report as "suddenly I get into the zone"? Ceja and Navarro (2009, 2011, 2012) departed from previous conceptualizations of flow and proposed that the variations of subjective experience at work conform to nonlinear dynamic models. They also provided empirical evidence in support of their claim estimating various forms of nonlinear models on experience sampling data.

Linear models assume that the change of outcome variables (e.g., concentration, absorption, and merging of action and awareness) as a function of the change of predictor variables (i.e., challenges, skills, and their relative balance) is smooth and continuous. In contrast, nonlinear models assume that, as the system departs from an equilibrium point its behavior becomes increasingly unstable to the extent that change in the outcome variable as a function of predictor variables becomes abrupt and discontinuous. The simplest instance of such abrupt changes is provided by Ceja and Navarro's (2012; Navarro & Ceja, 2011) *cusp catastrophe model of flow*, which is shown in Fig. 8.4.

The key feature of the model is the presence of a bifurcation edge, which is the source of instability. When "walking" on the edge of the cusp, a minimal change in levels of challenges and/or skills results in either a sharp enhancement (i.e., a climb on the surface) or a sharp deterioration (i.e., a descent on the surface) of experience. This means that when in the cusp zone, the approach to flow is an inherently unstable process that could fail abruptly, and its instability is not due to random error but to a deterministic mechanism. In particular, being in the cusp zone implies both the highest probability of experiencing flow suddenly and the highest probability of experiencing the opposite of flow suddenly, and hence the greatest variability of experiential outcomes. A key question is: could the existence of a cusp zone in the model of flow explain why and when expert problem solvers decide to abort a five-stage loop of creative thinking to seek a radical restructuring of the problem at hand?

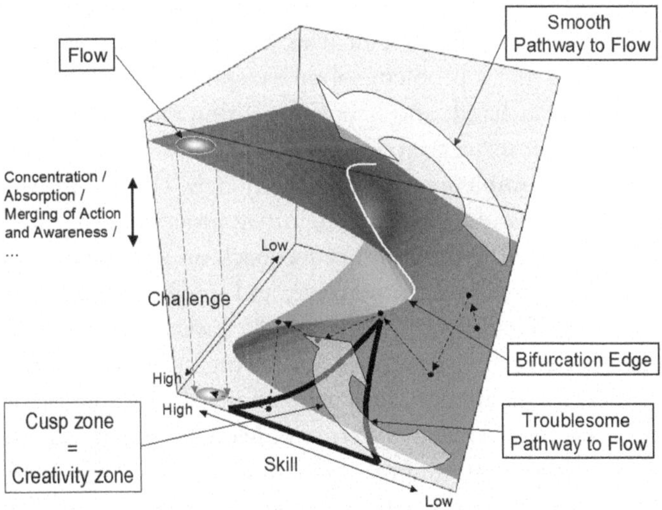

Fig. 8.4 Cusp catastrophe model of flow showing **a** the bifurcation edge, **b** the cusp zone, and **c** smooth and troublesome pathways to flow (adapted from Ceja & Navarro, 2012, and Navarro & Ceja, 2011)

The question invites to explore the different pathways a problem solver may follow to reach the flow state.

The nonlinearity of the cusp model of flow influences the way one can achieve flow. The figure shows the two extreme cases: smooth pathway and troublesome pathway to flow. On the one hand, the smooth pathway begins with low challenges and low skills, proceeds by just increasing skills till the point one feels extremely skillful in handling low challenges, and finally proceeds by just increasing challenges to reach the high-challenge, high-skill state of flow. On the other hand, the troublesome pathway begins with high challenges and low skills, proceeds by just increasing skills till the point one can progress toward the flow state if and only if one somehow manages to "climb" the steep inner wall of the cusp. As such, the smooth passage to flow avoids the instability of the cusp, the troublesome pathway faces it fully, and any other path in between the two faces intermediate levels of instability.

The two extreme pathways to flow are likely to impose differing demands on cognitive and emotional processes. On the one hand, the troublesome pathway to flow requires the ability to "survive" in the cusp zone and manage to come out of it as a winner. The cusp experience essentially means that a problem solver recognizes that old tricks do not work for the task at hand, and hence something radically new has to be figured out in order to succeed. In that context flow can be achieved only by conceiving and implementing a radically new, creative idea. As such, it is reasonable to assume that the cognitive processes that are required in the cusp zone are the provision of feedback on how one is doing, the ability and willingness to seek, perceive, and understand such feedback, problem finding (Getzels, 1964; Getzels & Csikszentmihalyi, 1976) as well as all other cognitive processes underlying creativity, such as information gathering, incubation, idea generation, idea evaluation, and idea implementation (see review by Palermo & Moneta, 2016). Moreover, the emotional processes that are probably required in the cusp zone are the initial experience of negative affect derived from failure and frustration in conducting ordinary ("algorithmic" in Teresa's terminology) problem solving, followed by an affective shift characterized by a decrease of negative affect and an increase of positive affect that support idea generation, idea evaluation, and idea implementation as represented in the *Phoenix*

Model of Creativity (Bledow, Rosing, & Frese, 2013). In this specific sense, the cusp zone could be labeled as the *creativity zone.*

On the other hand, the smooth pathway to flow requires ordinary learning processes and self-regulation that support understanding of the problem at hand and step-by-step acquisition and deployment of the new skills that would allow solving the problem. This does not mean that creativity cannot occur, but rather that it is optional and limited by context to a lesser and more ordinary form often referred to as "little-c" (Davis, 2004), "everyday" (Richards, Kinney, Benet, & Merzel, 1988), "small" (Feldman, Csikszentmihalyi, & Gardner, 1994), and "inherent" (Runco, 1995) creativity. Moreover, the emotional processes that are required in the non-cusp zone are those that support any well-paced and mostly progressive learning endeavor. In this specific sense, the non-cusp zone could be labeled as the *non-creativity zone.*

The existence of a range of pathways to flow can account for the complex role played by affective states in the creative process. Research conducted by Amabile and coworkers on the TEAM study (Amabile, Barsade, Mueller, & Staw, 2005; Amabile & Kramer, 2011) has shown that positive affect supports creative work by feeding the *progress loop* (Amabile & Kramer, 2011), wherein progress in meaningful work enhances positive affect and intrinsic motivation, which in turn foster more progress in meaningful work in an upward spiral fashion. However, Amabile and Pratt (2017) reviewed the mixed evidence on the link between negative affect and creativity, and suggested that both positive and negative affective states may facilitate creativity at different stages of the creative process. In particular, they proposed that negative and ambivalent affective states might turn out useful in task preparation and response validation because they support critical thinking, narrowed focus on details, and hence more objective evaluation. In this connection, the troublesome pathway to flow implies a clear perception of incumbent risk of failure, and hence inevitably involves some level of negative or ambivalent affect. As such, facing the cusp over and over again in a work project is grounded on a problem solver's ability to create "meaningfulness," i.e., "the ability to provide a compelling account – a justification – of why one's work is worth doing." (Amabile & Pratt, 2017, p. 14).

The model is consistent with the notion that flow is a universal experience, as any person during an endeavor could reach a high-challenge/high-skill condition by following the troublesome pathway. However, Ceja and Navarro (2012; Navarro & Ceja, 2011) found that for a minority of study participants the flow model has no cusp. For these participants experience conforms to linear models such as the one represented in Fig. 8.3. For any such linear model there is no difference between pathways to flow in that no pathway crosses a cusp or other form of turbulence area. Ceja and Navarro's study indicates that there are individual differences in the degree of nonlinearity of the flow model, ranging from strong nonlinearity and pronounced cusp to linearity and absence of cusp. In other words, there are individual differences in the degree of symmetry of the flow model, with "nonlinear individuals" exhibiting strong asymmetry and "linear individuals" exhibiting perfect symmetry. This implies that for "linear individuals" there is no troublesome pathway to flow, and hence they are structurally prevented from experiencing flow through the troublesome path. The key questions are: what are the causes of individual differences in linearity-nonlinearity, and what are the consequences of such individual differences on creative achievement?

Linearity implies the absence of the cusp area in an individual's flow model. The likely reason for the absence of the cusp area is that an individual is unable and/or unwilling to appropriately recognize and assess disconfirming feedback from the activity, i.e., the systematic failure derived from deploying algorithmic problem solving. The likely consequence of the absence of the cusp area is that an individual will be unable to activate those cognitive and emotional processes that are involved in heuristic creative problem solving. In all, only "nonlinear individuals"—those with a cusp area in their flow model—will have a chance to seek and correctly read signs of systematic failure in algorithmic problem solving, realize the need for a shift to a heuristic approach, and activate those cognitive and emotional resources—including negative and ambivalent affect—that are necessary for a radical restructuring of the problem at hand. As such, the difference between nonlinearity and linearity would seem to be a key factor for understanding the metacognitive processes underlying the deployment and tuning of creative problem solving skills to a given task.

As Kaufman and Beghetto (2013) humorously put it, whereas it is important to teach individuals to be creative, it is equally important to teach them when not to be creative. For example, it is not uncommon that a paragraph in an essay or report uses multiple terms to refer to the same concept or variable, creating unnecessary confusion in the reader. Probably, it is only by receiving appropriateness feedback over a long learning period of time in any given domain of activity that individuals can develop the metacognition of creativity and the ability to read the contextual cues that constrain the deployment of creativity. A nonlinear individual has the full potential to realize at a metacognitive level when in a work project it is appropriate to shift from an ordinary, algorithmic problem solving approach to a more radical, heuristic approach that requires a radical restructuring of the problem.

Toward and Understanding of the "Roller Coaster" of Creative Achievement

Building on the lessons learned, this essay presented an adaptation of the nonlinear dynamic model of flow (Ceja & Navarro, 2012) to explain the "roller coaster" of creative achievement by integrating flow and creative thinking within the same conceptual framework. The model sheds some new insight into the componential model of creativity (Amabile, 1983, 1988, 1996, 2017). First, the existence of a cusp zone in the model of flow can explain why and when expert problem solvers decide to abort a five-stage loop of creative thinking to seek a radical restructuring of the problem at hand. The model suggests that a return to the drawing table requires a strongly nonlinear individual flow model, whereas a linear individual flow model would lead the problem solver to keep approaching the problem in an algorithmic mode, resorting to well known tools that proved effective in the past. Second, the model suggests that problem finding coincides with entering the cusp zone in the course of problem solving, and hence appears to be an "accident" or setback that only the discriminating mind of nonlinear problem solvers can perceive and react emotionally to. Finally, the model suggests that problem finding may after all not be an independent stage of the creative process—as theorized in some models of the creative process but not in the componential model—but rather a dynamic and somewhat chaotic pattern through which the problem solver generates ideas, changes the task representation, provides a partial, pilot implementation of new ideas, followed by pilot evaluations of those ideas with the aim of understanding whether at lest one of them is worth pursuing—the overarching goal always being that of re-emerging from the cusp zone as a winner. As such, coming in and out of flow—and hence undergoing sudden shifts or even reversals in affective experience—may be the key process through which a problem solver identifies opportunities for creativity and is capable of recursive, prolonged engagement in meaningful work projects. In all, these suggestions call for identifying those personal and environmental factors that may facilitate the degree of nonlinearity in achieving flow among individuals who conduct creative work.

References

Amabile, T. M. (1983). The social psychology of creativity: A componential conceptualization. *Journal of Personality and Social Psychology, 45*(2), 357–376.

Amabile, T. M. (1988). A model of creativity and innovation in organizations. In B. S. Cummings (Ed.), *Research in organizational behavior* (pp. 123–167). Greenwich: JAI Press.

Amabile, T. M. (1996). *Creativity in context*. Boulder, CO: Westview Press.

Amabile, T., & Kramer, S. (2011). *The progress principle: Using small wins to ignite joy, engagement, and creativity at work*. Cambridge: Harvard Business Press.

Amabile, T. M., Barsade, S. G., Mueller, J. S., & Staw, B. M. (2005). Affect and creativity at work. *Administrative Science Quarterly, 50*, 367–403.

Amabile, T. M., & Pratt, M. G. (2017). The dynamic componential model of creativity and innovation in organizations: Making progress, making meaning. *Research in Organizational Behavior, 37,* 157–183.
Bledow, R., Rosing, K., & Frese, M. (2013). A dynamic perspective on affect and creativity. *Academy of Management Journal, 56*(2), 432–450.
Ceja, L., & Navarro, J. (2009). Dynamics of flow: A nonlinear perspective. *Journal of Happiness Studies, 10,* 665–684.
Ceja, L., & Navarro, J. (2011). Dynamic patterns of flow in the workplace: Characterizing within-individual variability using a complexity science approach. *Journal of Organizational Behavior, 32,* 627–651.
Ceja, L., & Navarro, J. (2012). 'Suddenly I get into the zone': Examining discontinuities and nonlinear changes in flow experiences at work. *Human Relations, 65,* 1101–1127.
Csikszentmihalyi, M. (1975/2000). *Beyond boredom and anxiety: Experiencing flow in work and play* (1st/2nd ed.). San Francisco: Jossey Bass.
Csikszentmihalyi, M., & LeFevre, J. (1989). Optimal experience in work and leisure. *Journal of Personality and Social Psychology, 56,* 815–822.
Davis, G. A. (2004). *Creativity is forever* (5th ed.). Dubuque, IA: Kendall/Hunt.
Feldman, D. H., Csikszentmihalyi, M., & Gardner, H. (1994). *Changing the world: A framework for the study of creativity.* Westport, CT: Praeger.
Getzels, J. W. (1964). Creative thinking, problem solving, and instruction. In E. R. Hilgard (Ed.), *Theories of learning and instruction: 63rd yearbook of the national society for the study of education* (pp. 240–276). Chicago: University of Chicago Press.
Getzels, J. W., & Csikszentmihalyi, M. (1976). *The creative vision: A longitudinal study of problem finding in art.* New York: Wiley.
Kaufman, J. C., & Beghetto, R. A. (2013). In praise of Clark Kent: Creative metacognition and the importance of teaching kids when (not) to be creative. *Roeper Review, 35,* 155–165.
Moneta, G. B., & Csikszentmihalyi, M. (1996). The effect of perceived challenges and skills on the quality of subjective experience. *Journal of Personality, 64,* 275–310.
Moneta, G. B., & Csikszentmihalyi, M. (1999). Models of concentration in natural environments: A comparative approach based on streams of experiential data. *Social Behavior and Personality, 27,* 603–637.
Navarro, J., & Ceja, L. (2011). Dinámicas complejas en el flujo: Diferencias entre trabajo y no trabajo [Complex dynamics of flow: Differences between work and non-work activities]. *Revista de Psicología Social, 26,* 443–456.

Palermo, G., & Moneta, G. B. (2016). Cognitive processes underlying creativity at work. In G. B. Moneta & J. Rogaten (Eds.), *Psychology of creativity: Cognitive, emotional, and social processes* (pp. 21–48). New York: Nova Science.

Pfister, R. (2002). Flow im Alltag: Untersuchungen zum Quadrantenmodell des Flow-Erlebens und zum Konzept der autotelischen Perso ̈nlichkeit mit der Experience Sampling Method (ESM) [*Flow in everyday life: Studies on the quadrant model of flow experiencing and on the concept of the autotelic personality with the experience sampling method (ESM)*]. Bern: Peter Lang.

Richards, R., Kinney, D. K., Benet, M., & Merzel, A. P. (1988). Assessing everyday creativity: Characteristics of the lifetime creativity scales and validation with three large samples. *Journal of Personality and Social Psychology, 54*(3), 476–485.

Runco, M. A. (1995). Insight for creativity, expression for impact. *Creativity Research Journal, 8*(4), 377–390.

9

Toward (Eventually) Expanding the Componential Model: Integrating Theory on the Bias Against Creativity

Jennifer S. Mueller

I began my career as a graduate student studying Health Psychology at Brandeis University. I will never forget the day when my advisor at the time, Joan Tucker, asked me how I was planning to make money during my first summer in graduate school—and whether I would be interested in working for Teresa Amabile. Teresa, she explained, used to be on the faculty at Brandeis, but had just taken a position at Harvard Business School. Joan told me that Teresa was looking for a student who could help with her research. I asked Joan why Teresa didn't just hire a Harvard student. Joan replied, "the pay is pretty low and Harvard students probably wouldn't work for so little, so I thought you would be perfect!" Little did Joan know that even though Teresa was no longer a faculty at Brandeis, the Brandeis graduate students still swooned at the idea of having a chance to work for her. I was no different.

J. S. Mueller (✉)
University of San Diego, San Diego, CA, USA
e-mail: jmueller@sandiego.edu

R. Reiter-Palmon et al. (eds.), *Creativity at Work*,
Palgrave Studies in Creativity and Innovation in Organizations,
https://doi.org/10.1007/978-3-030-61311-2_9

I was lucky that Teresa hired me that summer. And even luckier that she was able to hire me on for the next three years to work on the TEAM study almost full time. Later, when Joan left to another job at the RAND corporation, Teresa took on the primary responsibility for developing and training me as a scholar, working tirelessly to help me hone my dissertation. While her efforts to shape me as a scholar were critical to my development, at the time, I could not have predicted how working on the project she had architected to study creativity at work—the TEAM study—would also change the way I thought about creativity.

The TEAM study followed 238 employees in seven companies, prompting them to fill out daily diary entries about the events they experienced at work. This yielded a narrative database of around 12,000 events—and I remember reading through all of them several times. Having a window into employees' inner work lives was incredibly valuable, but even more valuable was being able to discuss them with Teresa. I would routinely bring her ideas and each time she would say the same thing, "that's very interesting. You should do some analyzes to flesh that idea out." To Teresa, every idea was an opportunity. This is perhaps why, it was so striking to me when I started to identify a very different pattern in the data—more often than not, when employees shared their ideas with others, they were met with derision.

In 2005, Teresa, Sigal Barsade, Barry Staw, (2005) and I published a paper in *Administrative Science Quarterly* on affect and creativity—which provided some evidence verifying my hunch around others' tendency to reject creative ideas. The theoretical contribution of this paper was to unveil the temporal dynamics of the relationship between affect and creativity, identifying that feeling positive affect can increase the likelihood of having a creative idea the next day and even the day after that. We also included qualitative analysis of daily diary events and identified an interesting cyclical relationship between affect and creativity; having a creative idea evoked a positive affective response, which in turn influenced more creativity. Alongside this virtual cycle of creativity, we saw a cycle of creative decline which was usually precipitated by sharing the idea with somebody else. Of the 20 total cases when employees described sharing their ideas with somebody else, 80% (16 cases) were characterized by others having a negative response to the idea. Importantly, all the employees in the sample came from companies and positions where creativity was lauded and encouraged. This observation began a line of questions that would help me shape my identity as a scholar. In particular, what could explain why, in a context that supported creativity, sharing ideas with others was generally met with negativity? And why were employees reacting so negatively to ideas that other employees believed were creative?

When I later asked Teresa why people desire but reject creativity, she asked a question I found surprising given that Teresa had devoted most of her life to studying creativity. She said, "why would anybody love creativity?" I believe her work partially answers this question. In the paper on affect and creativity I published with Teresa, Sigal, and Barry, we identified that people experienced joy immediately after having a creative idea. This could at least partially be explained by Teresa's theory of intrinsic motivation, which identifies that enjoyment and challenge in the work spur creative thinking (Amabile, 1985). That is, people are driven to create from a place of enjoyment, and one enjoyable aspect of working on a challenging puzzle is the belief that you may have solved it. Hence, Teresa's own work provides theory and some evidence that people are likely to feel positive affect subsequent to generating their "own" creative ideas—partially because they enjoy the process of generating them. But this question around why people would routinely react negatively to ideas that others view as creative was a bit more difficult to answer.

At the time I was asking this question "why don't people react positively to others creative ideas," the field had converged on the view that creative ideas were novel and useful and could be assessed by expert judges. Specifically, Teresa's consensual assessment technique (CAT) developed a clever way of creating a reliable measurement of creativity by assessing agreement between independent judges evaluating a set of ideas (Amabile, 1982). I believe Teresa's goal in creating the CAT was to help the field develop a reliable and shared approach to measuring and writing about something as seemingly amorphous as creativity. However, the need for the CAT also revealed to me another interesting possibility, that expert judges might not always agree about what is creative.

Teresa also authored another paper which sparked my imagination in a similar direction, but the paper did not relate to creativity per se. In the early 80 s, Teresa co-authored a paper showing that people who were intellectually insecure exhibited what she called a negatively bias—a tendency to evaluate others more negatively (Amabile & Glazebrook, 1982). That is, people could have differing views of the same person depending upon the psychological state they experienced—the more insecure people were, the more negatively they evaluated others. For me, I started to wonder if this general pattern might also reflect how people evaluate creative ideas. Simonton and others had long noted that the more novel an idea, the more uncertainty exists about its value and ability to solve a given problem (Simonton, 2003). Decades of research shows that people find uncertainty to be an aversive state. Again, I began asking questions. Irrespective of their level of expertise, could people's evaluations of the same creative idea depend, at least in part, upon their psychological experience of uncertainty? And in the back of my mind I heard Teresa's voice "That's very interesting. You should do some analyses to flesh that idea out."

I must admit that I struggled for years to answer these questions. My experience was that if you asked people if they valued creativity, they would tell you that they did. In fact, after years of interviewing hundreds of employees and managers, I did not encounter a single instance when a person expressed disdain for creativity. There was one instance though, that I found particularly puzzling. I interviewed a manager in the pharmaceutical division of a large consumer products company. When I asked him if he valued creativity he said, "*creative?* I'm not an artist. If I do something crazy it could kill a patient." When I then asked a follow-up question, "so does that mean you do not value creativity?" he exclaimed, "I take offense to that, I have to be innovative. If I'm not innovative every day, patients could die." This comment made me wonder why my question was viewed as offensive by the manager. It was almost as if, by suggesting he might not value creativity, I was accusing him of doing something wrong or breaking a norm. This made me wonder whether there was a social norm around valuing creativity in US culture that made it harder for people to admit their dislike of creative ideas.

To continue exploring these questions my colleagues Shimul Melwani and Jack Goncalo and I devised an experiment (Mueller, Melwani, & Goncalo, 2012). The three of us had a hunch built from an analogy: just as people have implicit biases against people of a certain age, race, or gender that are not necessarily overt (Greenwald & Banaji, 1995), people may also hold deeply rooted negative views of creativity that are not openly acknowledged. We employed the IAT—Implicit Attitude Test, a reaction time test, used to identify whether participants exhibit an implicit preference for creativity or practicality. In the paradigm of the IAT, an implicit preference for creativity would be indicated if participants exhibited faster reaction times when pairing positive words like "heaven" more quickly with words like "creativity" relative to words like "practicality" and pairing negative words like "rotten" more quickly with words like "practicality" relative to words like "creativity." We assessed explicit preferences as the extent to which a participant self-reported valuing creativity versus practicality. Importantly, we found that participants exhibited an explicit preference for creativity relative to practicality in all conditions. We also showed that in the control condition, participants exhibited an *implicit positive* association with creativity relative to practicality as well. However, people who experienced an intolerance to uncertainty explicitly told us that they valued creativity, but their reaction times indicated a negative association with creativity and resulting downgrading of a creative idea.

For me, this study provided one possible explanation of why participants in the TEAM study would have experienced so much negativity from others when sharing their ideas even in a context that generally supported creativity. People could simultaneously hold an authentic explicit positive association with creativity while also harboring an implicit negative belief around creativity when they are in specific situations where uncertainty is less tolerable. So, my next question was, are there certain situations or contexts which routinely evoke an intolerance to uncertainty, but that is a key part of how creativity managed in organizations? To answer these questions, I went back to the events in the TEAM study. When reading through the TEAM study events, it was clear that most if not all of the study participants loved engaging in creative problem-solving. When these participants had ideas, they expressed emotions akin to joy and elation. So there was very little evidence that people whose role it was to generate ideas were experiencing a bias against creativity. I also noticed that when TEAM study participants reported experiencing negative affect when sharing their idea, this was often in the context of the idea being evaluated by someone with the authority to resource the idea like a decision-maker (e.g., manager, supervisor or leader). This led to a second line of inquiry. Could being placed in a decision-maker role evoke an intolerance to uncertainty and resulting bias against creativity?

Because there was no theory at the time to help us justify hypotheses, it took Shimul Melwani and I (who were later joined with Jeff Lowenstein and Jennifer Deal) more than 10 years to develop and test a theoretical model explaining why those in a decision-making role might exhibit a tendency to reject creative ideas (Mueller, Melwani, Loewenstein, & Deal, 2018). First, we showed that when we placed people in a decision-maker role, by giving them responsibility for resourcing an idea, they experienced more accountability and responsibility and a higher economic mindset, than when we placed participants in a role where they were merely evaluating an idea. Second, when people are in an economic mindset, they look to features of any idea which indicate proven value and the likelihood of making an accurate and correct decision—thereby attempting to reduce uncertainty. One such feature involves social approval metrics—Facebook likes, investor interest, downloads, or other numerical indicators of the extent to which an idea has gained endorsement from a given group of people. Importantly though, creative ideas are often too early stage to have acquired social approval metrics (Schilling & Hill, 1998), and even so, research shows that social approval metrics are noisy and misleading indicators of idea quality when ideas are also new (Rao, Greve, & Davis, 2001). Surprisingly, we found that those in a decision-making role were more likely to rate an idea with low social approval as less creative relative to those who were not in a decision-making role. This evidence suggests that those in a decision-making role may have a different and potentially misguided view of creativity relative to those who do not have decision-making responsibility (e.g., idea generators, designers, consumers), such that they are more likely to downgrade the very kinds of ideas others view as highly creative.

To me, our findings suggested several important points about how the bias against creativity might manifest in organizations. First, the bias against creativity is not necessarily evoked by the mere act of evaluating an idea, but rather the mindset one adopts when evaluating ideas. Second, because decision-making roles come with responsibility to choose good ideas as well as the need to justify choices if they are later deemed poor, merely assigning a person a decision-making role can evoke the kind of mindset that harms creative idea recognition. We also showed that the more time people spent in an actual decision-making role, the more likely they were to adopt an economic mindset, suggesting that these mindsets evoked by a person's role might be more sticky and so unlikely to be altered by priming, nudges, or other more subtle approaches. Importantly though, all the decision-makers we studied in the field were in leadership positions, the more time in this role, the higher level the leader. This raises the question of whether leaders generally are more likely to exhibit a bias against creativity. One IBM survey of over 1500 C-suite executives identified the ability to recognize values in new and creative approaches as the leadership skill most needed to navigate the current complex, global, and volatile environment (Kern, 2010). Critically, however, over 50% of the executives in the sample admitted difficulty mastering this skill. Taken together, the bias against creativity may be baked into the structure of how we organize for creativity and innovation. You can have leaders who say they desire creativity, but reject creative ideas when they arrive.

Downstream Implications for the Componential Model of Creativity

Where I hope this work will eventually go is to add another layer to Teresa's componential model of creativity (Amabile, 1988; Amabile & Pratt, 2016). Teresa's componential model of creativity is perhaps one of the most widely employed, and valuable theories of creativity in organizational contexts—in no small part because it is broad enough to apply to a large variety of organizations, but also specific enough to offer actionable advice for companies hoping to stimulate more creativity. Importantly though, the componential model focuses on the generation of creative ideas as a key outcome. While this model does not preclude evaluation from key decision-makers or gate-keepers as a critical process influencing the development of creative ideas, it also does not provide a clear framework around how evaluation from those in decision-making roles might relate to the development of any idea over time and potentially bridge the process of creativity and downstream innovation. Said differently, the model adopts the perspective of the employee generating the creative ideas, but not the perspective of the decision-maker evaluating the ideas. This perspective is also important to adopt because those in decision-maker roles determine if employee ideas have impact and gain resources for implementation.

In her 1988 Research in Organizational Behavior article, Teresa initially mapped out a Componential Model of Organizational Innovation (Amabile, 1988). In this model she describes factors at the individual level that link to the organizational level. She notes that there are three organizational components that can help individuals and groups link their own creative endeavors to organizational level outcomes, namely: organizational motivation to innovate (the orientation of the organization toward innovation), resources in the task domain (the resources an organization has available to aid the work), and skills in innovation management (managerial skills and styles that are conducive to innovation). I hope to eventually contribute the idea that another way to link individual-level creative idea generation efforts with organizational level innovation outcomes is to examine the components that aid the ability of decision-makers to overcome a bias against novelty. As I'm in the process of developing this model now, I have very little to contribute beyond noting that I am certain that if I told Teresa my ideas she would say, "that's a very interesting idea. You should do some analyses to flesh that idea out." I am also certain she would help along the way, at any point, in any way should could, and it would never occur to her that I might devalue her perspective by adding to it. On the contrary, I am certain she would be pleased and delighted if I did.

References

Amabile, T. (1988). A model of creativity and innovation in organizations. In B. K. Staw (Ed.), *Research in organization behavior*, Vol. 10 (pp. 123–167). Greenwich, CT: JAI Press.

Amabile, T. M. (1982). Social psychology of creativity: A consensual assessment technique. *Journal of Personality and Social Psychology, 43*(5), 997–1013.

Amabile, T. M. (1985). Motivation and creativity: Effects of motivational orientation on creative writers. *Journal of Personality and Social Psychology, 48*(2), 393–397.

Amabile, T. M., Barsade, S. G., Mueller, J. S., & Staw, B. M. (2005). Affect and creativity at work. *Administrative Science Quarterly, 50,* 367–403.

Amabile, T. M., & Glazebrook, A. H. (1982). A negativity bias in interpersonal evaluation. *Journal of Experimental Social Psychology, 18*(1), 1–22.

Amabile, T. M., & Pratt, M. G. (2016). The dynamic componential model of creativity and innovation in organizations: Making progress, making meaning. *Research in Organizational Behavior, 36,* 157–183.

Greenwald, A. G., & Banaji, M. R. (1995). Implicit social cognition: Attitudes, self-esteem, and stereotypes. *Psychological Review, 102*(1), 4–27.

Kern, F. (2010). What chief executives really want. *Bloomberg Businessweek.*

Mueller, J., Melwani, S., Loewenstein, J., & Deal, J. J. (2018). Reframing the decision-makers' dilemma: Towards a social context model of creative idea recognition. *Academy of Management Journal, 61*(1), 94–110.

Mueller, J. S., Melwani, S., & Goncalo, J. A. (2012). The bias against creativity: Why people desire but reject creative ideas. *Psychological Science, 23,* 13–17.

Rao, H., Greve, H. R., & Davis, G. F. (2001). Fool's gold: Social proof in the initiation and abandonment of coverage by Wall Street analysts. *Administrative Science Quarterly, 46*(3), 502–526.

Schilling, M. A., & Hill, C. W. (1998). Managing the new product development process: Strategic imperatives. *The Academy of Management Executive, 12*(3), 67–81.

Simonton, D. K. (2003). Scientific creativity as constrained stochastic behavior: The integration of product, person, and process perspectives. *Psychological Bulletin, 129*(4), 475–494.

10

Local Safety Versus Global Risk: Models of the Creative Work Environment

Michael D. Mumford and Mark W. Fichtel

Creative achievement, or innovation, the development and fielding of new products or services, ultimately depends on the creative problem solution, the new ideas, of people (Mumford & Gustafson, 1988). Of course, creative problem-solving is influenced by many variables including effective execution of key creative problem-solving processes such as problem definition, conceptual combination, and idea generation (Mumford, Medeiros, & Partlow, 2012). Motivation, or task engagement, also seems critical to creative problem-solving (Tierney & Farmer, 2002), as is divergent thinking and intelligence (Runco, in press).

Among these varied influences on creative thought, however, climate appears of special significance. In a meta-analysis, Hunter, Bedell, and Mumford (2007) found climate perceptions to be among the strongest predictors of both idea generation and creative performance. In fact,

M. D. Mumford (✉) · M. W. Fichtel
University of Oklahoma, Norman, OK, USA
e-mail: mmumford@ou.edu

R. Reiter-Palmon et al. (eds.), *Creativity at Work*,
Palgrave Studies in Creativity and Innovation in Organizations,
https://doi.org/10.1007/978-3-030-61311-2_10

this observation is not especially unique. Amabile and her colleagues (Amabile & Conti, 1999; Amabile & Gryskiewicz, 1989; Amabile, Conti, Coon, Lazenby, & Herron, 1996) have long stressed the importance of peoples' work environment in shaping their engagement in, and capability for, creative problem-solving.

Climate

Climate refers to peoples' perceptions of certain aspects of their work environment. If only one person sees a certain feature, or aspect, of their work environment, we attribute such perceptions to the person rather than the shared, quasi-objective, features of the work environment we refer to as climate (James & Jones, 1974). Thus in appraising climate our concern is shared, agreed upon, features of the work environment (Joyce & Slocum, 1984).

Work environments, however, are complex, multi-faceted, phenomena. Thus there is not one climate, instead climate studies focus on shared perceptions of different aspects, or features, of the environment confronting people at work. Accordingly, we might speak of climate for safety (Griffin & Neal, 2000) or service climate (Schneider, White, & Paul, 1998). What should be recognized here, however, is people do not experience just one climate. They virtually always are exposed to multiple climates—often climates operating at different levels of analysis (Glisson & James, 2002).

Creative Climate

Creative work, of course, is a complex, multi-level, phenomenon (Mumford & Hunter, 2005). Accordingly, it is not at all surprising that models of creative climate have been developed to account for attributes of the work environment shaping creative performance at different levels of analysis. For example, Ekvall and Ryhammar (1999) focus on individual-level variables, for example, trust, debate, and playfulness, in their model of creative climate. West et al. (2003) examine environmental attributes operating at the team level that contribute to creative performance such as participative safety, support for innovation, challenging objectives, and task orientation. Lapierre and Giroux (2003), in contrast, focus on attributes of the organizational environment contributing to creative performance such as resources, risk taking, and product focus.

Amabile and her colleagues (e.g. Amabile & Gryskiewicz, 1989), in defining creative climate, took a multi-level approach focused on the work group as it operates within a broader organizational context proposing an eight dimensional model: (1) work group support, (2) challenging work, (3) organizational support, (4) supervisory support, (5) organizational impediments, (6) freedom, (7) workforce pressure, and (8) sufficient resources. Amabile et al. (1996) have provided compelling evidence that peoples' perceptions of these environmental attributes are strongly, positively, related to creative performance in real-world work settings.

Amabile and Kramer (2011) expanded this initial line of work in a search for a general model as to how firms should seek to establish an environment likely to contribute to creative work. Teams working for a number of firms focused on providing innovative new products were interviewed and team members were asked to complete daily event logs. Although a number of noteworthy findings emerged from this effort seven catalysts, or climate dimensions, were identified contributing to creative performance: (1) setting clear goals, (2) allowing autonomy, (3) providing resources, (4) giving enough time, (5) helping with the work, (6) learning, and (7) allowing ideas to flow. More broadly, they interpret these dimensions as establishing a climate of psychological safety with respect to the work being done.

Indeed, at a team level, the notion that psychological safety is a critical feature of a creative climate has found support in a number of other studies. For example, Carmeli, Reiter-Palmon, and Ziv (2010) found perceptions of psychological safety mediated the impact of inclusive leadership on creative performance. Kessel, Kratzer, and Schultz (2012) found psychological safety encourages information sharing in healthcare teams. Hirak, Peng, Carmeli, and Schaubroeck (2012) found psychological safety encourages people to learn from failure. Taken as a whole, it seems clear, a psychologically safe team environment contributes to creativity—put differently Amabile and Kramer (2011) appear to be correct about the team climate contributing to creative performance.

Professional Climate

Of course, the team represents only one aspect of the environment confronting the person doing creative work. Csikszentmihalyi (1999) notes another key aspect of the environment confronting people doing creative work is the field or profession in which they are working. In fact, creative people appear to draw much of their identity from the professional field in which they are working (Root-Bernstein, Bernstein, & Garnier, 1995). Not only does the profession provide information, and the collegial exchange of information, held to be crucial to creative achievement (Mumford & Hunter, 2005), evaluation of the value of the work being conducted is often professionally based (Bennich-Björkman, 2017).

Although the professional environment appears as important, if not more important, to creative people as the team in which they are working, the professional environment is different, very different, from the psychologically safe environment characterizing creative teams. The professional environment is a sharply critical environment where peer criticism is used to both improve ideas and, often, to reject ideas (Gibson & Mumford, 2013). Professions, moreover, selectively allocate resources and rewards with few, very few, people receiving professional accolades (Simonton, 1999). And, creative people are often involved in intense competition to receive these rewards and accolades (Clydesdale, 2006). Put more directly, the professional environment is not a nice, safe, place.

Although we lack viable studies examining the specific aspects of the professional environment that do, or do not, contribute to creative achievement, we do know something about the personality of creative people working in professional environments. Feist (1999) in a review of extant studies of creative scientists found they are open and flexible but also driven, ambitious, domineering, arrogant, self-confident, introverted, and independent. Although not the most attractive personality profile, it is a personality profile likely to contribute to adaptation in a critical, competitive, professional environment. Indeed, Fernham (in press) notes creative people are persistent and obsessed—again, characteristics that would contribute to success in a demanding professional environment.

In fact, Hunter, Bedell, and Mumford (2007) in their meta-analysis of creative climate found some evidence pointing to both the importance of the professional environment and the team environment. They found, in keeping with the importance of the professional environment, that mission clarity and intellectual stimulation were especially important aspects of the creative climate. They also found, in keeping with the team environment, that positive interpersonal exchange and positive supervisory relationships were especially important aspects of creative climate.

Integration

When one considers these observations a key dichotomy emerges. On the one hand a psychologically safe interpersonal, immediate, work environment contributes to creative performance. On the other hand, creative work occurs in a competitive, conflict laden, professional environment. This dichotomy poses a fundamental question: why do creative people need a safe local environment when working in a demanding, conflict laden, professional environment?

The simple answer to this question is creative work in a professional sense is a high risk venture where success is not insured. Indeed, as Huber (1998) reminds us most creative efforts are doomed to failure. To accept this risk, and pursue creative work, however, people must find support from somewhere—apparently, as Amabile has argued (Amabile & Kramer, 2011), in their local work environment. Thus creative people see local safety as protecting them from the global risk which characterizes the professional environment.

Although this observation may seem quite straightforward, it poses a number of noteworthy questions. For example, when is the risk of the professional environment more salient than the safety of the local environment? What work events make the professional environment as opposed to the local environment a key consideration in guiding the behavior of people doing creative work? How do people manage, or think about, concerns with safety and concerns with risk as they start work on creative tasks?

We do not know the answers to any of these questions, or a host of other questions, broached by the need for local safety when dealing with global risk. By the same token, however, we would argue that in attempts to facilitate creative work we must begin to look for mechanisms that promote integration of the professional and team environments. Indeed, Amabile, Schatzel, Moneta, and Kramer (2004) have argued leaders may play a key role in structuring creative teams so as to serve professional domains. Damanpour and Aravind (2012) have argued that organizations should structure themselves in such a way as to ensure a safe albeit professional work environment. Mumford and Hunter (2005) have argued that team process may prove critical to the effective integration of these two environmental pressures.

Although it is too soon to know exactly how such integrative research will play out, we do need to begin asking how we might manage creative people for local safety as they confront global risk. By bringing to fore the importance of psychological safety Amabile has defined half the equation. The key question confronting us in the future is how the two sides of this equation, the team and the profession, interact and what these interactions imply for the management of creative work.

Acknowledgements We would like to thank Sam Hunter, Logan Watts, Logan Steele, and Kelsey Medeiros for their contributions to the present effort. Correspondence should be addressed to Dr. Michael D. Mumford, Department of Psychology, The University of Oklahoma, Norman, Oklahoma 73019 or mmumford@ou.edu.

References

Amabile, T. M., & Conti, R. (1999). Changes in the work environment for creativity during downsizing. *Academy of Management Journal, 42*, 630–641.

Amabile, T. M., Conti, R., Coon, H., Lazenby, J., & Herron, M. (1996). Assessing the work environment for creativity. *Academy of Management Journal, 39*, 1154–1184.

Amabile, T. M., & Gryskiewicz, N. D. (1989). The creative environment scales: Work environment inventory. *Creativity Research Journal, 2*, 231–253.

Amabile, T., & Kramer, S. (2011). *The progress principle: Using small wins to ignite joy, engagement, and creativity at work*. Boston, MA: Harvard Business Review Press.

Amabile, T. M., Schatzel, E. A., Moneta, G. B., & Kramer, S. J. (2004). Leader behavior and the work environment for creativity: Perceived leader support. *The Leadership Quarterly, 15*, 5–32.

Bennich-Björkman, L. (2017). Academic leadership: Embracing uncertainty and diversity by building communication and trust. In M. D. Mumford & S. Hemlin (Eds.), *Handbook of research on leadership and creativity* (pp. 419–434). Cheltenham, UK: Elgar.

Carmeli, A., Reiter-Palmon, R., & Ziv, E. (2010). Inclusive leadership and employee involvement in creative tasks in the workplace: The mediating role of psychological safety. *Creativity Research Journal, 22*, 250–260.

Clydesdale, G. (2006). Creativity and competition: The Beatles. *Creativity Research Journal, 18*, 129–139.

Csikszentmihalyi, M. (1999). Implications of a systems perspective for the study of creativity. In R. T. Sternberg (Ed.), *Handbook of creativity* (pp. 312–338). Cambridge, UK: Cambridge University Press.

Damanpour, F., & Aravind, D. (2012). Organizational structure and innovation revisited: From organic to ambidextrous structure. In M. D. Mumford (Ed.), *Handbook of organizational creativity* (pp. 483–513). San Diego, CA: Academic Press.

Ekvall, G., & Ryhammar, L. (1999). The creative climate: Its determinants and effects at a Swedish University. *Creativity Research Journal, 12*, 303–310.

Feist, G. J. (1999). The influence of personality on artistic and scientific creativity. In R. J. Sternberg (Ed.), *Handbook of creativity* (pp. 273–296). Cambridge, UK: Cambridge University Press.

Fernham, A. (in press). Personality and creativity at work. In M. D. Mumford (Ed.), *Creativity and innovation in organizations.* New York: Taylor & Francis.

Gibson, C., & Mumford, M. D. (2013). Evaluation, criticism, and creativity: Criticism content and effects on creative problem solving. *Psychology of Aesthetics, Creativity, and the Arts, 7,* 314.

Glisson, C., & James, L. R. (2002). The cross-level effects of culture and climate in human service teams. *Journal of Organizational Behavior, 23,* 767–794.

Griffin, M. A., & Neal, A. (2000). Perceptions of safety at work: A framework for linking safety climate to safety performance, knowledge, and motivation. *Journal of Occupational Health Psychology, 5,* 347–358.

Hirak, R., Peng, A. C., Carmeli, A., & Schaubroeck, J. M. (2012). Linking leader inclusiveness to work unit performance: The importance of psychological safety and learning from failures. *The Leadership Quarterly, 23,* 107–117.

Huber, J. C. (1998). Invention and inventivity is a random, Poisson process: A potential guide to analysis of general creativity. *Creativity Research Journal, 11,* 231–241.

Hunter, S. T., Bedell, K. E., & Mumford, M. D. (2007). Climate for creativity: A quantitative review. *Creativity Research Journal, 19,* 69–90.

James, L. R., & Jones, A. P. (1974). Organizational climate: A review of theory and research. *Psychological Bulletin, 81,* 1096–1112.

Joyce, W. F., & Slocum, J. W. (1984). Collective climate: Agreement as a basis for defining aggregate climates in organizations. *Academy of Management Journal, 27,* 721–742.

Kessel, M., Kratzer, J., & Schultz, C. (2012). Psychological safety, knowledge sharing, and creative performance in healthcare teams. *Creativity and Innovation Management, 21,* 147–157.

Lapierre, J., & Giroux, V. (2003). Creativity and work environment in a high-tech context. *Creativity and Work Environment, 12,* 11–23.

Mumford, M. D., & Gustafson, S. B. (1988). Creativity syndrome: Integration, application, and innovation. *Psychological Bulletin, 103,* 27–43.

Mumford, M. D., & Hunter, S. T. (2005). Innovation in organizations: A multi-level perspective on creativity. In F. J. Yammarino & F. Dansereau (Eds.), *Research in multi-level issues* (Vol. IV, pp. 11–74). Oxford, UK: Elsevier.

Mumford, M. D., Medeiros, K. E., & Partlow, P. J. (2012). Creative thinking: Processes, strategies, and knowledge. *The Journal of Creative Behavior, 46,* 30–47.

Root-Bernstein, R. S., Bernstein, M., & Garnier, H. (1995). Correlations between avocations, scientific style, work habits, and professional impact of scientists. *Creativity Research Journal, 8,* 115–137.

Runco, M. A. (in press). Abilities for creative performance. In M, D. Mumford (Ed.), *Creativity and innovation in organizations.* New York: Taylor & Francis.

Schneider, B., White, S. S., & Paul, M. C. (1998). Linking service climate and customer perceptions of service quality: Tests of a causal model. *Journal of Applied Psychology, 83,* 150–163.

Simonton, D. K. (1999). Creativity from a historiometric perspective. In R. J. Sternberg (Ed.), *Handbook of creativity* (pp. 116–136). Cambridge, UK: Cambridge University Press.

Tierney, P., & Farmer, S. M. (2002). Creative self-efficacy: Its potential antecedents and relationship to creative performance. *Academy of Management Journal, 45,* 1137–1148.

West, M. A., Borrill, C. S., Dawson, J. F., Brodbeck, F. C., Shapiro, D. A., & Howard, B. (2003). Leadership clarity and team innovation in health care. *Leadership Quarterly, 14,* 393–410.

11

Reflections on the Impact of Teresa Amabile on the Development of the Field of Group Creativity

Paul B. Paulus

I first met Teresa Amabile at a dinner hosted in 1984 at the Eastern Psychological Association by Robert Kidd, the advisory editor of the Springer Series in Social Psychology. I remember sitting next to Kenneth Gergen as we discussed the importance of the series and its potential influence. Of the 11 volumes in the series at that time, *The Social Psychology of Creativity* (Amabile, 1983) turned out to be the most successful by far in terms of citations and impact. My edited volume on *Basic Group Processes* (Paulus, 1983) had many fine chapters but was not a big hit. There are a lot of factors that may have been responsible for the difference in the success of the books such as the type of volume, the area of focus, or the degree of creative novelty and usefulness. I think most would agree that the Amabile volume greatly broadened attentional focus of creativity research, which had up to that time focused

P. B. Paulus (✉)
University of Texas at Arlington, Arlington, TX, USA
e-mail: paulus@uta.edu

R. Reiter-Palmon et al. (eds.), *Creativity at Work*,
Palgrave Studies in Creativity and Innovation in Organizations,
https://doi.org/10.1007/978-3-030-61311-2_11

mostly on personal characteristics related to creativity. Interestingly, the term "group" was not found in the subject index of *The Social Psychology of Creativity* and the term "creativity" was not in the subject index of *Basic Group Processes*. Therefore, as Amabile was linking creativity with social processes, there was little recognition of the link between groups and creativity. Although there was some hype in popular books about the creative potential of teams (see review by Paulus, Brown, & Ortega, 1999) and discussions of the topic in the scholarly literature (Stein, 1975), systematic studies of group creativity using the brainstorming paradigm had found that groups were less productive in creative efforts than similar size collectives of individuals. Amabile in the 1983 volume and the 1996 revision noted this research as evidence for the low creative potential of groups. This perspective was solidly supported by a couple of subsequent reviews by Diehl & Stroebe (1987) and Mullen, Johnson and Salas (1991). Mullen et al. (1991) concluded that "..the long-lived popularity of brainstorming techniques is unequivocally and substantively misguided" p. 18.

The paper by Diehl & Stroebe (1987) stimulated my students and I to begin a program of research to examine in more detail the processes involved in group creativity and the creative potential of groups. Interestingly, at that time we found very few studies with the term "group creativity" in the literature. Our intellectual process involved immersing ourselves in the individual creativity literature and "inhaling" the *Social Psychology of Creativity*. In the beginning of this process, I found the work by Amabile and colleagues a great source of inspiration. They had legitimized the study of social creativity, laid a foundation for the evaluation of creative products, and provided a sophisticated theoretical perspective that could potentially be applied to group creativity. The componential model developed by Amabile provides a clear road map for research on group creativity. The group context requires task presentation and tapping one's own cognitive networks and that of group members to produce potentially creative products. The extent to which groups are effective in this process should depend on their collective motivation, domain relevant skills of the group members, and their creativity relevant skills, including skills for effective working on group contexts. Our research and that of others has provided evidence for the importance of all these factors in group creativity (cf., Paulus & Nijstad, 2019).

Our first published efforts revealed the importance of social influence processes in group creativity and led to the development of a social influence model of group creativity which highlighted the importance of social comparison processes. When Vincent Brown, a cognitive psychologist, became my colleague at the University of Texas at Arlington, we explored in detail the cognitive processes related to group creativity (e.g., Brown & Paulus, 1996; Brown, Tumeo, Larey, & Paulus, 1998). He was ahead of his time in developing sophisticated computational simulations of the group creative process and linking these to the various outcomes of our research. We also explored personal characteristics related to group creativity. We ended up with a broad perspective of group creativity that was similar in a number of ways to the broad scope of the componential model of creativity (Paulus & Brown, 2007; Paulus, Dugosh, Dzindolet, Coskun, & Putman, 2002). In our intellectual process, we did not consciously follow the componential perspective. Creativity can be hindered by premature fixation on the ideas of others and building on the ideas from others may work best when we intellectually appropriate those ideas into our own intellectual framework (John-Steiner, 2000; Wicklund, 1989). That is, making something intellectually our own may be an important factor in increasing one's intrinsic motivation to pursue certain areas or topics of research. However, we did build on the componential model, and it is clear that we owe a great intellectual and motivational debt to Teresa Amabile's ground breaking efforts and that of her students and colleagues. In fact, in the paper by Kurtzberg and Amabile (2001) it is clear that they anticipated the potential synergistic effects of group creativity.

There is now considerable evidence for the creative potential of groups and detailed models have highlighted the various cognitive and motivational processes involved (Nijstad & Stroebe, 2006; Paulus & Brown, 2007). There are of course unique aspects that come into play in a collaborative setting. The composition of the group in terms of its diversity relevant to the task is important (Paulus, van der Zee, & Kenworthy, 2019). The method of group interaction is also critical in determining the outcome for groups. Methods that facilitate efficient exchange of ideas such a by writing or electronic procedures are most likely to demonstrate the synergistic benefit of group creativity—groups exceeding the creative productivity of similar size collectives on individuals (Dennis, Minas, & Williams, 2019; Paulus & Kenworthy, 2019). The negative research cited on brainstorming in the *Social Psychology of Creativity* and in the papers by Diehl & Stroebe (1987) and Mullen et al. (1991) involved verbal interaction paradigms which limit the ability for effective exchange of ideas. Research has also demonstrated that group interaction can be quite useful for building on the ideas of others (Kohn et al., 2011) and that some degree of alternation of group and solitary creativity may be optimal (Korde & Paulus, 2017).

There is now a solid empirical and theoretical foundation for the field of group creativity (Paulus & Nijstad, 2003, 2019). Interestingly, most of the chapters included in these group creativity volumes cite the work by Amabile. It is clear that the development of that field was greatly facilitated by the social psychological perspective of Amabile. Group creativity research also benefited from the consensual assessment technique. Most studies use the number of ideas generated as one measure of creativity, but this is typically supplemented by measures of quality such as the average novelty and feasibility of the ideas. The acceptance of the consensual method as a reasonable and valid approach to evaluating creative outcomes greatly facilitated the ability of group creativity researchers to showcase the various outcomes of creative interactions. It is not surprising that this methodological contribution is one key basis for the continuing high level of citations of Amabile. It is often the case that useful methods contribute significantly to theory development (Greenwald, 2012).

We typically assess both the novelty and feasibility of ideas using consensual assessment. Assessment of these dimensions is obviously also important for practical considerations, certainly in a business environment. However, one negative side effect of this emphasis on the development of high-quality products in short-term sessions is the failure to appreciate and enjoy novelty for its own sake (Kaufman, 2018). I think researchers have taken this guideline too seriously. It should not be a requirement for every study. Premature fixation on feasibility or utility or impact by individuals or groups is likely to constrain the process of generating truly novel ideas and might even reduce intrinsic motivation. Feasibility, utility, and impact can come later in the more convergent phase of the creative process (see also Litchfield, Gilson, & Gilson, 2015). It is also true that novelty and feasibility are often negatively correlated, and that typically the feasible ideas win out in the selection process. Therefore, a lot of creativity can be lost or not effectively tapped. However, there are some who argue that a simultaneous focus on both novelty and feasibility may be optimal (Bledow, Frese, Anderson, Erez, & Farr, 2009; Harvey & Kou, 2013). This is obviously an interesting area for further exploration.

Amabile's body of work and theoretical efforts also can be a platform for future efforts in group creativity. In the beginning of her 1983 book, Teresa describes how her experiences in first grade with constraints on her artistic efforts may have reduced her motivation for that type of activity. This helped fuel her interest in creativity "killers." I wonder if a similar pattern of "loss" can be found for collaborative creativity. I have observed much creative play in young children, including my grandchildren. However, this seems to dissipate as they get older. This may be due to the creativity killer impact of external constraints but also could reflect developmental issues such as the process of developing one's unique identity and may be one reason for the relatively low level of collaborative problem-solving skills in secondary school students (Graesser et al., 2018) Since there appears to be very little research on collaborative creativity in children, this is an area wide open for exploration.

Another issue of interest is the relationship of intrinsic motivation to group creativity. This potential application of the componential theory was suggested in several of Amabile's papers (Amabile, Conti, Coon, Lazenby, & Herron, 1996; Kurtzberg & Amabile, 2001). Although intrinsic motivation was a central focus in the research program of Amabile, as far as I am aware this issue has not been examined systematically in group contexts (cf., Chen, Farh, Campbell-Bush, Wu, & Wu, 2013; Cooper & Jayatilaka, 2006). There has been a recognition of the collective motivation of pairs of creative collaborators—people who are on the same page, who complement each other beautifully, and who experience conceptual synchrony (John-Steiner, 2000). Marie and Pierre Curie, Watson and Crick, and Tversky and Kahneman are just a few examples. Many high-tech companies have been founded by a pair of highly motivated and compatible individuals. There may be a joint level of intrinsic motivation that binds such efforts.

Bennis and Biederman (1997) highlight what it takes to attain collective genius by examining such organizations as Xerox PARC, the Manhattan Project and Disney Animation. Their list includes member characteristics and leadership, but they also mention that these top groups "think they are on a mission from God," have a high degree of autonomy, and deem their creative work as its own reward in that group members appear to be intrinsically motivated for creative problem-solving. This of course fits nicely with Amabile's social influence perspective of creativity. Bennis & Biederman (1997) note that most great groups last only a short time, and that "few groups rise to greatness, while most flounder." (p. xvi). They note that the intensity of such groups is one reason for their inevitable demise. However, I wonder if some extrinsic pressures that may impinge on successful groups may eventually reduce their strong intrinsic motivation. The Beatles are one example that comes to mind. The many pressures that resulted from their success and the constant demands for large concerts may have been factors that reduced the intrinsic pleasure they experienced from their collective work in their early days. They stopped touring after only four years together and broke up officially in 8 years. Unfortunately, intrinsic motivation may also be a factor in the impact of hate groups. These groups have obviously involved a high degree of self-selection and are highly motivated to develop new ways to promote their cause. The persistence of such groups may in part be based on the persistence of their shared hate for other groups and the lack of impact of external factors on this type of motivation.

A research program on intrinsically motivated groups would face many challenges. It would have to explore the role of self-selection. Dynamic creative dyads typically find their compatible partners. It will be harder for this to occur at the group level. Can such groups be made? Some examples of groups that might fit that category are the New England Patriots, the Bletchley Park code breakers, and special operations groups. Putting together such exceptional groups requires careful selection of its members and experiences that allow for the development of both a strong sense of cohesion and the development of group level mental maps for effective collaborations.

The componential model of creativity could be expanded to serve as a platform to highlight critical factors for the development of great and highly motivated creative groups. The social environment will be an important factor. Is it an environment that encourages innovation, provides psychological safety, and facilitates both structured and casual group interactions? Both domain relevant skills, complementarity and integration of skills, and effective creative group processes are required. How influential will be the creativity killers highlighted for individual creativity such as lack of autonomy, external pressures, etc.? Will it have the same impact on groups or will groups be able to maintain their intrinsic motivation through mutual influence processes? The key requirement in this type of research would be to develop some type of measure of group intrinsic motivation in addition to measures of group member synchrony, complementarity, and intellectual and conceptual integration, shared meanings and co-construction of knowledge (John-Steiner, 2000; Schrage, 1990; Vygotsky 1978).

Amabile and others recognized the importance of combining individual and group creativity for optimal outcomes (Amabile, 1996; Csikszentmihalyi, 1996; Kurtzberg & Amabile, 2001). Evidence for this comes from examination of the lives of highly creative people and experimental studies (e.g., Korde & Paulus, 2017; Paulus & Yang, 2000). This is an important area for future exploration. The appropriate balance will vary for type of activity, type of person, and phase of the creative process. A comprehensive model of this balancing process would likely involve some integration of the componential model with group creativity models.

Amabile's early research highlighted the negative effects of evaluation on creativity. Research on group creativity has also emphasized the importance of low degree of evaluation (Diehl & Stroebe, 1987). For example, Osborn (1963) and others (e.g., Puccio, et al., 2018; Rosing et al., 2018) have noted that it is best if evaluation is deferred during the divergent creativity stage. However, others have argued for the benefit of mixing idea generation and evaluation processes (Bledow et al., 2009;

Harvey & Kou, 2013). In group contexts the number of ideas generated can be quite large in a short period of time. The evaluation process at the group level may be quite overwhelming. Mixing evaluation and generation sessions may allow for more careful evaluation processing and increase the likelihood of selecting novel ideas and building on them. Some additional theoretical development and research is required to explicate this issue and in the evaluation of those ideas there may be a bias toward feasibility

Another interesting issue is the role of gender composition in great groups. Those discussed by Bennis and Biederman (1997) were predominantly male, in large part because of a potentially limited pool available in the disciplines involved. However, recent research has found that collective intelligence in groups is enhanced by the inclusion of females (Woolley, Chabris, Pentland, Hashmi, & Malone, 2010). Even Osborn (1949) noted the effectiveness of mixed gender teams for creativity. Woolley et al. (2010) attribute the enhanced performance for groups with females to the social skills of female group members, but this effect may not hold for all-female groups. Does the mixing of gender and other task relevant diverse characteristics that are related to enhanced group performance have this positive impact in part due to the related increase in group level intrinsic motivation?

Isaac Newton and many others have suggested that we all stand on the shoulders of giants. My colleagues and I have built on the contributions of many giants in the creativity domain, but Teresa Amabile ranks as number one among these giants. I am grateful for all the groundwork she laid that helped pave the way for our work and enabling us to "jump off her shoulders."

References

Amabile, T. M. (1983). *The social psychology of creativity.* New York, NY: Springer-Verlag.

Amabile, T. M. (1996). *Creativity in context*. Boulder, CO: Westview Press.

Amabile, T. M., Conti, R., Coon, H., Lazenby, J., & Herron, M. (1996). Assessing the work environment for creativity. *Academy of Management Journal, 39*(5), 1154–1184. https://doi.org/10.2307/256995.

Bennis, W. G., & Biederman, P. W. (1997). *Organizing genius*. Reading, MA: Addison-Wesley.

Bledow, R., Frese, M., Anderson, N. R., Erez, M., & Farr, J. L. (2009). A dialectic perspective on innovation: Conflicting demands, multiple pathways, and ambidexterity. *Industrial and Organizational Psychology: Perspectives on Science and Practice, 2,* 305–337. https://doi.org/1754-9426/09.

Brown, V., & Paulus, P. B. (1996). A simple dynamic model of social factors in group brainstorming. *Small Group Research, 27,* 91–114.

Brown, V., Tumeo, M., Larey, T. S., & Paulus, P. B. (1998). Modeling cognitive interactions during group brainstorming. *Small Group Research, 29,* 495–526.

Chen, G., Farh, J., Campbell-Bush, E., Wu, Z., & Wu, X. (2013). Teams as innovative systems: Multilevel motivational antecedents of innovation in R&D teams. *Journal of Applied Psychology, 98*(6), 1018–1027.

Cooper, R. B., & Jayatilaka, B. (2006). Group creativity: The effects of extrinsic, intrinsic, and obligation motivations. *Creativity Research Journal, 18*(2), 153–172.

Csikszentmihalyi, M. (1996). *Creativity: Flow and the psychology of discovery and invention.* New York, NY: Harper Perennial.

Dennis, A., Minas, R. K., & Williams, M. L. (2019). Creativity in computer-mediated virtual groups. In P. B. Paulus & B. A. Nijstad (Eds.), *Handbook of group creativity and innovation* (pp. 253–269). New York: Oxford University Press.

Diehl, M., & Stroebe, W. (1987). Productivity loss in brainstorming groups: Toward the solution of a riddle. *Journal of Personality and Social Psychology, 53,* 497–509.

Graesser, A. C., Fiore, S. M., Greiff, S., Andrews-Todd, J., Foltz, P. W., Friedrich, W., et al. (2018). Advancing the science of collaborative problem solving. *Psychological Science in the Public Interest, 19*(2), 59–92.

Greenwald, A. G. (2012). There is nothing so theoretical as a good method. *Perspectives on Psychological Science, 7*(2), 99–108.

Harvey, S., & Kou, C. Y. (2013). Collective engagement in creative tasks: The role of evaluation in the creative process in groups. *Administrative Science Quarterly, 58*(3), 346–386.

John-Steiner, V. (2000). *Creative collaboration.* New York, NY: Oxford University Press.

Kaufman, J. C. (2018). Finding meaning with creativity in the past, present, and future. *Perspectives on Psychological Science, 13*(6), 734–749.

Kohn, N. W., Paulus, P. B., & Choi, Y. (2011). Building on the ideas of others: An examination of the idea combination process. *Journal of Experimental Social Psychology, 47,* 554–561.

Korde, R., & Paulus, P. B. (2017). Alternating individual and group idea generation: Finding the elusive synergy. *Journal of Experimental Social Psychology, 70,* 177–190.

Kurtzberg, T. R., & Amabile, T. M. (2001). From Guilford to creative synergy: Opening the black box of team-level creativity. *Creativity Research Journal, 13*(3–4), 285–294.

Litchfield, R. C., Gilson, L. L., & Gilson, P. W. (2015). Defining creative ideas: Toward a more nuanced approach. *Group and Organization Management, 40*(2), 238–265.

Mullen, B., Johnson, C., & Salas, E. (1991). Productivity loss in brainstorming groups: A meta-analytic integration. *Basic and Applied Social Psychology, 12*(1), 3–23.

Nijstad, B. A., & Stroebe, W. (2006). How the group affects the mind: A cognitive model of idea generation in groups. *Personality and Social Psychology Review, 10,* 186–213.

Osborn, A. (1949). *Your creative power: How to use imagination.* New York: Charles Scribner's Sons.

Osborn, A. F. (1963). *Applied imagination* (2nd ed.). New York: Scribner.

Paulus, P. B. (Ed.). (1983). *Basic group processes.* New York: Springer-Verlag.

Paulus, P. B., & Brown, V. R. (2007). Toward more creative and innovative group idea generation: A cognitive-social motivational perspective of brainstorming. *Social and Personality Compass, 1,* 248–265.

Paulus, P. B., Brown, V., & Ortega, A. H. (1999). Group creativity. In R. E. Purser & A. Montuori (Eds.), *Social creativity* (Vol. 2, pp. 151–176). Cresskill, NJ: Hampton Press.

Paulus, P. B., Dugosh, K. L., Dzindolet, M. T., Coskun, H., & Putman, V. L. (2002). Social and cognitive influences in group brainstorming. Predicting production gains and losses. *European Review of Social Psychology, 12,* 299–325.

Paulus, P. B., & Kenworthy, J. (2019). Effective brainstorming. In P. B. Paulus & B. A. Nijstad (Eds.), *Handbook of group creativity: Innovation through collaboration* (pp. 287–306). New York: Oxford University Press.

Paulus, P. B., & Nijstad, B. A. (Eds.). (2003). *Group creativity: Innovation through collaboration*. New York: Oxford University Press.
Paulus, P. B., & Nijstad, B. A. (Eds.) (2019). *The Oxford handbook of group creativity and innovation*. New York: Oxford.
Paulus, P. B., van der Zee, K. I., & Kenworthy, J. (2019). Diversity and group creativity. In P. B. Paulus & B. A. Nijstad (Eds.), *Handbook of group creativity and innovation* (pp. 33–49). New York: Oxford University Press.
Paulus, P. B., & Yang, H. (2000). Idea generation in groups: A basis for creativity in organizations. *Organizational Behavior and Human Decision Processes, 82*(1), 76–87.
Puccio, G. J., Burnett, C., Acar, S., Yudess, J. A., Holinger, M., & Cabra, J. F. (2018). Creative problem solving in small groups: The effects of creativity training on idea generation, solution creativity, and leadership effectiveness. *The Journal of Creative Behavior, 0,* 1–19. https://doi.org/10.1002/jocb.381.
Rosing, K., Bledow, R., Frese, M., Baytalskaya, N., Lascano, J. J., & Farr, L. (2018). The temporal pattern of creativity and implementation in teams. *Journal of Occupational and Organizational Psychology, 91,* 798–822.
Schrage, M. (1990). *Shared minds: The new technologies of collaboration*. Bloomington and Indianapolis: Indiana University Press.
Stein, M. J. (1975). *Stimulating creativity. Volume II-Group procedures*. New York: Academic Press.
Vygotsky, L. S. (1978). *Mind in society: The development of higher psychological processes*. Cambridge, MA: MIT Press.
Wicklund, R. A. (1989). The appropriation of ideas. In P. B. Paulus (Ed.), *Psychology of group influence* (pp. 393–423). Hillsdale, NJ: Lawrence Erlbaum Associates Inc.
Woolley, A. W., Chabris, C. F., Pentland, A., Hashmi, N., & Malone, T. W. (2010). Evidence for a collective intelligence factor in the performance of human groups. *Science, 330*(6004), 686–688.

12

An Intellectual Journey: The Path from Creativity in Context to a Social Network Perspective of Creativity

Jill Perry-Smith

We live in an era where creativity is a vibrant and robust field of research within the organizational sciences. At a recent conference, a small group of creativity researchers debated whether or not the field has matured. My perspective is that it is not mature in the sense that we have not run out of ideas; many puzzles remain, and more reveal themselves every day. However, from the perspective of scope, the field is mature. The body of creativity research and the active scholars for whom creativity is central to their identity are both broad. At the 2019 Annual Meeting of the Academy Management, for instance, there were twenty sessions with a creativity theme. When I was a doctoral student, I only recall one! The distinction between now, and the creativity field when I first entered, is striking. At the heart of not only this context, but also my research, is Teresa Amabile. Her writings and research undergird my

J. Perry-Smith (✉)
Gozuieta Business School, Emory University, Atlanta, GA, USA
e-mail: jill.perry-smith@emory.edu

R. Reiter-Palmon et al. (eds.), *Creativity at Work*,
Palgrave Studies in Creativity and Innovation in Organizations,
https://doi.org/10.1007/978-3-030-61311-2_12

research program and were foundational even when creativity research was a niche field.

Imprinting

When I entered my doctoral program, I did not intend to study creativity. My initial ideas had little to do with the topic. This changed when I read some of my advisor, Christina Shalley's, published papers (e.g., Shalley, 1995). I did not yet identify as a creative person, nor did I recognize myself as having any experience with creativity. But, as I read, I realized that my prior professional experience as an engineer indeed required creative problem-solving. That is, coming up with novel and useful solutions to complex problems were key to my work. I was curious about what I read, and I wanted to learn more. When I expressed interest in working with Christina and researching creativity, she told me to read more. In particular, she directed me to read *Creativity in Context* by Teresa Amabile (1996).

This was a powerful imprinting experience for me. Imprinting research suggests that early influences endure and effect future attitudes and behavior (Bianchi, 2013; Higgins, 2005). In particular, I found Amabile's componential model and her focus on individual motivation, cognitive skills, and knowledge broad enough to be inclusive but parsimonious enough to be memorable. I say this from, at the time, the perspective of a new doctoral student who was bombarded with many theoretical perspectives, models, and domains. *Creativity in Context* became a theoretical Bible for me—a piece of text referred to again and again and again—as I began the journey of developing a research program.

Building and Extending

I describe my research journey from the perspective of three core aspects of Teresa's seminal research: intrinsic motivation, domain relevant knowledge, and creative process. I initially was fascinated by how social context can dampen intrinsic motivation. As my interests developed more centrally around social networks as a key contextual element, my fascination shifted to domain relevant knowledge, a less explored aspect of the componential model. My research progressed to theorizing about creativity over time, emphasizing the creativity and innovation process, and the winnowing of novelty as an idea moves and stalls between phases. I explain these three influences on my research program to date starting with intrinsic motivation.

Social Context & Intrinsic Motivation

In my first published paper (Shalley & Perry-Smith, 2001), Christina Shalley and I investigated the effect of controlling, informational evaluation, and creative models on creativity. At the center of our argumentation, the core to our theorizing, lay intrinsic motivation. Amabile's foundational insight was key to our research development, as our underlying assumption was that people must be intrinsically motivated to be creative. We also sought to disentangle conflicting results about expected evaluation and, in particular, the notion that expected evaluation undermines creativity and intrinsic motivation. Building on Amabile's (1979) and Shalley's (1995) prior work, we employed cognitive evaluation and social cognitive theories to predict that informational expected evaluation facilitated creativity, while controlling evaluation undermined it. In doing so, we extended Amabile's social contextual research to reveal how one contextual factor—evaluation—can be good or bad depending on type. This project was my first dive into creativity; Amabile's research clearly influenced its development and my emerging view of creativity as a social process.

Social Networks & Domain Relevant Knowledge

In parallel with my investigation of creativity, my interest in social networks emerged. Like creativity, I did not know that I would study networks when I entered graduate school. In fact, I was not aware that social networks were a domain of study. I recall my first introduction to a social network paper (Ibarra, 1992) in a research seminar; I was fascinated by the methodology and theories, and how the power of the informal social context aligned with my professional experience. At the same time, I was disappointed. I found various references to novelty and creativity (e.g., Ibarra & Andrews, 1993), but I considered them both intriguing and incomplete, given the rich theorizing of Amabile and others. From my vantage point, these references were important yet passing nods, rather than fully articulated reasonings or predictions. In short, social network research clearly recognized the role of creativity as a key advantage, but in an incomplete and simplified way that did not reflect creativity's complexity.

In the 1990s, most creativity research emphasized the intrinsic motivation component of Amabile's componential model. The domain-relevant knowledge component stood out to me as being central to how and when network characteristics influence creativity. The social network domain largely emanates from sociology and macro perspectives of organizations. As such, the social network field's initial emphasis on novelty largely centered on the transference of novel ideas and inventions through networks at the firm level (e.g., Rogers, 1983). Amabile's componential model describes how domain relevant knowledge is one of three key components that facilitates generating ideas. This prompted my interest in networks as helping or harming individuals who come up with new ideas, not just enhancing individuals' exposure to new ideas developed by others.

While Amabile's social-psychological approach set up the notion of creativity as influenced by social factors, in a paper with Christina Shalley (Perry-Smith & Shalley, 2003) and a paper based on my dissertation (Perry-Smith, 2006), I went beyond the componential model to explore social context's richness as expressed by social networks. I spring-boarded from creativity as a social process to creativity as an interpersonal, social-network one. At the core of my research are the influences of direct and indirect relationships, as well as network structure, while I simultaneously stay true to the social-psychological perspective of creativity. I have sought to apply theoretical principles and methodologies from the creativity field, with Teresa Amabile's clear influence, to the social network field. This research theorizes that network ties and structures that provide exposure to a breadth of knowledge equip individuals with a deeper reservoir of knowledge, which aids novel combinations. Weak ties and central network positions provide this type of breadth, my findings suggested, but are not expected to enhance intrinsic motivation, although other ties and structures may. This perspective adds to Teresa's view that the work environment influences creativity primarily through intrinsic motivation by suggesting that it also may influence creativity through domain relevant skills.

Later, I pushed more on the domain relevant knowledge component of Amabile's componential model. I noticed network scholars who emphasized networks' role in facilitating nonredundant knowledge, or knowledge that is unique relative to what other network ties provide, and theorized about the benefits primarily for individual outcomes such as individual performance, salary, and promotion. Creativity was often included as another byproduct, rather than its own central outcome (e.g., Mehra, Kilduff, & Brass, 2001). It struck me that core to domain relevant knowledge for creativity was having the appropriate foundation to generate and assess the viability of novel ideas. The articulation of knowledge in the network literature did not account for the cognitive or psychological needs associated with creativity.

In Perry-Smith (2014), I extended the domain relevant knowledge component of Amabile's core theory by investigating the kind of knowledge received from network ties, information (i.e., facts or data) versus frames (i.e., interpretations or impressions), that facilitates creative ideas. In her theorizing, Amabile (1983) described how knowledge accumulation is good, but more important is how it effects the organization of content in the mind. Although network scholars primarily emphasized the transfer of nonredundant knowledge, there were some hints that network ties also change perspectives. Thus, individuals come out of interactions and are affected by them in terms of their vantage point. Here, I provided evidence of self-generating novel ideas versus merely adopting other's ideas by using an experimental design, atypical in network research, where participants generated solutions, and creativity was assessed using Amabile's consensual assessment technique.

Social Networks & Creative Process

In addition, in a paper with Pier Mannucci (Perry-Smith & Mannucci, 2017) we built on Amabile's definition of creativity. Although receiving less attention than the four phases of the idea journey, a very interesting aspect of the paper is that we disentangle the novel and useful components of creativity as an idea progresses or stalls between phases. We outline the ideal linear progression of an idea through phases, but we also describe the impact of continuous cycling between phases, and interactions with the wrong types of ties, on the delicate balance between novelty and usefulness. In particular, we argue that as an idea cycles back to an earlier journey phase, that idea is likely to be stripped of its novelty as creators work to make the idea more viable and thus more useful. This compliments Amabile and Pratt's (2017) process model by describing how later phases of the process and how linear versus cyclical progression through phases may actually decrease novelty. I continue to be intrigued by the novelty and usefulness components of Amabile's definition of creativity, and I hope to see more theoretical and empirical work push on the ebb and flow of these components.

As shown by these examples, Amabile's work has been foundational to my social-network view of creativity. Her research shaped my vantage point and influenced the way I consumed the social-network research I read as a doctoral student. Now, as an experienced organizational scholar, rather than a newcomer to the field, I shift to my thoughts on Amabile's work from the perspective of where I am today.

Research Values and Impact

Though I admire how her theorizing and empirics influenced my research program, Teresa Amabile's scholarly footprint, values, and identity, or the ways in which she tackles research and contributes to the field, are truly impactful. Her boundary-spanning role brought approaches from social psychology and the study of children (e.g., Amabile, 1989) firmly into the organizational realm. She went from an outsider reshaping the field to an insider central to a robust community of organizational creativity scholars, and she transformed the way organizational behaviorists study creativity. It is difficult to imagine a creativity paper that does not cite Teresa Amabile's research. Whether her definition of creativity, her articulation of creativity's contextual view, or aspects of her componential model, recognizing Amabile's research as foundational is necessary. While we can see the success of this now, it is not easy to be a boundary-spanner of different research domains. I have observed doctoral students struggle with spanning research boundaries, and I have been challenged with this as well. Identifying an audience from disparate domains, and, once identified, speaking firmly to each domain in ways true to their unique cores, are just a few examples of this difficulty. I admire Teresa Amabile's success in tackling such challenges. I hope my research will serve a similar bridge between social-network research and creativity research.

I also respect and appreciate Amabile's willingness to reflect on the messiness of creativity. I see in her theorizing a key skill of breaking down something complex and messy in ways that bring order and are testable, but that also leave room for new questions, answers, and extensions. I often repeat Amabile's view from many of her papers (e.g., Amabile, 1982, 1988) that creativity is something that is difficult to articulate; experts "know it when they see it." For some, this is not a satisfying point of view, because it is more difficult to come up with an objective indicator. However, the beauty of the consensual assessment technique is that it reflects the inherent messiness of creativity. Amabile, Barsade, Mueller & Staw's empirical paper (2005) conveys this point of reflecting the messiness of creativity in a different way. The data are drawn from a large diary study that allowed for both qualitative and quantitative analysis, which yielded insights about the tricky role of affect over time and across days. Given the organizational context and varied data, the study distilled this complexity into a cyclic perspective of affect and creativity.

Conclusion

Without Amabile's guiding work, so much creativity research, including my own, would be very different. My social-network view of creativity is birthed from her notions of creativity as a social-psychological versus intraindividual perspective. As my research program continues and my ideas morphs and develops, I imagine Amabile's work as a continual foundation. Beyond being foundational to my research, Amabile's approach to research and her success in shaping a field offers many guiding posts for scholars beyond creativity.

References

Amabile, T. M. (1979). Effects of external evaluation on artistic creativity. *Journal of Personality and Social Psychology, 37,* 221–233.

Amabile, T. M. (1982). The social psychology of creativity: A consensual assessment technique. *Journal of Personality and Social Psychology, 43,* 997–1013.

Amabile, T. M. (1983). The social psychology of creativity: A componential conceptualization. *Journal of Personality and Social Psychology, 45,* 357–377.

Amabile, T. M. (1988). A model of creativity and innovation in organizations. In B. M. Staw & L. L. Cummings (Eds.), *Research in organizational behavior* (Vol. 10). Greenwich, CT: JAI Press.

Amabile, T. M. (1989). *Growing up creative*. New York: Crown.

Amabile, T. M. (1996). *Creativity in context*. Boulder, CO: Westview Press.

Amabile, T. M., Barsade, S. G., Mueller, J. S., & Staw, B. M. (2005). Affect and Creativity at Work. *Administrative Science Quarterly, 50,* 367–403.

Amabile, T. M., & Pratt, M. G. (2017). The dynamic componential model of creativity and innovation in organizations: Making progress, making meaning. In B. Staw & A. Brief (Eds.), *Research in Organizational Behavior, 37,* 157–183.

Bianchi, E. (2013). The bright side of bad times: The affective advantages of entering the workforce in a recession. *Administrative Science Quarterly, 58,* 587–623.

Higgins, M. (2005). *Career imprints: Creating Leaders across an industry*. San Francisco: Wiley.

Ibarra, H. (1992). Homophily and differential returns: Sex differences in network structure and access in an advertising firm. *Administrative Science Quarterly, 37,* 422–447.

Ibarra, H., & Andrews, S. B. (1993). Power, social influence, and sense making: Effects of network centrality on employee perceptions. *Administrative Science Quarterly, 38,* 277–303.

Mehra, A., Kilduff, M., & Brass, D. J. (2001). The social networks of high and low self-monitors: Implications for workplace performance. *Administrative Science Quarterly, 46,* 121–146.

Perry-Smith, J. E. (2006). Social yet creative: The role of social relationships in facilitating individual creativity. *Academy of Management Journal, 49,* 85–101.

Perry-Smith, J. E. (2014). Social network ties beyond non-redundancy: An experimental investigation of the effect of knowledge content and tie strength on creativity. *Journal of Applied Psychology, 99,* 831–846.

Perry-Smith, J. E., & Mannucci, P. V. (2017). From creativity to innovation: The social network drivers of the four phases of the idea journey. *Academy of Management Review, 42,* 53–79.

Perry-Smith, J. E., & Shalley, C. E. (2003). The social side of creativity: A static and dynamic social network perspective. *Academy of Management Review, 28,* 89–106.

Rogers, E. M. (1983). *Diffusion of innovations.* New York: Free Press.

Shalley, C. E. (1995). Effects of coaction, expected evaluation, and goal setting on creativity and productivity. *Academy of Management Journal, 38,* 483–503.

Shalley, C. E., & Perry-Smith, J. E. (2001). Effects of social-psychological factors on creative performance: The role of informational and controlling expected evaluation and modeling experience. *Organizational Behavior and Human Decision Processes, 84,* 1–22.

13

Meaningful Work and Creativity: Mapping Out a Way Forward

Greg Fetzer and Michael G. Pratt

The componential model has been, and continues to be, a foundational piece of the research on creativity. Through several updates (Amabile, 1983, 1988, 1996; Amabile & Pratt, 2016) the componential model remains dynamic and open to changes based on the most recent research. These updates, done "in a spirit of creative inquiry" (Amabile & Pratt, 2016: 2), are a testament to the impact of Teresa's work, as well as her passion for continuing to advance the study of creativity in organizations. One of the authors, Mike, was included in the latest revision of the componential model, where he and Teresa included several new elements, including the progress principle (Amabile & Kramer, 2011), synergistic motivation (Amabile, 1993), and affect (Amabile et al., 2005). Given that the progress principle was about progress in meaningful work, the two also added additional details about the role of meaningful work, and

G. Fetzer · M. G. Pratt (✉)
Carroll School of Management, Chestnut Hill, MA, USA
e-mail: prattmg@bc.edu

R. Reiter-Palmon et al. (eds.), *Creativity at Work*, Palgrave Studies in Creativity and Innovation in Organizations, https://doi.org/10.1007/978-3-030-61311-2_13

particularly, work orientations, in motivating and keeping the creative process going. Although Amabile and Pratt (2016) posit several ways in which meaningful work may influence the creative process, this part of the model remains the most speculative. In our chapter, we build on these initial insights from the revised componential model to discuss two important areas for future research at the intersection of creativity and meaningful work. In particular, we suggest:

1. Moving beyond whether certain work orientations are more or less likely to be creative, and toward uncovering conditions that motivate different orientations to be creative; and
2. Moving beyond the role of meaningfulness in relatively short-term persistence (e.g., the progress principle) to better understand how creative workers persist over the long term.

For each of these directions we raise questions and suggestions for fruitful theorizing and future empirical research.

Meaningful Work and Creativity

Meaningful work is, at the broadest level, work that is perceived as purposeful and significant for the individual(s) doing it (Pratt & Ashforth, 2003). Meaningfulness can be derived from many sources, including: (1) from work itself, such as the types of tasks people engage in (Grant, 2008; Hackman & Oldham, 1976); (2) from our selves: such as beliefs about the role work should play in our lives, including seeing our work as a calling (Bunderson & Thompson, 2009; Dik & Duffy, 2009; Wrzesniewski et al., 1997); (3) and more broadly, from social and cultural accounts, such as how the media portrays "good" work, that provide a justification for why one's work is worth doing (Boova et al., 2019; Lepisto & Pratt, 2017). An important way of exploring meaningful work that is central to the latter two approaches involves the notion of work orientations. Work orientations are "internalized evaluations about what makes work worth doing" (Pratt, Pradies, & Lepisto, 2013: 175). As noted by Pratt and colleagues (2013), although the concept of work orientations has evolved over time (Wrzesniewski et al., 1997), the initial seed came from Teresa's work on intrinsic (i.e., working for its own sake) or extrinsic (i.e., working for something outside the work) motivational orientations (Amabile, 1993; Amabile et al., 1994). Thus, it seems very appropriate that work orientations in their current form have found their way back into the componential model.

Work Orientations

The most comprehensive model of work orientations posits at least six primary orientations: *utilitarian*, sometimes known as *job*, where work is a means to an end (e.g., a paycheck that I use to support my family); *status*, sometimes known as *career*, where work allows me advancement or achievement; *passion*, where work allows me to do what I love; *kinship*, where work allows me to help my workplace "family"; *service*, where work allows me to help others or a greater cause; and *craftsmanship*, where work allows me to continuously improve, to achieve quality (Boova et al., 2019; Pratt et al., 2013). The dynamic componential model (Amabile & Pratt, 2016) presents some preliminary ideas regarding how meaningful work should influence the creative process, especially through its effect on motivation. It suggests some ways in which work orientations, in particular, may influence how persistent individuals are in their creative work—which is conceptualized in terms of a progress loop where individuals find making progress in meaningful work highly motivating on a day-to-day basis (Amabile & Kramer, 2011). Although these suggestions provide a solid foundation for future research, they represent only a fraction of the research possibilities at the intersection of meaningful work and creativity.

Teresa and colleagues' (Amabile et al., 2005; Amabile & Kramer, 2011) comprehensive daily diary study—following 26 teams in seven organizations over five months—illuminated the importance of what they call "the progress principle" (Amabile & Kramer, 2011). Positive inner work life—positive emotions, perceptions, and intrinsic motivation experienced at work—is sustained by the perception that one is making progress in something meaningful every day (Amabile &

Kramer, 2011; Ariely et al., 2008; Fishbach & Finkelstein, 2012). Making progress can set off a virtuous cycle, the progress loop, which allows individuals to sustain positive affect and motivation over time, helping them persist in creative projects (Amabile & Kramer, 2011). Progress in meaningful work is construed differently, however, across individuals and contexts; indeed, what is meaningful in one setting may not be meaningful in another (Rosso et al., 2010). For a scientist trying to develop a treatment for a rare disease, for example, meaningful progress may involve finding a new pattern in data which allows them to develop a novel drug compound; such small wins (Weick, 1984) help the scientist feel they are helping others. By contrast, work on an ad campaign may involve coming up with the "big" idea and then refining it in incremental ways over time. In short, these perceptions of progress in meaningful work are shaped by the individual perceptions around what makes work worth doing in a particular context.

As internalized evaluations about what makes work meaningful, work orientations should shape how individuals persist in creative projects in at least three major ways. First, Amabile and Pratt (2016: 171) suggest that perceptions of meaningful work mediate the relationship between "leaders' statements and actions about innovation and intrinsic motivation." One's work orientation likely plays a key role in this mediation process. Put another way, the degree of "fit" between organizational discourse about work and a given employees' work orientation is likely to predict whether that employee finds the work to be intrinsically motivating or not.[1] More research is needed, however, to understand the complexities of this "fit" process, and what may thwart it. To illustrate, do work orientations change over time to fit with strong organizational cultures? If they are more stable, do individuals self-select out of organizations whose justifications of work do not fit their work orientations, or do they engage in a type of job crafting "fit work" to reflect their own work orientations?

Second and similarly, work orientations should influence the way employees are motivated by incentives. Teresa and others' work has

[1]At present, scholars have not posited a "creative" work orientation. However, if work orientations do start in broader cultural narratives about work (Boova, et al., 2019), then it is possible that the increasing valorization of creativity could lead to such an orientation.

shown that extrinsic rewards can interact synergistically or not with intrinsic motivation (Amabile, 1993; Amabile & Pratt, 2016) and that work orientations provide a lens for understanding "the meanings people attach to extrinsic motivators" (Amabile & Pratt, 2016: 20). Financial incentives, such as bonuses, for example, are likely to be most effective for individuals who have utilitarian orientations; they may also be effective for those with a status orientation, especially in industries where money is a symbol of being a high performer (e.g., finance). For individuals with kinship or service orientations, on the other hand, contact with beneficiaries, both inside and outside the organization should be the most meaningful (Grant et al., 2007). For those with craftsmanship and passion orientations, the work itself is the best incentive, so the key is likely removing barriers that prevent creative workers from deep engagement with tasks (see Pratt et al., 2013). Leaders who provide opportunities for personal self-expression, or who allow learning and improvement opportunities are likely to help make work meaningful for these individuals. Although empirical research has focused on calling and service work orientations (Dik & Duffy, 2009; Grant & Berry, 2011; Wrzesniewski et al., 1997), there remains a paucity of research exploring other orientations (e.g., kinship, job, craftsmanship) and how meaningfulness unfolds and little to no research on how work orientations and leader messaging play out within the context of creative work.

Third, work orientation should shape the ways that individuals collaborate with other organizational members. Recent research shows that teammates can have an important influence on a sense of meaningful work (Buis et al., 2019); this is likely to be especially salient in collaborative creative work. Since work orientation is believed to strongly influence motivation, groups and teams that are heterogeneous with regards to work orientation may be challenged in how they talk about, justify, and ultimately perform their work. For example, team members with craftsmanship and kinship orientations are likely to focus on different aspects of a project: the craftsmanship-oriented member will likely focus on the quality of the work itself, while the kinship-oriented member will be focused on the team's dynamic and interpersonal climate. Such differences could be especially acute when doing creative work where goals can be nebulous or vague as such conditions may make the justification process for "why work is worth doing" up for grabs. Such differences in perspective are likely to have an upside, given the benefits of cognitive diversity for creativity (e.g., Hoever et al., 2012; Shin et al., 2012); however, the contingencies and boundary conditions of when work orientation diversity can be fruitful rather than detrimental for creativity is an important topic for future study. In this way, exploring work orientations can contribute to a relatively under-developed part of the componential model: group creativity.

Persistence in Creative Work

A second important area for future research is understanding the impact of meaningfulness in long-term creative work. Consistent with our discussion above, Amabile and Kramer's (2011) progress principle explains persistence toward proximal creative goals, which are relatively immediate and concrete (e.g., finishing a project). However, individuals can also persist toward more distal creative goals—goals that are more long-term and abstract (e.g., making AI emotionally intelligent, developing a cure for a rare disease, etc.). Such goals are often the drivers of radical innovations (Gilson & Madjar, 2011). Although there has been relatively little research on persistence toward these long-term goals (see Bateman & Barry, 2012 for an exception), we believe that a useful starting point is considering whether such work goals are anchored in the past or the future, when examining the issue of creative persistence.

Although most people think about distal creative goals as being oriented toward the future, our work with bespoke shoemakers (Fetzer & Pratt, 2020), who often have a craftsmanship orientation, opened our eyes to the possibility that some creative work is about bringing the past into the present. For these workers, creativity is necessary but is also shaped and constrained by goals to preserve traditional techniques. For other creative workers (e.g., scientists, cutting-edge technologists, etc.), the goal is to bring the future closer to the present (rather than bringing the past into the present).[2] As we considered the challenges faced by these different types of creative workers (those focused on the past vs. those focused on the future), we began to think about the impact of different temporal orientations toward creative work.

We argue that long-term creative work, in general, is attuned to temporal dynamics associated with both proximal (e.g., what I am making now) and distal (e.g., what do I ultimately hope to achieve) goals. Although concrete, proximal creative goals are focused on the immediate future (e.g., the end of the current project), more distal goals about what a creator hopes to ultimately accomplish may have a qualitatively different effect. The nature of these effects likely depends on whether one's long-term creative goals are to bring the future to the present (*future-anchored goals*) or to bring the past into the present (*past-anchored goals*). More specifically, each goal brings with it certain challenges that we believe should be explored more fully.

The purpose of such *future-anchored goals* is to imagine and elaborate future possibilities. Creativity is essential to long-term, future-oriented work (Hagtvedt, 2019), yet the characteristics of such work seem to pose challenges that make them less conducive to creative ideas. A wealth of evidence points to the importance of intrinsic motivation to creative engagement and performance (e.g., Amabile, 1993, 1996; Amabile & Pratt, 2016). However, future-anchored projects are often high in ambiguity and uncertainty. When an individual does not know where they are going to end up (i.e., what the final product will look like) or when they will arrive, it can be difficult to maintain intrinsic motivation (Amabile, 1985; Bateman & Barry, 2012). This is echoed by research on goal setting which shows that the most motivating goals are one which is specific, concrete, and attainable (Locke et al., 1981, 1988; Locke & Latham, 2004). Future-anchored projects thus present something of a paradox: although motivation is needed to continue pushing forward, the ambiguity around goals and possible outcomes may make such motivation difficult to maintain.

---

[2]One of the authors, Greg, was so enamored with the challenges of bringing the future to the present in creative work that he decided to study these types of creative workers in his dissertation.

Past-anchored work, such as those of bespoke shoemakers and other craft workers, faces a very different set of challenges. On the one hand, what is most meaningful for those who make shoes by hand is to preserve those techniques from the past that would otherwise be lost (Fetzer & Pratt, 2020). On the other hand, current conditions such as differences in shoe styles—as well as limited access to traditional materials and tools—means that creative changes to traditional techniques must somehow be made. The challenge is to balance needed innovations with preserving traditional techniques. Although temporal orientations, such as past- and future-anchored work, came from our research on meaningful work, the connection between temporal orientations and work orientations has yet to be fully fleshed out. We feel that such relationships are likely to be particularly critical, however, in creative work that has more long-term goals than those found in lab-based studies of creativity (see Rouse & Pratt, 2020, for further critiques).

Finally, issues of persistence in meaningful work over the long haul beg the question of what "fuel" can motivate individuals to overcome these various temporally related tensions, as well as other obstacles workers will confront over time. Although Amabile and Kramer (2011) emphasize the importance of positive affect in maintaining the progress loop, the inclusion of meaningful work opens the door to another possibility: the influence of eudaimonic forces in maintaining such progress. Although not explicitly defined as such, positive emotions in creativity research seem to be conceptualized hedonically—as emotions that bring pleasure to the creator. Some perspectives on meaningful work, however, build on eudaimonia rather than hedonia (Lepisto & Pratt, 2017). Like hedonia, eudaimonia is often utilized in conceptualizing well-being. However, eudaimonia also refers to a "process of fulfilling or realizing one's daimon or true nature—that is, of fulfilling one's virtuous potentials and living as one was inherently intended to live" (Deci & Ryan, 2008: 2). Thus, one may be driven not by positive affect, but rather by desires for self-realization (Huta & Waterman, 2014) in the creative process. Taking a more eudaimonic perspective on the progress principle has the potential to fundamentally change how we think about the drive to be creative. For example, Amabile and Kramer (2011: 92) note, "the power of setbacks to diminish happiness is more than twice as strong as the power of progress to boost happiness." Eudaimonia may be important for carrying creative workers over such abysses of frustration or failure that are part of doing highly innovative work. A meaningful (eudaimonic) purpose—one that invokes a person's self-realization and unique potential—may be a stronger sustainer of motivation than hedonic feelings of pleasure which appear to be transitory (e.g., the hedonic treadmill; Brickman & Campbell, 1971).

Conclusion

Inspired by the latest evolution of the componential model (Amabile & Pratt, 2016) in relation to our own work, we have discussed several pathways for future research at the intersection of creativity and meaningful work. In particular, we explore how work orientations can be better integrated into research on creativity both at the individual- and team-level. Moreover, we build from the proximal goal-oriented focus at the heart of "progress from meaningful work" (Amabile & Kramer, 2011) toward exploring more distal goals and their temporal orientations. As noted in our introduction, the revised componential model introduces the potential for research on meaningful work and creativity, and although we have gone further down this path, we realize that we have barely scratched the surface of the richness this blending of theoretical perspectives can produce.

References

Amabile, T. M. (1983). The social psychology of creativity: A componential conceptualization. *Journal of Personality and Social Psychology, 45*(2), 357.

Amabile, T. M. (1985). Motivation and creativity: Effects of motivational orientation on creative writers. *Journal of Personality and Social Psychology, 48*(2), 393.

Amabile, T. M. (1988). A model of creativity and innovation in organizations. *Research in Organizational Behavior, 10*(1), 123–167.

Amabile, T. M. (1993). Motivational synergy: Toward new conceptualizations of intrinsic and extrinsic motivation in the workplace. *Human Resource Management Review, 3*(3), 185–201.
Amabile, T. M. (1996). *Creativity in context*. Boulder: Westview press.
Amabile, T. M., Barsade, S. G., Mueller, J. S., & Staw, B. M. (2005). Affect and creativity at work. *Administrative Science Quarterly, 50*(3), 367–403.
Amabile, T. M., Hill, K. G., Hennessey, B. A., & Tighe, E. M. (1994). The work preference inventory: Assessing intrinsic and extrinsic motivational orientations. *Journal of Personality and Social Psychology, 66*(5), 950.
Amabile, T. M., & Kramer, S. J. (2011). *The progress principle: Using small wins to ignite joy, engagement, and creativity at work*. Cambridge: Harvard Business Press.
Amabile, T. M., & Pratt, M. G. (2016). The dynamic componential model of creativity and innovation in organizations: Making progress, making meaning. *Research in Organizational Behavior, 36,* 157–183.
Ariely, D., Kamenica, E., & Prelec, D. (2008). Man's search for meaning: The case of Legos. *Journal of Economic Behavior & Organization, 67*(3–4), 671–677.
Bateman, T. S., & Barry, B. (2012). Masters of the long haul: Pursuing long-term work goals. *Journal of Organizational Behavior, 33*(7), 984–1006.
Boova, L., Pratt, M. G., & Lepisto, D. A. (2019). Exploring work orientations and cultural accounts of work: Toward a research agenda for examining the role of culture in meaningful work. In *Oxford handbook of meaningful work*.
Brickman, P., & Campbell, D. T. (1971). Hedonic relativism and planning the good science. In. M. H. Appley (Ed.), *Adaptation level theory: A symposium* (pp. 287–302). New York: Academic Press.
Buis, B. C., Ferguson, A. J., & Briscoe, J. P. (2019). Finding the "I" in "Team": The role of groups in an individual's pursuit of calling. *Journal of Vocational Behavior, 114,* 88–99.
Bunderson, J. S., & Thompson, J. A. (2009). The call of the wild: Zookeepers, callings, and the double-edged sword of deeply meaningful work. *Administrative Science Quarterly, 54*(1), 32–57.
Deci, E. L., & Ryan, R. M. (2008). Hedonia, eudaimonia, and well-being: An introduction. *Journal of Happiness Studies, 9*(1), 1–11.
Dik, B. J., & Duffy, R. D. (2009). Calling and vocation at work: Definitions and prospects for research and practice. *The Counseling Psychologist, 37*(3), 424–450.
Fetzer, G., & Pratt, M. G. (2020). *Craftsmanship and meaningful work*. Working paper, Boston College

Fishbach, A., & Finkelstein, S. R. (2012). How feedback influences persistence, disengagement, and change in goal pursuit. *Goal-Directed Behavior*, 203–230.

Gilson, L. L., & Madjar, N. (2011). Radical and incremental creativity: Antecedents and processes. *Psychology of Aesthetics, Creativity, and the Arts, 5*(1), 21.

Grant, A. M. (2008). The significance of task significance: Job performance effects, relational mechanisms, and boundary conditions. *Journal of Applied Psychology, 93*(1), 108.

Grant, A. M., & Berry, J. W. (2011). The necessity of others is the mother of invention: Intrinsic and prosocial motivations, perspective taking, and creativity. *Academy of Management Journal, 54*(1), 73–96.

Grant, A. M., Campbell, E. M., Chen, G., Cottone, K., Lapedis, D., & Lee, K. (2007). Impact and the art of motivation maintenance: The effects of contact with beneficiaries on persistence behavior. *Organizational Behavior and Human Decision Processes, 103*(1), 53–67.

Hackman, J. R., & Oldham, G. R. (1976). Motivation through the design of work: Test of a theory. *Organizational Behavior and Human Performance, 16*(2), 250–279.

Hagtvedt, L. P. (2019). *Creating artificial intelligence: An inductive study of how creative workers forecast the future and manage present emotions.* Unpublished doctoral dissertation, Boston College.

Hoever, I. J., Van Knippenberg, D., Van Ginkel, W. P., & Barkema, H. G. (2012). Fostering team creativity: Perspective taking as key to unlocking diversity's potential. *Journal of Applied Psychology, 97*(5), 982.

Huta, V., & Waterman, A. S. (2014). Eudaimonia and its distinction from hedonia: Developing a classification and terminology for understanding conceptual and operational definitions. *Journal of Happiness Studies, 15*(6), 1425–1456.

Lepisto, D. A., & Pratt, M. G. (2017). Meaningful work as realization and justification: Toward a dual conceptualization. *Organizational Psychology Review, 7*(2), 99–121.

Locke, E. A., & Latham, G. P. (2004). What should we do about motivation theory? Six recommendations for the twenty-first century. *Academy of Management Review, 29*(3), 388–403.

Locke, E. A., Latham, G. P., & Erez, M. (1988). The determinants of goal commitment. *Academy of Management Review, 13*(1), 23–39.

Locke, E. A., Shaw, K. N., Saari, L. M., & Latham, G. P. (1981). Goal setting and task performance: 1969–1980. *Psychological Bulletin, 90*(1), 125.

Pratt, M. G., & Ashforth, B. E. (2003). *Fostering meaningfulness in working and at work* (pp. 309–327). Positive Organizational Scholarship: Foundations of a New Discipline.

Pratt, M. G., Pradies, C., & Lepisto, D. A. (2013). Doing well, doing good, and doing with: Organizational practices for effectively cultivating meaningful work. In *Purpose and meaning in the workplace* (pp. 173–196). American Psychological Association.

Rosso, B. D., Dekas, K. H., & Wrzesniewski, A. (2010). On the meaning of work: A theoretical integration and review. *Research in Organizational Behavior, 30,* 91–127.

Rouse, E. D., & Pratt, M. G. (forthcoming). Using qualitative methods to generate divergence in creativity theory. In *Handbook of research on creativity and innovation.* Cheltenham: Edward Elgar Publishing.

Shin, S. J., Kim, T.-Y., Lee, J.-Y., & Bian, L. (2012). Cognitive team diversity and individual team member creativity: A cross-level interaction. *Academy of Management Journal, 55*(1), 197–212.

Weick, K. E. (1984). Small wins: Redefining the scale of social problems. *American Psychologist, 39*(1), 40.

Wrzesniewski, A., McCauley, C., Rozin, P., & Schwartz, B. (1997). Jobs, careers, and callings: People's relations to their work. *Journal of Research in Personality, 31*(1), 21–33.

14

Polarities in Creativity: Revisiting Amabile's Componential Model

Gerard J. Puccio

Introduction

Sternberg and Lubart's (1995) investment theory of creativity holds that the path to creativity lies in the discovery of original ideas that possess great promise and then convincing others to accept those ideas. Of course, the challenge with original ideas is that they are often perceived as a threat (Mueller, 2018), thus, creative individuals must work hard to get others to adopt their new ideas. Like successful investors, successful creatives "buy low and sell high" (Sternberg & Lubart, 1995). Teresa

I wish to express my appreciation to Dr. Christine Boyko-Head and Dr. Marsha Huber and for their helpful feedback on an earlier draft of this chapter.

G. J. Puccio (✉)
Creativity & Change Leadership Department,
SUNY Buffalo State, Buffalo, NY, USA
e-mail: PUCCIOGJ@buffalostate.edu

R. Reiter-Palmon et al. (eds.), *Creativity at Work*,
Palgrave Studies in Creativity and Innovation in Organizations,
https://doi.org/10.1007/978-3-030-61311-2_14

Amabile's work in the field of creativity serves as a quintessential example of the investment perspective on creativity.

In the 1970s, when Amabile began her research, the field of creativity could best be described as fledgling. Despite this fact, Amabile expressed a desire to focus her dissertation work on creativity and persuaded her committee to support this idea. Since that time, Amabile has embarked on an ambitious vision to establish a social psychology of creativity (Amabile, 1983). Today, a casual glance at the reference section of most creativity publications demonstrates the widespread influence of Amabile's work. She bought low and sold high, and the acceptance of her work has helped to uplift an entire field of study.

The purpose of this chapter is twofold. First, to highlight the crucial contribution polarity thinking, that is the integration of opposite qualities and characteristics, makes to creative achievement. Second, to revisit Amabile's (1996) seminal work and consider how polarities might operate within her componential model.

The Case for Polarities in Creativity

It is my contention that the assimilation of characteristics and qualities that, at first glance, appear to be contradictory is essential to creative achievement. Moreover, I believe that examples of contradictions are embedded across the four fundamental facets of creativity, that is the creative person, process, product, and environment (Rhodes, 1961). Perhaps, the facet of creativity where such contradictions are most apparent is in the composition of the creative personality. The landmark studies carried out at the Institute of Personality Assessment and Research (IPAR) are rife with examples of socially recognized individuals who possess contradictory personality traits. For instance, MacKinnon (1978) found that America's most creative architects to be both unconventional yet civilized, spontaneous and at the same time planful, and egotistical while prone to be forgiving.

While the IPAR unearthed a wide range of personality traits that included apparent contradictory characteristics, Csikszentmihalyi's (1996) analysis of the creative person specifically called out polarities within the creative personality. Csikszentmihalyi's work revealed ten pairs of contrasting personality traits that contribute to the formation of a complex personality. Examples of Csikszentmihalyi's contradictory personality pairs included: high energy yet often quiet and at rest; tendencies toward both extroversion and introversion; and an ability to engage in both divergent and convergent thinking. Csikszentmihalyi explained how the uncommon integration of contradictory traits promotes creativity when he stated:

> ...what is important to keep in mind is that these conflicting traits–or any conflicting traits–are usually difficult to find in the same person. Yet without the second pole, new ideas will not be recognized. And without the first, they will not be developed to the point of acceptance. Therefore, the novelty that survives to change a domain is usually the work of someone who can operate at both ends of these polarities–and this is the kind of person we call "creative." (p. 76)

Where Csikszentmihalyi's work focused on personality, Rothenberg's work revealed the presence of polarities in the creative process. Rothenberg's (1999) analysis of artists and scientists showed that those who produced breakthrough insights were more likely to simultaneously entertain antithetical concepts when engaged in the creative process. Rothenberg referred to this phenomenon as the janusian process which he described as "Antitheses and opposites during the course of the janusian process are held in tense apposition; they operate side by side and lead to subsequent new and valuable constructions" (p. 105).

A final example of polarities in creativity comes from the work of Parnes and Biondi (1975). Parnes and Biondi described creativity as a life process in which a "delicate balance" is achieved by oscillating between extreme qualities, such as looseness and tightness, contemplation and action, and cognitive and affective approaches. To be clear, the purpose of the present essay is not to lay claim to the insight that creativity emerges from the intersection of opposites, but to extend the work of Csikszentmihalyi (1996), Parnes and Biondi (1975), and Rothenberg (1999) by offering an operational description of how and why the union of contradictory elements serves as a crucial catalyst to creative performance. And, furthermore, to present, by way of example, four specific polarities that contribute to creative achievement.

How Polarities Operate

What is polarity? A polarity is a continuum that contrasts pairs of opposites at either end of a single dimension. For a continuum to be considered a polarity it must meet the following four characteristics (Johnson, 1996; Jung, 1960; van der Steur, 2018):

- The opposing poles must be interdependent. Both poles are necessary for the system to function.
- The opposing poles must be value neutral. One pole is not inherently good or better than the other pole.
- The dimension represented by the polarity is enduring. Unlike problems that fade away once they are solved, polarities are ongoing.
- Emphasis on one pole over the other eventually leads to a breakdown of the whole.

Csikszentmihalyi's contradictory personality traits exemplify the characteristics associated with polarities. To illustrate, earlier it was noted that creative individuals are energetic yet also require rest. Higher energy and rest represent an interdependent relationship. One pole cannot exist without the other. Furthermore, one pole is not inherently better than the other; high energy and rest are value-neutral. The dimension of human activity, which vacillates between intense activity and quiet reflection, is an ongoing condition and not a problem to be solved once. Finally, emphasis on one pole, to the exclusion of the other, promotes dysfunction. It is the integration of these opposites that leads to creative success.

Johnson (1996) provided a framework useful in understanding the dynamics that unfold while an individual reconciles opposites. According to Johnson both positive and negative outcomes can be attributed to each pole. When polarities are managed well, an individual knows when to shift between the two poles so that he or she maximizes the benefits of each pole. However, when polarities are poorly managed, generally when one pole is favored over the other, the positive aspects of one pole gives way to negative outcomes. Returning to the energy-rest dialectic shared earlier, both high energy and rest have their inherent advantages; however, too much focus on either can produce negative consequences. High energy creates movement and engagement, but a rigid focus on high energy output eventually leads to burn out. Rest promotes reflection and rejuvenation; however, preoccupation with rest yields indolence and indecision. Creative individuals are consciously aware of the dynamics that play out between extreme poles and recognize when it is time to shift their attention or behavior from one pole to the other. Success is not found through a mediocre amalgam of opposite qualities, rather it is holding the poles as distinct and learning to vacillate between the two.

Revealing Further Creativity Polarities

I would contend that polarities are foundational to the creative experience and suggest that much greater attention should be given to the dynamics of polarities within the creative person, process, product, and environment. From a theoretical perspective an understanding of the dynamics of polarities might promote deeper insights into the complex nature of the creative person. And from a practical perspective the use of polarity management methodologies, such as those described by Johnson (1996), might enhance the alacrity and competence with which individuals, teams, and organizations address polarities essential to their creative potential. With these theoretical and practical goals in mind, I describe four creativity polarities. The first two polarities have been introduced elsewhere (Puccio, 2017; Puccio, Cabra, & Schwagler, 2018; Puccio, Klarman, & Szalay, in press) and are embellished here. The additional two polarities are based on Amabile's (1996) componential model of creativity.

Creativity–Conformity: A Macro Polarity

I begin with a dialectic dimension that I now refer to as a macro polarity for, in my view, it is a universal, innate, and a fundamental aspect of the human condition. From a biological perspective there are at least two competitive advantages that are innately found in the human species. And it is precisely the polarity between these two paradoxical qualities that has been essential to human survival (Puccio, 2017; Puccio et al., 2018). At one end of the human survival continuum is the creativity pole and at the other is the conformity pole (see Fig. 14.1). Human beings, as a result of biological and cultural evolution, are predisposed to both create, seek the production of new and useful ideas to complex problems, and to conform, act in accordance to a standard or authority. While creativity and conformity are often described as rival qualities, in reality it is their paradoxical and interdependent relationship that has allowed humans to flourish.

I have witnessed some creativity professionals, as they are positively disposed toward the benefits of creativity, cast conformity in a pejorative light. According to polarity theory (Johnson, 1996), when a preference is given to one pole (e.g., creativity), the natural inclination is to narrowly describe the other pole by focusing only on that pole's downside (e.g., conformity). Thus, resulting in the misguided belief that conformity is a threat to creativity. This is fundamentally untrue. Instead, creativity and

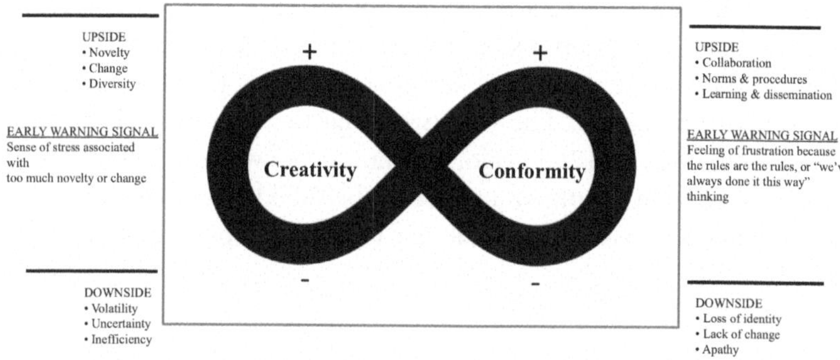

Fig. 14.1 Macro polarity: creativity–conformity dimension

conformity are paradoxical partners that promote the growth of a civilization. Creativity is helped by conformity in that new and useful ideas are disseminated through humans' propensity to conform. To be sure, conformity may result in initial doubt as a creative idea can be perceived as a threat to established practices, but through persistence and persuasion the value of a creative idea can facilitate broad adoption. Figure 14.1, which illustrates the creativity–conformity polarity, includes lists of the upside and downside to each pole, along with the early warning signals that help individuals, teams, and organizations recognize when it might be time to shift between poles.

Divergence-Convergence: The Creative Process Polarity

In biological evolution variations are generated with the most adaptive being selected and retained. Similarly, the creative process involves oscillating phases of novelty and evaluation. Indeed, a hallmark of the Creative Problem-Solving process (Puccio, Mance, & Murdock, 2011), cited as one of the most effective creativity training programs (Scott, Leritz, & Mumford, 2004), features the balance between divergent thinking, the ability to generate many, varied, and original options, along with convergent thinking, the ability to select, evaluate, and develop the most valuable options. Csikszentmihalyi (1996) summarized the benefits of this process dialect when he observed that "people who bring acceptable novelty in a domain seem able to use well two opposite ways of thinking: the convergent and the divergent" (p. 60). Previously, Puccio et al. (in press) have formalized divergent and convergent thinking into a polarity (see Fig. 14.2).

Divergent thinking promotes original concepts (novelty), a wide range of possibilities (flexibility), and a nonjudgmental attitude (openness). Convergent thinking results in coherence (clarity), decision-making (direction), and a deeper understanding (insight). A bias toward one form of thinking over the other results in suboptimal thinking and problem-solving. What follows are two examples, the first educational

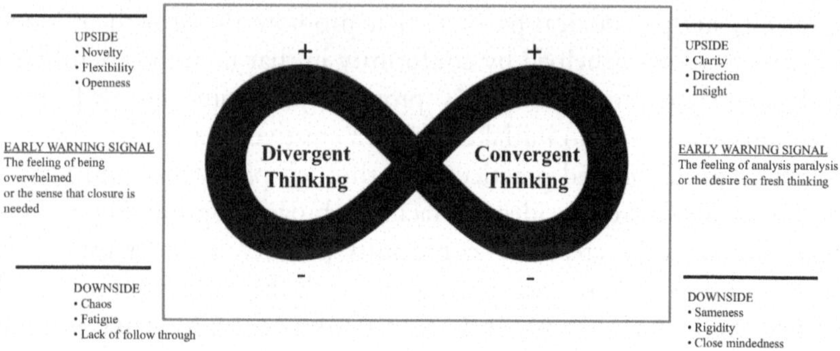

Fig. 14.2 Process polarity: divergent–convergent thinking

and the second organizational, that highlight the consequences associated with a bias towards convergent thinking.

Despite the fact that many current-day reports tout the importance of creativity as a twenty-first-century skill (Puccio, 2017); it would seem that educational practices do not provide the necessary balance between divergent and convergent thinking to facilitate this crucial competence. As Runco (2007) pointed out, "Most educational efforts emphasize convergent thinking, and may do very little, if anything, for creative potential" (p. 5). Sadly, this emphasis on convergent thinking may result in students becoming stuck in the downside of convergent thinking (i.e., sameness, rigidity, and close-mindedness) and may explain the erosion of divergent thinking in a population over time (see Kim, 2011).

Meetings are a common collaboration tool in organizations, as such meetings are often used for the purpose of problem-solving (Schwarz, 1994). Unfortunately, meetings can be unproductive and dysfunctional (Rogelberg, Shanock, & Scott, 2012). A significant contributing factor to unproductive problem-solving meetings is the imbalance between divergent and convergent thinking. Meetings steeped in convergent thinking are seen as dull, stifling, unengaging, and run the risk of producing mediocre outcomes. A study by Puccio et al. (2020) demonstrated that by introducing a balanced process agenda in a problem-solving meeting, divergent thinking first followed by a convergent phase, significantly more productive outcomes are achieved.

The Intrinsic–Extrinsic Motivation Polarity

The previous two creativity polarities are drawn from my prior work, in revisiting Amabile's (1996) componential theory of creativity (i.e., Task Motivation, Domain-Relevant Skills, and Creativity-Relevant Skills) two further polarities crucial to creative performance might be considered. The first relates to Amabile's research into motivation and creative performance (Amabile, 1987). The second polarity emerges from the relationship between domain and creativity-relevant skills.

Amabile's (1993) recast of the relationship between intrinsic and extrinsic motivation provided impetus for me to revisit the task motivation continuum as a polarity. As Amabile (1993) observed, "It does not seem that intrinsic and extrinsic motivation operate in a simple additive fashion *or* in simple opposition" (p. 193). As a consequence, Amabile described the synergistic relationship between intrinsic and extrinsic motivation. To this I add the polarity framework illustrated in Fig. 14.3. By conceiving of intrinsic and extrinsic motivation as a polarity, where both poles are value-neutral, the synergistic interplay between the two can be further understood. Where intrinsic motivation provides an emotional foundation for work, encouraging exploration and persistence, extrinsic factors help to meet resource needs and provides assurances that outcomes are delivered. Conversely, as highlighted in Fig. 14.3, detrimental effects occur when an individual or team becomes

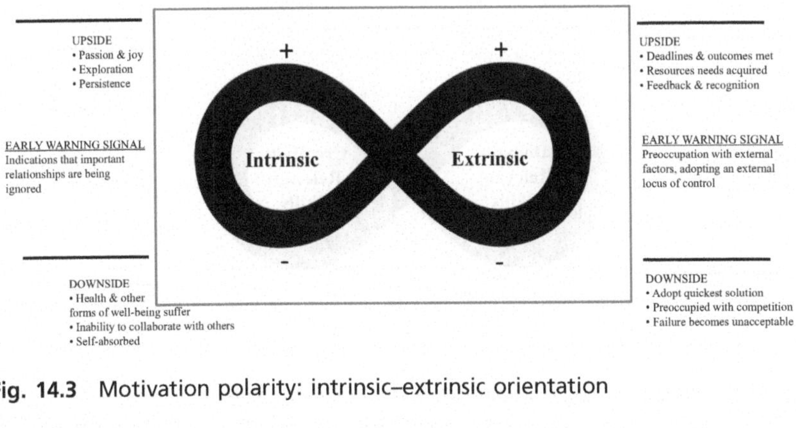

Fig. 14.3 Motivation polarity: intrinsic–extrinsic orientation

overly focused on one form of motivation to the exclusion of the other. Perhaps reframing task motivation as a polarity further highlights the synergistic relationship between intrinsic and extrinsic orientations.

The Skills Polarity

Where the task motivation component of Amabile's model may be represented as a stand-alone polarity, the two remaining components could be portrayed as a unified polarity (see Fig. 14.4). Domain-relevant skills and creativity-relevant skills may be thought of as a continuum in which a bias toward one pole, to the exclusion of the other, is detrimental. Whereas, integration promotes creative work. As depicted in Fig. 14.4, both domain and creativity-relevant skills have their respective benefits.

Conceiving of domain and creativity-relevant skills as a polarity further clarifies the dynamics that can play out when a bias exists toward one pole. For instance, Amabile (1996) provided a warning against those who favor the creativity pole when she stated, "the popular notion that a great deal of knowledge in a given domain can be detrimental to creativity is incorrect" (p. 87). Using polarity thinking to interpret this quote, those who favor the creativity pole run the risk of focusing exclusively on the downside of the domain-relevant skills pole. Instead, as Amabile's componential model underscores, there must be an integration between domain and creativity-relevant skills. By viewing these elements

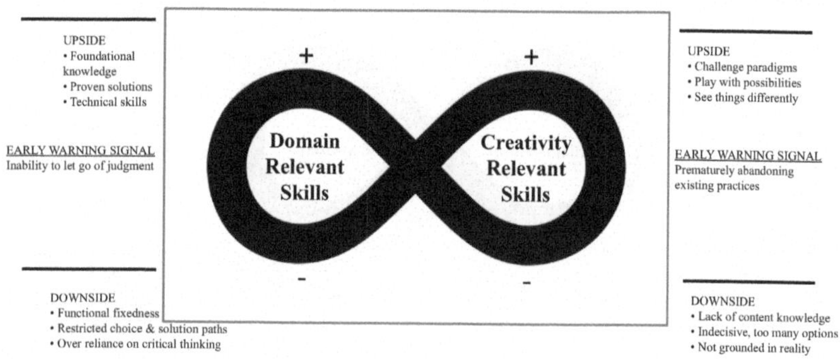

Fig. 14.4 Skills polarity: domain–creativity relevant skills

of the componential model as a polarity a 'both-and' relationship is promoted over an 'either-or' choice.

Conclusion

The overarching goal of this chapter was to call attention to the important contribution polarities make to our understanding of creativity. To that end, four sample polarities were described. The four polarities are not meant to be exhaustive. Instead, as Csikszentmihalyi so astutely observed about his own list of contradictory personality pairs. While these personality contradictions are important, what may be more crucial is the transcendent process individuals experience by learning to rectify contradictory perspectives. By learning to manage polarities, the creative person progresses from 'either-or' thinking, a singular reality, to 'both-and thinking', dual reality, to 'yes-and' thinking, a new reality. In short, the successful integration of polarities in the creative personality leads to ever-expanding levels of consciousness (Jung, 1960; Miller, 2004; van der Steur, 2018). In turn, expanded levels of consciousness could serve to enhance an individual's ability to engage in Rothenberg's janusian process, thus increasing the probability of producing creative breakthroughs. Initial empirical evidence for the benefits of priming individuals with paradoxical frames can be found in the work of Miron-Spektor, Gino, and Argote (2011).

References

Amabile, T. M. (1983). *The social psychology of creativity*. New York, NY: Springer-Verlag.

Amabile, T. M. (1987). The motivation to be creative. In S. G. Isaksen (Ed.), *Frontiers of creativity research: Beyond the basics* (pp. 223–254). Buffalo, NY: Bearly Limited.

Amabile, T. M. (1993). Motivational synergy: Toward new conceptualizations of intrinsic and extrinsic motivation in the workplace. *Human Resource Management Review, 3*(3), 185–201.

Amabile, T. M. (1996). *Creativity in context*. Boulder, CO: Westview.

Csikszentmihalyi, M. (1996). *Creativity: Flow and the psychology of discovery and invention*. New York, NY: HarperCollins.

Johnson, B. (1996). *Polarity management: Identifying and managing unsolvable problems*. Amherst, MA: HRD Press.

Jung, C. G. (1960). The transcendent function In R. F. C. Hull (Trans.), *The collected works of C. G. Jung* (Vol. 8). Princeton, NJ: Princeton University Press (Original work published in 1947).

Kim, K. H. (2011). The creativity crisis: The decrease in creative thinking scores on the Torrance Tests of Creative Thinking. *Creativity Research Journal, 23,* 285–295.

MacKinnon, D. W. (1978). *In search of human effectiveness*. Buffalo, NY: Creative Education Foundation.

Miller, J. C. (2004). *The transcendent function: Jung's model of psychological growth through dialogue with the unconscious*. Albany: State University of New York Press.

Miron-Spektor, E., Gino, F., & Argote, L. (2011). Paradoxical frames and creative sparks: Enhancing individual creativity through conflict and integration. *Organizational Behavior and Human Decision Processes, 116,* 229–240.

Mueller, J. (2018). *Creative change: Why we resist it…how we can embrace it*. New York, NY: Mariner Books.

Parnes, S. J., & Biondi, A. M. (1975). Creative behavior: A delicate balance. *The Journal of Creative Behavior, 9,* 149–158.

Puccio, G. J. (2017). From the dawn of humanity to the 21st century: Creativity as an enduring survival skill. *The Journal of Creative Behavior, 51,* 330–334. https://doi.org/10.1002/jocb.203.

Puccio, G. J., Burnett, C., Acar, S., Yudess, J. A., Holinger, M., & Cabra, J. F. (2020). Creative problem solving in small groups: The effects of creativity training on idea generation, solution creativity, and leadership effectiveness. *The Journal of Creative Behavior, 54,* 453–471. https://doi.org/10.1002/jocb.381.

Puccio, G. J., Cabra, J. F., & Schwagler, N. (2018). *Organizational creativity: A practical guide for innovators & entrepreneurs*. Thousand Oaks, CA: Sage.

Puccio, G. J., Klarman, B., & Szalay, P. (in press). *Creative problem solving*. In V. Glăveanu (Ed.), *Encyclopedia of the possible*. New York: Palgrave Macmillan.

Puccio, G. J., Mance, M., & Murdock, M. C. (2011). *Creative leadership: Skills that drive change* (2nd ed.). Thousand Oaks: Sage.

Rhodes, M. (1961). An analysis of creativity. *Phi Delta Kappan, 42,* 305–310.

Rogelberg, S. G., Shanock, L. R., & Scott, C. W. (2012). Wasted time and money in meetings: Increasing return on investment. *Small Group Research, 43,* 236–245.

Rothenberg, A. (1999). Janusian process. In M. A. Runco & S. R. Pritzker (Eds.), *Encyclopedia of creativity* (pp. 103–108). San Diego, CA: Academic Press.

Runco, M. A. (2007). *Creativity. Theories and themes: Research, development, and practice.* Oxford, UK: Elsevier.

Scott, G. M., Leritz, L. E., & Mumford, M. D. (2004). The effectiveness of creativity training: A meta-analysis. *Creativity Research Journal, 16,* 361–388.

Schwarz, R. M. (1994). *The skilled facilitator: Practical wisdom for developing effective groups.* San Francisco: Jossey-Bass.

Sternberg, R. J., & Lubart, T. I. (1995). *Defying the crowd: Cultivating creativity in a culture of conformity.* New York, NY: The Free Press.

van der Steur, J. (2018). *The power of polarities: An innovative method to transform individuals, teams, and organizations. Based on Carl Jung's theory of the personality.* Austin, TX: Polarity Institute.

15

The Consensual Assessment Technique: Refinement and Further Development

Roni Reiter-Palmon

Teresa Amabile's 1982 paper on the Consensual Assessment Technique (CAT) provided a breakthrough in the study of creativity. Prior to this paper, the study of creativity was limited. Researchers have focused on eminent individuals, evaluating creativity through peer nominations or awards (Batey, 2012). Alternatively, to study creativity in the general population, the metric used was that of divergent thinking. However, divergent thinking tests measure only one aspect of the creative process, that of ideation (Reiter-Palmon, Forthmann, & Barbot, 2019), and are better viewed as measure of creative potential than actual creativity.

The availability of a new approach to measure and evaluate creativity opened the door for increasing research on creativity including experimental studies and using normal adult populations. In fact, the CAT has been viewed as the "gold standard" for creativity researchers (Cseh &

R. Reiter-Palmon (✉)
Department of Psychology, University of Nebraska Omaha, Omaha, NE, USA
e-mail: rreiter-palmon@unomaha.edu

R. Reiter-Palmon et al. (eds.), *Creativity at Work*,
Palgrave Studies in Creativity and Innovation in Organizations,
https://doi.org/10.1007/978-3-030-61311-2_15

Jefferies, 2019). Without the development of the CAT, my own research would look very different. My research started as a graduate student, focusing on problem construction as part of the creative process, only a few years after the publication of the 1982 paper. In our lab (directed by Mike Mumford), we used the CAT to evaluate a range of products such as solutions to problems, problem restatements, marketing plans, and short stories (Arreola & Reiter-Palmon, 2016; Byrne, Shipman, & Mumford, 2010; Mobley, Doares, & Mumford, 1992; Reiter-Palmon & Arreola, 2015; Reiter-Palmon, Mumford, & Threlfall, 1998). While many researchers have used the CAT, over the years, many have engaged in modifications to this approach (Cseh & Jefferies, 2019). In this chapter, I would like to detail some of the modifications and refinements that we have implemented in my own lab, and discuss the reasoning for these modifications and refinement. In the end, I believe that these changes make the CAT more reliable and valid for the study of creativity as I approach it.

Before discussing some of the modifications that have been implemented, it is important to briefly discuss the original formulation of the CAT as presented by Amabile (1982). Specifically, Amabile called for the use of experts in a domain to provide evaluation of creativity. According to Amabile, individuals who have familiarity with the domain and products can agree with one another with respect to judgments of creativity. Further, Amabile called for the rating of creativity overall. Finally, judges should provide ratings without training. Rather, the judgments of creativity are based on familiarity with the domain.

One important modification that we implemented was the differentiation between quality/usefulness and originality. While the original work from Amabile called for ratings of creativity, we have looked to evaluate the two components of creativity separately. Over the years we have found that the two components do not always correlate highly (Reiter-Palmon, Mumford, Boes, & Runco, 1997), and if fact, may have different relationships with other constructs (Morral-Robinson & Reiter-Palmon, 2013; Reiter-Palmon, Illies Young, Kobe, Buboltz, & Nimps, 2009). It is precisely for that reason that it is important to study the two factors independently. For example, Morral-Robinson and Reiter-Palmon (2013) found that creative self-efficacy was correlated with the originality of the solution, but not with quality. Reiter-Palmon and Schoenbeck (2020) have found that tolerance for ambiguity was related to solution quality but not originality. Finally, Reiter-Palmon et al. (2009) found that the specific parameters of the problem can influence the quality and originality of the solutions generated. These studies suggest that it is beneficial to evaluate the two components of creativity separately to determine their antecedents and correlates.

In addition, as we have started to study malevolent creativity, we have found that ratings for creativity or quality were not appropriate. Malevolent creativity is an idea or act that is creative or original, but has harmful effects. Ratings of quality typically include evaluation of feasibility (which implies legality and ethicality). As a result, we have suggested that malevolent creativity should be evaluated as the combination of valence, that is, negativity or harmfulness and originality (Harris, Reiter-Palmon, & Kaufman, 2013). As a result, we have developed a rating scale for valence, and used the CAT to rate solutions on this dimension as well (Harris et al., 2013; Harris & Reiter-Palmon, 2015).

As I started my own stream of research focusing on the role of problem construction in creative problem-solving, an additional issue emerged. In order to study problem construction effectively using a college student population, the content of the problem had to be one that students would be familiar with. As expertise has been identified as critical for creativity (Amabile, 1996; Weisberg, 2018), it was important to develop problems that would be familiar to students, and that students could be considered to have some degree of expertise. As a result, I have designed a number of problem scenarios reflecting problems that students would be familiar with, problems regarding student leadership, school performance, or relationships. However, the use of everyday problem scenarios presented a different difficulty. Amabile's CAT approach requires the use of experts, but is unclear who is considered an expert for everyday problems. The solution that we developed was to use the graduate students in the lab as raters. These graduate students had knowledge regarding the problems in question, as they were students themselves. Moreover, they had knowledge of the creativity literature, so could apply that knowledge to provide ratings. I have found that both graduate and undergraduate students could be effective raters for the solutions generated to the type of problems we have used.

This led to an interest in identifying what would be required for high quality and high agreement to emerge for rating creative products. While the CAT calls for the use of expert judges and rating of creativity as a holistic construct, my own research has diverged from this, but I was still able to obtain effective ratings. This combined with my own interest in measurement has led to an interesting study on the whether experts, quasi-experts, and novices can be effective raters (Kaufman, Baer, Cropely, Reiter-Palmon, & Sinnett, 2013). In this paper we evaluated two different types of creative activities. In one sample, participants engaged in writing a poem. Expert raters were professional writers, quasi-experts were graduate students trained either in writing or in creativity, and novice raters were undergraduate students. In this sample, we have found that both expert and quasi-experts had reliable ratings of poems, with a sample of about 10 raters. However, novice raters were unreliable. Sufficient levels of reliability were obtained only when reaching 100 raters, a number that is not realistic for most studies. A second study evaluated the suitability of quasi-expert raters in a different domain, that of engineering design. Here the findings suggested that exerts (professional engineers) were reliable raters, quasi-experts (first-year engineering students) were moderately reliable, and novices (undergraduate students outside of engineering) were not as reliable. This study suggests that the use of quasi-experts, depending on the domain, maybe an appropriate substitute for using experts for CAT.

Based on this research, and the fact that the problems I use in creative problem-solving exercises are everyday problems familiar to many, the use of graduate and undergraduate students that have domain knowledge of creativity and the CAT, is appropriate, and provides reliable results. This is an important modification and refinement to the original CAT. As noted, in many cases, experts are difficult to obtain, so using quasi-experts allows us to conduct research effectively and efficiently. In my own case, it is hard if not impossible to really identify experts, so the focus shifted to having knowledge with regards to the rating process and understanding of creativity.

That led to another refinement and modification of the rating process. All of the students in the lab start by reading papers on the topic of creativity in general, and specifically about the CAT. In addition, students familiarize themselves with the research conducted in the lab specifically. Finally, students participate in a discussion with one or more advanced students regarding the process of CAT and the nature of creativity ratings. Once student raters are provided with this initial training focusing on creativity in general and creativity ratings specifically, they can engage in rating process. However, this by itself cannot guarantee reliable ratings. As these raters are quasi-experts, additional procedures have been put in place to ensure that raters approach the problem and solutions with the same frame of reference. Having a shared mental model and shared understanding of the actual problem and its parameters should help facilitate agreement among the raters regarding the quality and originality of the solution (LeBreton & Senter, 2008). Therefore, prior to starting the rating process, the raters get together to discuss the problem itself and their understanding of the problem. In addition, the raters are provided with a reminder of the guidelines suggested by Amabile (1982) such as evaluating the solutions in context by reviewing all solutions prior to rating. We instruct raters to attend to the content of the solution and not focus on typos or grammatical errors when evaluating. In addition, we instruct the raters not to read into the solution what is not clearly stated. That is, to avoid a situation where different raters make different assumptions about the intent of problem solver, we instruct them to focus on what is explicitly stated.

Another way to ensure that all raters are viewing the materials with the same mindset and approach is to provide raters with more information regarding the rating scale. While Amabile (1982) suggested that experts will understand what creativity means, I do provide more detail for my raters. That is, I provide raters with a detailed definition of quality and originality and their components. Quality focuses on the extent to which a solution is (a) complete and addresses multiple aspects of the problem and (b) to what extent is the solution viable, practical, and appropriate. For originality, raters are instructed to evaluate (a) the degree of novelty in the solution, (b) whether the solution presents an imaginative or humorous approach, and (c) the extent to which the solution is structured and limited by the problem content. These provide additional information to the raters as they make judgments regarding quality and originality of the solutions.

Finally, to ensure a similar understanding of quality and originality and how those relate to the problem and solutions in each study, we conduct rater training specific to the problems and solutions in the study under consideration. This rater training lasts about an hour, and includes discussion of the problem for a better understanding of problem parameters. The raters then further discuss the rating scale—either quality and originality. After the problem and rating scales have been discussed, the raters rate a random sample (typically about five solutions) of solutions. If solutions to the same problem are available from a previous study, we try to use those as the sample solutions. The raters then discuss the reasoning for the ratings they provided, allowing them to uncover differences in how they apply the rating scale to the solutions presented and identify and discuss potential points of disagreement. This discussion, in turn, allows the rater to reach a shared understanding of the definition, the rating scale, and its application to the solutions presented (Cannon-Bowers, 2007). During the rater training meeting, the process of rating independently and then a discussion is repeated two–three times, until the raters seem to converge and have a shared understanding. At that point, raters are asked to rate a sub-sample of the solutions independently. Once that sub-sample is rated, we evaluate inter-rater reliability. If the inter-rater reliability index is sufficient, raters are then asked to rate the entire corpus of solutions. However, if the inter-rater reliability is too low (below .7), we meet again to rate and discuss solutions ratings to improve the shared understanding.

Conclusion

In this chapter I detail some modifications and refinements to the CAT that I have engaged in the last 30+ years of studying creativity. These modifications and refinements are not unique. However, only limited research has evaluated their efficacy or reasoning (Cseh & Jefferies,

2019). Further, in many published articles it is unclear what modifications have taken place. Here, I have provided a discussion of the modifications and refinements in detail, and also provided the rational for these changes relative to Amabile's (1982) original suggestions. Most of the changes stem from the need to account for both the nature of the task as well as the availability of experts. My own work extending and modifying the CAT allows for the study of everyday creative problem-solving with a wide variety of populations. While this work extends the use of the CAT, additional research on the CAT and these modifications is necessary. For example, while past research has suggested that quality and originality may have different antecedents, that is not always the case. It would be beneficial to understand the relationship between quality and originality as well when and under what conditions predictors differ or are the same. In addition, while research on the use of quasi-experts suggests that quasi-experts can be an effective substitution to experts, additional research is needed.

References

Amabile, T. M. (1982). Social psychology of creativity: A consensual assessment technique. *Journal of Personality and Social Psychology, 43*(5), 997–1013. https://doi.org/10.1037/0022-3514.43.5.997.

Amabile, T. M. (1996). *Creativity in context: The social Psychology of creativity*. London: Taylor & Francis.

Arreola, N., & Reiter-Palmon, R. (2016). The effect of problem construction creativity on solution creativity across multiple real-world problems. *Psychology of Aesthetics, Creativity, and the Arts, 10*, 287–295.

Batey, M. (2012). The measurement of creativity: From definitional consensus to the introduction of a new heuristic framework. *Creativity Research Journal, 24*, 55–65.

Byrne, C. L., Shipman, A. S., & Mumford, M. D. (2010). The effects of forecasting on creative problem solving: An experimental study. *Creativity Research Journal, 22*, 119–138.

Cannon-Bowers, J. (2007). Fostering mental model convergence through training. In F. Dansereau & F. J. Yammarino (Eds.), *Multi-level issues in organizations and time*. Research in Multi-Level Issues (Vol. 6, pp. 149–157). Bingley: Emerald Group Publishing Limited. https://doi.org/10.1016/S1475-9144(07)06006-7.

Cseh, G. M., & Jefferies, K. K. (2019). A scattered CAT: A critical evaluation of the Consensual Assessment Technique for creativity research. *The Psychology of Aesthetics, Creativity, and the Arts, 13,* 159–166.

Harris, D. J., & Reiter-Palmon, R. (2015). Fast and furious: The influence of implicit aggression, premeditation, and provoking situations on malevolent creativity. *Psychology of Aesthetics, Creativity, and the Arts, 9,* 54–64.

Harris, D. J., Reiter-Palmon, R., & Kaufman, J. C. (2013). The effect of emotional intelligence and task type on malevolent creativity. *Psychology of Aesthetics, Creativity and the Arts, 7,* 237–244.

Kaufman, J., Baer, J., Cropely, D., Reiter-Palmon, R., & Sinnett, S. (2013). Furious activity vs. understanding: How much expertise is needed to evaluate creative work? *Psychology of Aesthetics, Creativity and the Arts, 7,* 332–341.

LeBreton, J. M., & Senter, J. L. (2008). Answers to 20 questions about interrater reliability and interrater agreement. *Organizational Research Methods, 11,* 815–852.

Mobley, M. I., Doares, L., & Mumford, M. D. (1992). Process analytic models of creative capacities: Evidence for the combination and reorganization process. *Creativity Research Journal, 5,* 125–155.

Morral-Robinson, E., & Reiter-Palmon, R. (2013). The interactive effects of self-perceptions and job requirements on creative problem solving. *Journal of Creative Behavior, 47,* 200–214.

Reiter-Palmon, R., & Arreola, N. J. (2015). Does generating multiple ideas lead to increased creativity? A comparison of generating one idea vs. many. *Creativity Research Journal, 27,* 1040–1049.

Reiter-Palmon, R., Forthmann, B., & Barbot, B. (2019). Scoring divergent thinking tests: A review and systematic framework. *The Psychology of Aesthetics, Creativity, and the Arts, 13,* 144–152.

Reiter-Palmon, R., Illies Young, M., Kobe, L., Buboltz, C., & Nimps, T. (2009). Creativity and domain specificity: The effect of task type of multiple indices on creative problem solving. *The Psychology of Aesthetics, Creativity, and the Arts, 3,* 73–80.

Reiter-Palmon, R., Mumford, M. D., Boes, O. J., & Runco, M. A. (1997). Problem construction and creativity: The role of ability, cue consistency, and active processing. *Creativity Research Journal, 10,* 9–24.

Reiter-Palmon, R., Mumford, M. D., & Threlfall, V. K. (1998). Solving everyday problems creatively: The role of problem construction and personality type. *Creativity Research Journal, 11,* 187–197.

Reiter-Palmon, R., & Schoenbeck, M. (2020). Creativity equals creativity—Or does it? How creativity is measured influences our understanding of creativity. In M. Stierand & V. Dorfler (Eds.), *Handbook of research methods of creativity*. Edward Elgar.

Weisberg, R. A. (2018). Expertise and structured imagination in creative thinking: Reconsideration of an old question. In K. A. Erriccson, R. R. Hoffman, A. Kozbelt, & A. M. Williams (Eds.), *The Cambridge handbook of expertise and expert performance* (pp. 812–834). Cambridge: Cambridge University Press.

16

A Hobby Out of Control: Festschrift for Teresa Amabile

Mark A. Runco

In 1981 the artist known as Wyland painted a large mural of a pair of whales on a large outdoor wall, facing Pacific Coast Highway, in Laguna Beach, California. It was a beautiful tribute to the magnificent animals and accomplished Wyland's goal of raising consciousness about the threats to their livelihood and the survival of their species. Wyland went on to paint dozens of what came to be known as "whaling walls." People like me travel miles and miles to view whaling walls. Significantly, Wyland donates all proceeds. He makes no money from them.

This essay begins with a paragraph about Wyland because it allows me to say something about the need to protect whales, and other endangered species, and thus allows acknowledgment of what may be the most

An earlier version of this chapter was presented at Harvard Business School August 14, 2019.

M. A. Runco (✉)
Southern Oregon University, Ashland, OR, USA
e-mail: runcom@sou.edu

R. Reiter-Palmon et al. (eds.), *Creativity at Work*,
Palgrave Studies in Creativity and Innovation in Organizations,
https://doi.org/10.1007/978-3-030-61311-2_16

important area of creativity research, namely that focused on *benevolent creativity*. In addition, Wyland's work exemplifies something that has been clearly demonstrated in Teresa Amabile's research. This was implied by what was just said about proceeds from the whaling walls, for obviously Wyland worked on his paintings without receiving monetary rewards. On the same point consider Wyland's statement in 2019, as he worked on the newest mural. He was quoted as saying that painting whales "is a hobby that got out of control" (quoted by Pinho, 2019, 22 July). Photos of the newest whaling wall and additional background can be found at https://enewspaper.latimes.com/desktop/latimes/default.aspx?pubid=50435180-e58e-48b5-8e0c-236bf740270e.

Wyland exemplifies one of Amabile's concepts, namely the concept of intrinsic motivation. I will discuss this concept in some detail below but also explore a few other contributions found in Amabile's work. Given that this is a Festschrift, and I must first say something about context, and in particular about the state of the art when we both started and about how significantly Teresa's efforts contributed to my work and the progress in the field. I have had the great honor of working with her for over 30 years. Amabile has been on the Editorial Board of the *Creativity Research Journal (CRJ)* since it was inaugurated in 1988, and I have often pointed out that the *CRJ* was successful largely because that Editorial Board included all the luminaries in the field. At about the same time as the *CRJ* inauguration Amabile participated in the Pitzer Creativity Conference, which resulted in the 1990 volume, *Theories of Creativity* (Albert & Runco, 1990; Amabile, 1990). In July of 2019 she gave the Lego Creativity Keynote Address to the 2nd Annual Southern Oregon Creativity Conference. I was co-executive Director of both conferences and can say the same thing about them that I said about the *CRJ*: the successes were due to the participation of Amabile and the other big names.

Given this history, going back to the late 1980s, the present chapter understandably takes a long view. This chapter appears in a volume where others also identify Amabile's contributions to the field so the present chapter needs not be comprehensive. It merely highlights several aspects of intrinsic motivation, the Consensual Assessment Technical, and Amabile's useful distinctions about the creative process and product.

Intrinsic Motivation

Like many researchers studying creativity, I have probably cited Amabile's work on *intrinsic motivation* just about as much or more than I have cited any other research (e.g., Rubenson & Runco, 1992, 1995; Runco, 1993, 2014b, 2020). That is in part because motivation is a prerequisite to creative behavior—*all* creative behavior, even though creative behavior is a fairly diverse and varied thing (e.g., domain differences). A person can have tons of creative talent, including all of the cognitive skills necessary, but if they are not interested, it is unlikely that those talents and skills will be expressed.

This is an enormously important idea. It is vital in the cognitive research on creativity, including investigations of divergent thinking (Runco, 1991, 2013; Runco & Acar, 2012). To bring the point home: to be realistic, the cognitive research on creativity must acknowledge extracognitive processes, and in particular intrinsic motivation.

Outside of the creativity research cognition is usually viewed as involving thinking processes, and only thinking processes. In fact, more often than not controls are used in the cognitive research is isolate thinking processes and exclude all else. Extracognitive factors, such as emotion and motivation, have usually been treated as confounds. That makes no sense when it comes to the creative process. Both cognition and motivation play a role in creative thinking, and the latter is required or the former may lead to naught. More precisely, when the motivation for originality is lacking, cognition may not be activated or mindful, or, more likely, it may not focus on or involve creative processes. It may gravitate to routine instead of creative thinking. Amabile's research demonstrated the importance of motivation, and unlike earlier research on intrinsic motivation, such as that done at the Institute for Personality Assessment and Research (IPAR; e.g., Barron, 1995), Amabile used experimental rather than observational or correlational designs in her research. This was much more rigorous than any other mention of intrinsic motivation. Amabile's conclusions about intrinsic motivation are highly reliable, but of course she was careful and qualified the findings, noting, for example, the possibility that extrinsic motivation could also come into play.

The two-tier model offered by Chand and Runco (1992), captures most of these ideas and certainly reflects the influence of Amabile. This model has a primary tier for creative thinking, with problem finding, ideation, and judgment or evaluation, but it also recognizes influences on those three processes. Both information and motivation are on this second tier.

Figure 16.1 shows that the information that influences creative thinking may be declarative or procedural. The former is conceptual and often factual and the latter is know-how. Motivation is also of two sorts, namely extrinsic or intrinsic. Extrinsic motivation may be responsive to rewards, bonuses, grades (in school), and similar things found in or given by someone in the environment. Intrinsic motivation comes from within.

Amabile has demonstrated how very important intrinsic motivation is for education and business. She has also (a) delineated extrinsic factors so they are not all clumped together (e.g., evaluation, expected feedback, surveillance) and (b) explored alternative relationships between intrinsic and extrinsic motivation. Both (a) and (b) exemplify how Amabile's research evolved over the years. Early on the emphasis was on intrinsic motivation as distinct from extrinsic motivation, for example, but Amabile soon pointed out that this is a simplification and unrealistic. Sometimes extrinsic factors do influence the creative process, and sometimes intrinsic and extrinsic factors both play a role. Rubenson and Runco (1992, 1995) also described situations where both were involved.

(secondary tier)

Motivation
Intrinsic / Extrinsic

Knowledge
Procedural/ Declarative

(Primary tier)

Problem Finding
Problem Identification/ Problem Definition

Ideation (Divergent Thinking)
Fluency/ Originality/ Flexibility

Evaluation
Valuation/ Criticism

Fig. 16.1 The two tier model of the creative process (*Source* Chand and Runco 1992)

Consensual Assessment

Amabile has contributed more than just a refinement of the concept of intrinsic motivation to the field of creative studies. She has, for instance, developed and refined a very useful methodology (the Consensual Assessment Technique, or CAT). The CAT asks participants in research to create a product, which is often a collage or poem (e.g., Ruscio, Whitney, & Amabile, 1998). These products are then evaluated by judges, which is why the method is labeled consensual. One requirement of the CAT is that judges each use their own definition of "creativity" to rate the products. Also, the CAT procedure calls for all judges to begin by examining all products so they are aware of the full range of what the entire sample of participants has produced and they can rate anyone object relative to all others. This is important because samples may vary, and without the initial examination of all products in any one sample, judges might implicitly compare something from one sample with what they had seen previously, in another sample or context. In addition to rating the products for creativity, judges are asked to offer ratings for the technical skill and aesthetic appeal of the products. The CAT has proven to be useful in quite a number of empirical investigations, by Amabile and many others (see review in the *Encyclopedia of Creativity*).

Importantly, some of the research, done by teams not including Amabile, seems to have forgotten an important detail. The CAT was developed as a method that Amabile could use to study the impact of setting (including the presence or absence of extrinsic influences). Amabile was quite clear that the CAT was not developed as a measure of individual differences. Yet it is very often used in research that is focused on individual differences. This is problematic because it is one thing to use the CAT to draw inferences about groups in different settings but quite another thing to use it to discriminate between individuals. These are two different levels of analysis.

Like her work on intrinsic motivation, Amabile's CAT stimulates quite a bit of research. Just to name one example, I used an adaptation of the CAT in a project which examined the art of young children (Runco, 1989). The objectives of that research included determining inter-item reliabilities (i.e., correlations among products) and checking inter-rater reliabilities among the professional artists who evaluated the artwork. I was also interested in the generality of creative ability so asked the artists to rate three products: A crayon drawing the children did when asked to illustrate a particular limerick; a collage of a dragon constructed from colored paper, with glitter and crayon detailing; and a tempera painting that included additions and revisions using crayons and colored pencils and pens. Another objective of the research was to examine age differences within the sample of 4th, 5th, and 6th grade children. The final objective was to look closely at different aspects of creativity (i.e., how it was operationalized). With this in mind two of the professional artists just rated the artworks for creativity while the others rated the artwork for Aesthetic Appeal, Originality, and Technical Skill. Interestingly, the Aesthetic Appeal index showed the highest level of inter-rater agreement while the Creativity index had the lowest level of agreement (.63). An examination of the distribution of the ratings confirmed that the artists recognized that creativity is statistically rare. Correlations among the various works of art were quite low (median $r = .18$) which brings the idea of general creativity into question.

The distributions of the ratings got me thinking about the best judges for the CAT. In a subsequent investigation my colleagues and I obtained ratings of college student art from another group of professional artists but we also collected self- and peer-ratings. We again found differences among works of art, but the most important finding was that the ratings of the professionals differed from the self- and peer-ratings. The professionals gave the lowest ratings, which implied that they saw the least amount of creativity in the artwork. We concluded that the professionals might be too critical and that they may have been judging the students' art in terms of what it takes to be a professional. Findings like these have made me suspicious of the generalizability of judges' ratings (cf. Johnson, Runco, & Raina, 2003; Runco, 1989; Runco, McCarthy, & Svensen, 1994; Runco & Smith, 1992). Note that this is quite a different issue from the interrater reliability of judges' ratings that is typically reported. If a research project has judges who are in any way homogeneous (e.g., all professionals), the good inter-rater agreement may be found, even if their ratings do not generalize to other groups of judges.

The need for judges when using the CAT, and my concern about generalization from judges to judges, keeps me from agreeing that the claim that the CAT represents the gold standard for creativity measurement. In fact, I can't imagine any gold standard for creativity measurement. There is no one universally useful applicable creativity measure or assessment. Creativity can be expressed in so many ways, and it is a complex rather than a unitary thing. Certain measures work well for certain objectives and other measures for other objectives. An obvious example of this involves the difference between measures that are designed for creative products and assessments that focus on the creative personality, the creative process, or the creative place. The CAT was designed to assess products and offer information about how those are influenced by the place, or setting. Hennessey (1994) did explore the value of the CAT as a way of understanding the creative process.

Before moving on there is one other intriguing consideration. Recall here that when using the CAT Amabile does not define creativity for the judges. They are to use their own implicit definitions. This seems to work well, at least when you look at the reliabilities reported. Intrigue arises when this approach is juxtaposed to the debate that Paul Torrance had with J. P. Guilford (see Acar & Runco, 2019; Cramond, 1993). This debate involved what to tell participants in studies of creativity. It was not specifically about what to tell judges, but it does suggest that there are situations where it may be problematic to leave "creativity" undefined. Simplifying, Torrance wanted to tell individuals in his research to be creative. He felt that he would obtain the clearest picture of their creativity if they knew that he wanted creativity. In subsequent studies this approach involves explicit instructions where research participants may be told to be creative—and they may be told what creativity is (e.g., an idea that no one else will find) or even how to be creative (e.g., think of things that no one else will think of). Guilford, in contrast, did not want to tell research participants much at all. He felt that the more useful view of their behavior was unguided. He wanted them to be spontaneous, the assumption being that some individuals will be creative when left to their own devices. This is of course the part that relates to Amabile's approach. If the interest is in what people will do, spontaneously, without direction, then allow them to use their own notion of what creativity is. This makes a great deal of sense, at least if the interest is in research results that are indicative of what occurs in the natural environment. There is something to the other view, however. In particular, there is a line of research showing that maximal performances tend to be highly reliable. When people function at their highest level, they tend to behave in a very stable fashion. This in turn leads directly to reliability, which is unsurprising given that reliability is defined as stability and consistency (Anastasi, 2007). Those pros and cons—reliability vs results that generalize to the natural environment—may apply to the question of what judges should be told. Amabile's approach would seem to have the advantage of generalizing to the natural environment.

One of Amabile's (2019) latest chapters explores the theory of Graham Wallas (1926). Wallas is famous for his stage model of the creative process. It includes preparation, incubation, illumination, and verification. I won't summarize Amabile's fine treatment of this theory but do want to say something about one point from her chapter which really struck home. I am referring to her reporting that Wallas used the word *creative* only twice, and he never used the word *creativity*. This struck home because I have several times suggested that the word creativity be avoided (Runco, 2014a). It is too general, and as a noun implies that there is one thing that we can call creativity. Yet in the research someone may be measuring the creative personality and infer something about creativity, while someone else may measure a creative attitude, mood, or cognitive capacity but also infer something about creativity—yet the measures may target very different things. For this reason I have often suggested that it is wise to avoid the word creativity and much better to use the word "creative" because as an adjective it requires that a specific noun is also clearly presented. I just used creative above with personality, attitude, mood, and cognitive capacity, and "creative" can also be used with process, achievement, behavior, and so on. This specificity will allow us to avoid assumptions and communicate more precisely. That is especially important for recommendations about what to do (and what to avoid) and when conducting empirical research. I suspect that Wallas (1926), and maybe Amabile (2019), would go along with this. I will ask Teresa the next chance I get. I do hope to continue collaborating with her. The past 30 years, reading her research and talking turkey on occasion, have been intrinsically meaningful.

Conclusions

The research on creativity has evolved since I started my career, which was within a few years of Amabile's joining the fray. Dozens of influences on creative behavior have been identified in the research, but unlike most influences, it is likely that the intrinsic motivation studied by Amabile is a requirement, not a mere influence. People simply may not put any effort into being creative unless they are intrinsically motivated, and the work resulting when intrinsic motivation is absent may lack something such that it is not truly creative. One possibility is that behavior that is lacking intrinsic motivation is not authentic. Authenticity was tied to creativity long ago (Rogers, 1959) and is more and more recognized as playing a vital role (Runco, 2018; Tan, 2016). Alternatively, behavior that is not intrinsically motivated might be superficial. Individuals who are intrinsically motivated are more likely to be persistent and invest more time into the problem or task, and this in turn increases the likelihood of remote associates and incubation (Plucker, Runco, & Lim, 2006).

One enormously attractive aspect of Amabile's research is that it is quite clear about "creativity." What I mean by that is that she is precise about what is measured and where the action is. When she applied the CAT to collages and poems, for example, she was perfectly clear that she was looking at potentially creative products. When she validated her measure of organizational settings, she was quite clear that the focus was on environments and what have been called "press" factors. In that recent chapters examining the model of Wallas (1926), Amabile kept the focus on process. All of this implies that Amabile avoids an all-too-common pitfall in the creativity research. I am referring to what might be viewed as a kind of inappropriate generalization, where an investigation measures a creative product but slips into generalizations about what it took to make that product (that is, the underlying creative process) or slips into a discussion about the person who made it—when the data are only about the product.

It is very difficult to find any fault at all with Amabile's research. I did mention my concern about generalizing from one group of CAT judges to other groups, but that is not about the CAT nor the rigor of the research designs. It is a statement about how to best interpret results. This chapter also suggested that generalization might be increased by Amabile's technique which does not inform judges of how to define creativity. The other key points herein contrasted measuring situational influences vs individual differences, the varied relationship of intrinsic and extrinsic motives, and the problem of using a one-size-fits-all measurement. There is no gold standard, no one always a valid measure of creativity. Amabile knows this and has produced a corpus of research that is realistic and useful. It has itself been creative and we owe her an enormous debt.

References

Acar, S., & Runco, M. A. (2019). Divergent thinking: New methods, recent research, and extended theory. *Psychology of Aesthetics, Creativity, and the Arts, 13,* 153–158. http://dx.doi.org/10.1037/aca0000231.

Albert, R. S., & Runco, M. A. (1990). Observations, gaps, and conclusions. In M. A. Runco & R. S. Albert (Eds.), *Theories of creativity*. Newbury Park, CA: Sage.

Amabile, T. M. (1990). Within you, without you: The social psychology of creativity, and beyond. In M. A. Runco & R. S. Albert (Eds.), *Theories of creativity* (pp. 61–19). Norwood, NJ: Albex.

Amabile, T. M. (2019). The art of (creative) thought: Graham Walls on the creative process. In V. P. Glaveanu (Ed.), *The creativity reader* (pp. 15–32). New York: Oxford University Press.

Anastasi, A. (1982). *Psychological testing* (5th ed.). New York: Macmillan.

Barron, F. (1995). *No rootless flower: An ecology of creativity*. Cresskill, NJ: Hampton Press.

Chand, I., & Runco, M. A. (1992). Problem finding skills as components in the creative process. *Personality and Individual Differences, 14,* 155–162.

Cramond, B. (1993). The Torrance Tests of Creative Thinking: From design through establishment of predictive validity. In R. F. Subotnik & K. D.

Arnold (Eds.), *Beyond Terman: Contemporary longitudinal studies of giftedness and talent* (pp. 229–254). Norwood, NJ: Ablex.

Hennessey, B. A. (1994). The consensual assessment technique: An examination of the relationship between ratings of product and process creativity. *Creativity Research Journal, 7,* 193–208.

Johnson, D., Runco, M. A., & Raina, M. K. (2003). Parents and teachers' implicit theories of children's creativity: A cross-cultural perspective. *Creativity Research Journal, 14,* 427–438.

Pinho, F. E. (2019, July 22). Having a whale of a time. *Los Angeles Times.* https://enewspaper.latimes.com/desktop/latimes/default.aspx?pubid=50435180-e58e-48b5-8e0c-236bf740270e.

Plucker, J., Runco, M. A., & Lim, W. (2006). Predicting ideational behavior from divergent thinking and discretionary time on task. *Creativity Research Journal, 18,* 55–63.

Rogers, C. R. (1959). Toward a theory of creativity. In H. H. Anderson (Ed.), *Creativity and its cultivation* (pp. 69–82). New York: Harper & Row.

Rubenson, D. L., & Runco, M. A. (1992). The psychoeconomic approach to creativity. *New Ideas in Psychology, 10,* 131–147.

Rubenson, D. L., & Runco, M. A. (1995). The psychoeconomic view of creative work in groups and organizations. *Creativity and Innovation Management, 4,* 232–241.

Runco, M. A. (1989). The creativity of children's art. *Child Study Journal, 19,* 177–189.

Runco, M. A. (Ed.). (1991). *Divergent thinking.* Norwood, NJ: Ablex Publishing Corporation.

Runco, M. A. (1993). Operant theories of insight, originality, and creativity. *American Behavioral Scientist, 37,* 59–74.

Runco, M. A. (Ed.). (2013). *Divergent thinking and creative potential.* Cresskill, NJ: Hampton Press.

Runco, M. A. (2014a). *Creativity: Theories and themes: Research, development, and practice* (2nd ed.). San Diego, CA: Academic Press.

Runco, M. A. (2014b). *Creativity: Theories and themes: Research, development, and practice* (rev ed.). San Diego, CA: Academic Press.

Runco, M. A. (2018). Authentic creativity: Mechanisms, definitions, and empirical efforts. In R. J. Sternberg & J. Kaufman (Eds.), *The nature of human creativity* (pp. 246–263). New York: Cambridge University Press.

Runco, M. A. (2020). Behavioral view of creativity. In M. A. Runco & S. R. Pritizker (Eds.), *Encyclopedia of creativity* (3rd ed.). Cambridge, UK: Elsevier.

Runco, M. A., & Acar, S. (2012). Divergent thinking as an indicator of creative potential. *Creativity Research Journal, 24*, 66–75.

Runco, M. A., McCarthy, K. A., & Svensen, E. (1994). Judgments of the creativity of artwork from students and professional artists. *Journal of Psychology, 128*, 23–31.

Runco, M. A., & Smith, W. R. (1992). Interpersonal and intrapersonal evaluations of creative ideas. *Personality and Individual Differences, 13*, 295–302.

Ruscio, J., Whitney, D. M., & Amabile, T. M. (1998). Looking inside the fishbowl of creativity: Verbal and behavioral predictors of creative performance. *Creativity Research Journal, 11*, 243–263. https://doi.org/10.1207/s15326934crj1103_4.

Tan, C. (2016). Creativity and confucius. *Journal of Genius and Eminence, 1*, 79–84.

Wallas, G. (1926). *The art of thought*. New York: Harcourt Brace & World.

17

The Importance of the Componential Model of Creativity

Christina E. Shalley

Teresa Amabile's Componential Model of Individual Creativity (Amabile, 1983) set the stage for a new era in the study of creativity. Essentially, using a social psychological perspective, she moved the primary focus of much of the research from looking at more of a person-centric approach (e.g., examining highly creative individuals in order to understand why they are so creative) to looking at how the work context can have important effects on individual creativity. In addition, together with the interactionist perspective of creativity (Woodman, Sawyer, & Griffin, 1993), she discussed how personal factors, contextual factors, and their interaction can significantly affect employee creativity. The purpose of this chapter is to reflect on the influence of Teresa's

C. E. Shalley (✉)
Scheller College of Business, Georgia Institute of Technology, Atlanta, GA, USA
e-mail: christina.shalley@scheller.gatech.edu

R. Reiter-Palmon et al. (eds.), *Creativity at Work*,
Palgrave Studies in Creativity and Innovation in Organizations,
https://doi.org/10.1007/978-3-030-61311-2_17

Componential Model of Individual Creativity and her development of the consensual assessment technique for my own research.

By using the Componential Model in a literature synthesis (Shalley, Zhou, & Oldham, 2004), we were able to organize the literature in a cohesive fashion, and to discuss areas in need of future research going forward. For example, we noted that much of the literature that had been conducted was focused on individual creativity, with less research focusing on team creativity. Recently, we have seen significant progress on team creativity research (e.g., Hu, Erdogan, Jiang, Bauer, & Liu, 2017; Mannucci, 2017; Perry-Smith & Shalley, 2014). For example, Y. Li, N. Li, C. Li, and J. Li (2020) drew on a social model of team creativity and developed a dualistic model of the influence of team members who were creative stars on team creativity. They found that a creative star who occupies a central position in the team workflow network has both a positive direct effect on team creativity and a negative indirect effect on team creativity by reducing the learning of members who were nonstars. Also, they found that team coordination can buffer this negative indirect effect on team creativity.

The Componential Model consists of three important factors; that of, domain-relevant skills, creativity relevant skills, and intrinsic motivation. Both the domain-relevant skills and creativity relevant skills were more about the person in terms of their existing knowledge base, and their ability to engage in both divergent and convergent thinking in order to effectively produce creative outcomes. Furthermore, intrinsic motivation was argued to be a critical factor, and contextual factors were proposed to influence individuals' intrinsic motivation. Stressing the key role of intrinsic motivation for creativity has resulted in a body of creativity research that predicts and explains how contextual factors can influence individuals' creativity via its effect on their intrinsic motivation. Some of my work on goal setting, expected evaluation, and competition has strongly relied on this motivation principle (e.g., Shalley, 1991, 1995; Shalley & Oldham, 1997), and in general, the results of this research have been supportive.

A related factor to the above is that by emphasizing a motivational perspective, this has led researchers, including myself, to also look at the important role of other motivational factors. For example, we conducted a fairly recent meta-analysis (Liu, Jiang, Shalley, Keem, & Zhou, 2016) that examined the important role of motivation for creativity across 191 independent samples and over 50,000 employees. Specifically, four types of motivation were included, with three serving as the primary focus (i.e., self-efficacy, prosocial motivation, and intrinsic motivation) and controlling for one in the analysis (i.e., extrinsic motivation). Self-efficacy represents a person's belief that they can be effective on a task, and according to social cognitive theory it can serve as a motivational mechanism. Prosocial motivation is the motivation to focus on novel discoveries that are useful for others according to prosocial motivation theory. In this meta-analysis, we first looked at studies that included the role of creative self-efficacy or general self-efficacy and found significant effects on creativity. Second, the role of prosocial motivation was examined with this also having significant effects on creativity. Third, the role of intrinsic motivation was examined and it also had significant effects on creativity. In general, our results indicated that each of the three types of motivation (i.e., intrinsic motivation, self-efficacy, and prosocial motivation) all simultaneously contributed to creativity. Thus, by using the intrinsic motivation principle, we have expanded on the relationship between other motivational mechanisms for creativity by showing that each of these types of motivation can have an effect on creativity.

In the above-referenced meta-analysis (Liu, et al., 2016), we also found that various contextual and personal factors had different relationships with each of the three different types of motivation. Along this line, we conducted a recent piece (Wang, Liu, & Shalley, 2018) where we examined the effect of idiosyncratic work arrangements (i.e., i-deals) on individual creativity via creative self-efficacy (i.e., an individual's belief that they can be creative on a task). I-deals are individualized work arrangements that are offered to high performing employees either to attract or retain them. We found that i-deals fully mediated the effect for developmental i-deals (e.g., receiving training to enhance their career development), and only partially mediated the effect for flexibility i-deals (e.g., working from home during certain days or hours). In addition, in another study, we looked at whether people high on creative personality are more likely to behave unethically (Keem, Shalley, Kim, & Jeong, 2018). Specifically, research in this area has resulted in mixed findings.

We hypothesized and found that moral disengagement and moral imagination are two parallel mechanisms that encourage or inhibit unethical behavior, with which of these mediation processes occurring depending on moral identity. So, for example, our results across two studies indicated that employees high on dispositional creativity and moral identity were less likely to be morally disengaged and behave less ethically. In addition, those high on both dispositional creativity and moral identity were more likely to be morally imaginative and to behave less unethically. In summary, the specific personal and contextual factors that influence creativity are continuing to be discovered as we detail how and when various motivational mechanisms influence creativity.

In discussing her Componential Model of Creativity, Teresa also focused on how creativity should be defined and how it can be assessed. In terms of her definition, creativity is culturally and historically defined, but in general includes both novelty and usefulness (or appropriateness). This definition is widely accepted and has been used extensively in the literature. In addition, I believe that a major contribution that Teresa has made to the literature is in developing her consensual assessment technique (CAT) to use in order to reliably assess whether a product is creative. The CAT involves having knowledgeable others independently evaluate how creative an idea, product, or process is using the definition of creativity. Both the introduction of the requirement that a product needs to be both novel and useful, and the use of the CAT has led to great strides being made in developing the creativity literature since we can appropriately be able to determine what may or may not be considered to be creative in the field. I have used this technique many times and in a number of studies, and it is widely considered to be highly valid and reliable. In fact, in a recent paper (Koseoglu, Liu, & Shalley, 2017) we adapted the CAT in order to evaluate how creative managers are by having multiple subordinates of a manager rate their manager's level of creativity. That is, instead of taking the assessment of one employee or the manager's supervisor, we took the assessment of three or more of a manager's employees after ensuring that this was appropriate via statistical tests (i.e., Cronbach's alpha, ICC1 and ICC2). This is the first time that the CAT was used in this way, but I believe it could be helpful in the future as more work looks at the effect of subordinates or followers on their managers or leaders. Also, this approach could be used by having coworkers or team members assess the creativity of another employee or team member.

In summary, Teresa Amabile's introduction of the influential Componential Model of Individual Creativity has dramatically moved the field of creativity forward. As of today, creativity research is thriving with multiple researchers studying all different aspects of individual and team creativity. We now have learned quite a bit about individual creativity, in particular, but there is still much more that we need to learn about how to stimulate and support employee creativity. Moreover, we know less about how not to stifle or constrain individual or team creativity, and a great deal of work is still needed to study this issue.

References

Amabile, T. M. (1983). The social psychology of creativity: A componential conceptualization. *Journal of Personality and Social Psychology, 45*(2), 357–376.

Hu, J., Erdogan, B., Jiang, K., Bauer, T. N., & Liu, S. (2017). Leader humility and team creativity: The role of team information sharing, psychological safety, and power distance. *Journal of Applied Psychology, 103,* 313–324.

Keem, S., Shalley, C. E., Kim, E., & Jeong, I. (2018). Are creative individuals bad apples? A dual pathway model of unethical behavior. *Journal of Applied Psychology, 103,* 416–431.

Koseoglu, G., Liu, Y., & Shalley, C. E. (2017). Working with creative leaders: Exploring the relationship between supervisors' creativity and their employees' creativity. *The Leadership Quarterly, 28,* 798–811.

Li, Y., Li, N., Li, C., & Li, J. (2020). The boon and bane of creative "stars": A social network exploration of how and when team creativity is (and is not) driven by a star teammate. *Academy of Management Journal, 63,* 613–635.

Liu, D., Jiang, K., Shalley, C. E., Keem, S., & Zhou, J. (2016). Motivational mechanisms of employee creativity: A meta-analytic examination and theoretical extension of the creativity literature. *Organizational Behavior and Human Decision Processes, 137,* 236–263.

Mannucci, P. V. (2017). Drawing Snow White and animating Buzz Lightyear: Technological toolkit characteristics and creativity in cross disciplinary teams. *Organization Science, 28,* 711–728.

Perry-Smith, J. E., & Shalley, C. E. (2014). A social composition view of team creativity: The role of member nationality heterogeneous ties outside the team. *Organization Science, 25,* 1434–1452.

Shalley, C. E. (1991). Effects of productivity goals, creativity goals, and personal discretion on individual creativity. *Journal of Applied Psychology, 76,* 179–185.

Shalley, C. E. (1995). Effects of coaction, expected evaluation, and goal setting on creativity and productivity. *Academy of Management Journal, 38,* 483–503.

Shalley, C. E., & Oldham, G. R. (1997). Competition and creativity performance: Effects of competitor presence and visibility. *Creativity Research Journal, 10,* 337–345.

Shalley, C. E., Zhou, J., & Oldham, G. R. (2004). The effects of personal and contextual characteristics on creativity: Where should we go from here? *Journal of Management, 30,* 933–958.

Wang, S., Liu, Y., & Shalley, C. E. (2018). Idiosyncratic deals and employee creativity: The mediating role of creative self-efficacy. *Human Resource Management, 57,* 1443–1453.

Woodman, R. W., Sawyer, J. E., & Griffin, R. W. (1993). Toward a theory of organizational creativity. *Academy of Management Review, 18,* 293–321.

18

The Two Social Psychologies of Creativity: From Historiometric to Experimental (and the Latter to Stay)

Dean Keith Simonton

Teresa Amabile and I faced a similar problem when each of us entered our respective graduate programs in social psychology, I at Harvard in 1970 and she at Stanford in 1972. That problem was simply that we both wanted to study creativity when that subject was not then a recognized research topic in the subdiscipline. For example, the textbook assigned in my introductory social psychology course in college didn't even include "creativity" as an index entry (viz. Brown, 1965). In contrast, creativity was then considered a bona fide area in introductory psychology texts, including the one that I had studied in my sophomore year (viz. Hilgard & Atkinson, 1967). Yet it was then considered to belong to subdisciplines like educational, personality, and cognitive psychology—but definitely not social psychology.

D. K. Simonton (✉)
Department of Psychology, University of California, Davis, Davis, CA, USA
e-mail: Dksimonton@ucdavis.edu

R. Reiter-Palmon et al. (eds.), *Creativity at Work*,
Palgrave Studies in Creativity and Innovation in Organizations,
https://doi.org/10.1007/978-3-030-61311-2_18

Even so, I was somewhat more fortunate than Amabile insofar as my social psychology program was housed in the Department of Social Relations, which included sociology and cultural anthropology as well as personality and developmental psychology. Even though the department broke apart shortly after I entered the program, the faculty remained more open to alternative perspectives and methods than might hold in a more mainstream social psychology program. It also helped me that Harvard's program hired a brand new assistant professor, David A. Kenny, who was very open to new methodologies, having been the doctoral student of the eminent social psychologist Donald Campbell, a major proponent of quasi-experimental designs (e.g., Campbell, 1969). In fact, Kenny's supreme openness to methodological innovations much later led to his receiving the 2019 Distinguished Scientific Contributions Award from the American Psychological Association.

In any event, I managed to convince Kenny to chair my dissertation, resulting in a thesis entitled "The Social Psychology of Creativity: An Archival Data Analysis" (Simonton, 1974). Despite the fact that I was warned that my research was unpublishable in top-tier journals, I decided to submit a revised version of the core chapter to the *Journal of Personality and Social Psychology* (*JPSP*), then viewed as the premier journal in the field (see Simonton, 2002). Contrary to the warnings, the manuscript was accepted, pending the usual revise and resubmit (Simonton, 1975). Indeed, the responses from both editors and referees were surprisingly appreciative, apparently welcoming research that departed so dramatically from the mainstream. A few years later one of my *JPSP* submissions was even accepted without any requests for revisions from any of the reviewers, the editor even telling me that he had never seen that before—nor have I since! Admittedly, it was partly a matter of being at the right place at the right time, for social psychology back then was undergoing a "crisis of confidence" (Elms, 1975), a discontent even expressed by *JPSP*'s editor shortly before I began my career (McGuire, 1973). The feeling was widespread back then that the subdiscipline was stagnating, and thus overdue for an infusion of new topics and techniques.

By the time that my work started appearing, Amabile was formulating her research ideas within a much more traditional social psychology program. As she reported,

> When I told my graduate advisors that I wanted to research in the social psychology of creativity, they informed me that there was no such thing. But, just weeks after that conversation, I opened the new *Journal of Personality and Social Psychology* to find an article by Dean Simonton (1975) with the phrase "social psychology of creativity" splashed boldly about. That was all the encouragement I needed. (Amabile, 1990, p. 64)

The aftermath is well-known to everybody participating in this Festschrift: She made a big name for herself publishing research in the social psychology of creativity. But I want to go a step further by arguing that she, not I, deserves all of the credit for establishing creativity as a genuine topic within social psychology. To be sure, judging from database searches using PsycINFO and Google Scholar, I seem to have been the first to invent the expression "social psychology of creativity." Yet those words are only found in the main title of my 1974 dissertation. I never once repeated that title in any of my publications. Even my central thesis results were published under the title "Sociocultural Context of Individual Creativity: A Transhistorical Time-Series Analysis" (Simonton, 1975). Moreover, not a single one of my own graduate students ever used those words in any of their published titles either (cf. Ting, 1986). Indeed, "sociocultural context" came to replace "social psychology" (see also Glăveanu et al., 2020).

All this stands in striking contrast to Amabile's claim on the phrase. First of all, she actually used "social psychology of creativity" in the main tiles of major publications, starting with her *JPSP* article on the consensual assessment technique (Amabile, 1982) and then continuing with her very first book a year later (Amabile, 1983; see also Amabile, 1996). Better yet, she even succeeded in getting at least one graduate student to incorporate this expression in main title (e.g., Hennessey, 2003). Yet most importantly, her methods were more compatible with mainstream social psychology, which remains strongly orientated toward laboratory experiments. Contemporary researchers who claim to be doing the social psychology of creativity are in fact experimentalists, even if testing hypotheses far removed from Amabile's research program (Damian & Simonton, 2015). By comparison, the bulk of my empirical research on creativity has been strictly historiometric in character (Simonton, 2019a,

2019b). As in my doctoral dissertation, historical and biographical data are collected on hundreds, even thousands of creative geniuses, and then nomothetic hypotheses are tested by subjecting those data to objective quantification and statistical analyzes.

Amabile (1983) herself recognized early on that the two social psychologies are hardly the same, even when overtly addressing the same general phenomenon. She gave the example of the relation between social reinforcement and creativity, where I found no association whereas she "found that the relationship is sometimes positive and sometimes negative" (p. 176). She then provides three stark differences between her and my research programs: (a) there's little overlap between the independent variables investigated; (b) the independent variables are examined across rather contrasting time periods; and (c) the operational definitions of the dependent variable, creativity, are vastly divergent. It's like in the biomedical sciences where in vitro and in vivo studies do not necessarily yield the same outcomes.

To be sure, Amabile has by no means confined her research to laboratory experiments (e.g., Amabile & Kramer, 2011), and I myself must admit to conducting experimental research from time to time (e.g., Ritter et al., 2012; cf. Simonton, 1986). Yet when every consideration is given its proper weight, I believe that she, not me, should be identified as the true founder of the social psychology of creativity. I'm no more than a precursor.

References

Amabile, T. M. (1982). Social psychology of creativity: A consensual assessment technique. *Journal of Personality and Social Psychology, 43,* 997–1013.

Amabile, T. M. (1983). *The social psychology of creativity*. New York: Springer-Verlag.

Amabile, T. M. (1990). Within you, without you: The social psychology of creativity, and beyond. In M. A. Runco & R. S. Albert (Eds.), *Theories of creativity* (pp. 61–91). Newbury Park, CA: Sage.

Amabile, T. M. (1996). *Creativity in context: Update to the social psychology of creativity*. Boulder, CO: Westview.
Amabile, T. M., & Kramer, S. J. (2011). *The progress principle: Using small wins to ignite joy, engagement, and creativity at work*. Boston: Harvard Business Review Press.
Brown, R. (1965). *Social psychology*. New York: The Free Press.
Campbell, D. T. (1969). Reforms as experiments. *American Psychologist, 24,* 409–442.
Damian, R. I., & Simonton, D. K. (2015). Four perspectives on creativity. In R. A. Scott & S. M. Kosslyn (Eds.), *Emerging trends in the social and behavioral sciences* (pp. 1–15). Oxford, UK: Wiley.
Elms, A. C. (1975). The crisis of confidence in social psychology. *American Psychologist, 30,* 967–976.
Glăveanu, V. P., Hanchett Hanson, M., Baer, J., Barbot, B., Clapp, E., Corazza, G. E., … Sternberg, R. J. (2020). Advancing creativity theory and research: A sociocultural manifesto. *Journal of Creative Behavior, 54,* 741–745.
Hennessey, B. A. (2003). The social psychology of creativity. *Scandinavian Journal of Educational Research, 47,* 253–271.
Hilgard, E. R., & Atkinson, R. G. (1967). *Introduction to psychology* (4th ed.). New York: Harcourt, Brace, & World.
McGuire, W. J. (1973). The yin and yang of progress in social psychology: Seven koan. *Journal of Personality and Social Psychology, 26,* 446–456.
Ritter, S. M., Damian, R. I., Simonton, D. K., van Baaren, R. B., Strick, M., Derks, J., & Dijksterhuis, A. (2012). Diversifying experiences enhance cognitive flexibility. *Journal of Experimental Social Psychology, 48,* 961-964.
Simonton, D. K. (1974). *The social psychology of creativity: An archival data analysis* (Unpublished doctoral dissertation). Harvard University.
Simonton, D. K. (1975). Sociocultural context of individual creativity: A transhistorical time-series analysis. *Journal of Personality and Social Psychology, 32,* 1119–1133.
Simonton, D. K. (1986). Dispositional attributions of (presidential) leadership: An experimental simulation of historiometric results. *Journal of Experimental Social Psychology, 22,* 389–418.
Simonton, D. K. (2002). It's absolutely impossible? A longitudinal study of one psychologist's response to conventional naysayers. In R. J. Sternberg (Ed.), *Psychologists defying the crowd: Stories of those who battled the establishment and won* (pp. 238–254). Washington, DC: American Psychological Association.

Simonton, D. K. (2019a). The sociocultural context of exceptional creativity: Historiometric methods. In I. Lebuda & V. P. Glăveanu (Eds.), *Palgrave handbook of social creativity research* (pp. 13–25). London: Palgrave Macmillan.
Simonton, D. K. (2019b). The sociocultural context of exceptional creativity: Historiometric studies. In I. Lebuda & V. P. Glăveanu (Eds.), *Palgrave handbook of social creativity research* (pp. 177–189). London: Palgrave Macmillan.
Ting, S.-S. (1986). *The social psychology of Chinese literary creativity: An archival data analysis* (Unpublished doctoral dissertation). University of California, Davis.

19

The Legacy of Inner Work Life in the Progress Principle

Jeff Steiner

The Legacy of Inner Work Life in the Progress Principle

I first encountered Teresa Amabile's scholarship as a practitioner (a talent development director at a Wall Street firm) seeking novel, important, and prescriptive insights to share with new managers. Amabile's research, writing, and public speaking about the progress principle (Amabile & Kramer, 2011a) was precisely what I had been searching for. The concept was remarkable in three ways: its uniquely person-centric approach to management, its comprehensive and rigorous methods, and its relevance to practitioners. Upon commencing an academic career, my appreciation of how the progress principle's research simultaneously advanced social

J. Steiner (✉)
Harvard Business School, Boston, MA, USA
e-mail: jsteiner@hbs.edu

R. Reiter-Palmon et al. (eds.), *Creativity at Work*,
Palgrave Studies in Creativity and Innovation in Organizations,
https://doi.org/10.1007/978-3-030-61311-2_19

science theory, research methods, and management practice continued to increase.

In this chapter, I will elaborate on the uniqueness of the progress principle and its research program with special attention to the concept of *inner work life*. I will briefly define and summarize the contributions made in this work by Amabile and coauthor Steven Kramer, elaborate on its many contributions to the field, and discuss how it has influenced my own work. Lastly, I will discuss how the discovery of the progress principle paved the way for future research and what that future might hold.

The Progress Principle and Inner Work Life

The progress principle asserts that the best and most sustainable source of employee motivation is the psychological experience associated with making progress on tasks deemed meaningful (Amabile & Kramer, 2011a). This theory suggests that managers ought to focus more on how workers psychologically relate to making (and not making) progress on their work. Therefore, the role of a manager is to catalyze employees' progress and eliminate both objective and subjective barriers.

Amabile and Kramer discovered the progress principle during a longitudinal, mixed-methods field study that sought answers to basic questions about an individual's *inner work life*. The authors defined this term as the emotions, perceptions, and motivations that an individual experiences as they react to and make sense of events at work. According to Amabile and Kramer (2007), perceptions range from "immediate impressions to more fully developed theories about what is happening and what it means," while *emotions* refer to "sharply defined reactions (such as elation over a particular success or anger over a particular obstacle) or more general feeling states, like good and bad moods." Meanwhile, motivations are "your grasp of what needs to be done and your drive to do it at any given moment" (Amabile & Kramer, 2007). The authors' progress principle answered such questions as what affects a person's inner work life, how it relates to actual events at work, and its relationship to performance outcomes.

The progress principle research illuminated the dynamism of inner work life, showing that perceptions, emotions, and motivations interact in complex ways (as opposed to a more traditional view depicting an individual's thoughts and perceptions as mere antecedents to motivations and perceptions). Inner work life is a constant, ever-evolving stream: As events unfold at work, individuals automatically form and adjust perceptions of their colleagues, organization, work, and even themselves. Perceptions shape emotions that, in turn, affect moment-to-moment motivation regarding tasks, ultimately driving daily performance. Moreover, emotions, motivations, and performance also affect perceptions. Thus, inner work life is the product of a highly complex and ever-changing system consisting of multiple recursive relationships.

The complexity of inner work life suggests that no quick fix is available for managers to create enduring, positive inner work life experiences. However, essential practical implications remain. Amabile and Kramer (2011a) identified *catalysts* for a positive inner work life, such as setting clear goals, encouraging autonomy, providing sufficient resources, and providing help. The authors also defined *nourishers*, or acts of interpersonal support like respect, recognition, and emotional comfort. These suggested practices align with longstanding recommendations in the management literature (Hackman & Oldham, 1980; Herzberg, 1966) but provide a much deeper understanding of how they actually affect individual workers. More specifically, fostering a positive inner work life is vital because it can create a "progress loop" in which a positive inner work life drives progress on work, in turn enhancing inner work life, increasing motivation, and making future progress more likely. The greatest takeaway for managers is *not* to try to manipulate the feelings of others. Instead, they should seek to change the circumstances of the situation that make realizing objective progress on work likely. Amabile and Kramer's (2011a) book includes countless examples—taken directly from real data—of how managers can improve inner work life by making progress easier to achieve.

Skeptics might say that using the metaphorical microscope to scrutinize nearly 12,000 daily diaries submitted by employees, analyzing their relationship to work outcomes, might not have been necessary. Indeed, for management scholars, "progress at work" seems intuitive and obvious, leading them to speculate how they might have missed grasping the concept. Yet despite seeming so fundamental, the most essential and enduring teachings of management—whether frequently cited in academic publications, featured in Management 101 courses, or offered as timeless advice by business leaders—would suggest that managers have indeed overlooked this basic principle of managing others. As Amabile and Kramer proved empirically, even managers overlook the importance of progress. When asked to identify what motivates workers and what most affects employee emotions, 669 managers surveyed globally ranked "making progress in the work" *last* on a list that also included recognition for good work, incentives, interpersonal support, and clear goals. Amabile and Kramer wrote:

> If you are a manager, the progress principle holds clear implications for where to focus your efforts. It suggests that you have more influence than you may realize over employees' well-being, motivation, and creative output. Knowing what serves to catalyze and nourish progress—and what does the opposite—turns out to be the key to effectively managing people and their work. (2011b)

Thus, while the term "manager" does not evoke "nourisher of progress" for most, it ought to. A good manager is not merely upbeat, able to communicate a vision, and accustomed to holding others accountable—Amabile and Kramer provided data showing that the best managers focus on catalyzing progress, and positive outcomes follow from that. Astonishingly, researchers and practitioners alike have historically said little about the importance of helping workers make incremental progress on daily tasks. This dearth only makes the contribution of the progress principle more significant.

The Contributions and Legacy of the Progress Principle

Person-Centric Approach

The progress principle—and, in particular, its contribution of inner work life—helped to humanize the science and practice of management. Considering that a term for "inner work life" was even needed in the first place, it is telling that management scholars did not yet have a way to refer to the moment-to-moment subjective experience of working people. The history and traditions of management research offer a critical context for understanding the uniqueness of the progress principle's approach and its impact on the field. From its outset, management research sought to understand precisely how humans function best at work to optimize their performance (Taylor, 1911). While researchers problematized the human elements of work, inner experiences were only interesting insofar as they affected performance and could be manipulated by managers. The behaviorist paradigm that dominated psychology research (Mahoney, 1989) influenced management (Locke, 1977). Researchers therefore began to focus on objective aspects of the work environment and how these aspects could be altered. Job design theory (Hackman & Oldham, 1975), for example, championed the idea that an individual's psychology affected performance. To influence performance, the authors asserted, managers must design jobs to be conducive to universal human needs. In subsequent years, researchers considered a variety of constructs (e.g., motivation, engagement, commitment, sense of purpose, and others) interesting because their perceptions correlated with performance. Nevertheless, much of the research still failed to fully consider how each individual worker had unique moment-to-moment subjective experiences, and that feelings about work could vary widely even within a single day.

Through coining the term "inner work life" and studying its underlying structure with detailed self-reported data from workers, Amabile and Kramer put particular emphasis on the lived experience at work. They shifted an individual's unique experience at work from the background to the foreground. Hence, they contributed to management scholarship by humanizing its approach, emphasizing the necessity of moment-to-moment subjective experience and giving voice to the workers who live it.

Rigorous Methods

Inner work life is difficult to ascertain from an outside observer's perspective, undoubtedly one reason why so few have tried to study this topic. Workers regularly conceal their thoughts and feelings at work, which makes their inner experiences challenging to monitor in an organizational setting as well as difficult to scientifically interrogate. To paraphrase Amabile and Kramer (2011a), even if a hidden observer could scan one's work emails, observe one's interactions at work, and have insight into the quality of one's work, that outside observer would still not be able to observe *what the experience was like for the individual under consideration*, the worker performing the work.

The puzzle, then, was how to obtain access to this subjective experience and quantify the inner work lives of individuals. Amabile and Kramer adopted a much more rigorous method than the traditional one-time survey. Accordingly, they embraced the inherent complexity associated with studying the inner lives of working people. In the process, the authors designed a study that did not rely on the assumption that individuals could respond accurately and thoroughly to questions about a general, abstract account of a "typical" experience at work spanning an unspecified time horizon. Instead, they prompted individuals to report only on their actual experiences that day. After all, knowledge workers would certainly be unlikely to describe any given day as "typical."

Thus, Amabile and Kramer studied a discrete number of project teams to capture workers' daily experiences—in terms of actual, objective events and inner, subjective experiences—to understand the work contexts in which each individual operated. Workers responded to a daily survey that inquired about their perceptions of the work environment (supervisor, team, work environment, and the work), their mood, and their motivation throughout the day. Employees also responded to an open-ended question about an event that happened during the day, as well as quantitative items pertaining to that event. Such extensive data collection enabled the research team to generate a rich representation of each individual's daily experience on a given date.

The study ultimately analyzed the experiences of 238 employees across 26 teams inside seven companies: in other words, a total of 11,637 daily diary surveys were analyzed (of which, astonishingly, Amabile personally read each one). Using extensive analytical databases with strong inter-rater reliability, the researchers categorized events (and attributes of the events) in extensively detailed ways, enabling a deep understanding of how people related their experiences at work. The data illuminated the lives of workers with unprecedented detail and complexity. Unquestionably, the Progress Principle research program was ahead of its time in setting new standards for methodological rigor.

Relevance to Practitioners

The contributions of the Progress Principle are practitioner-relevant. Practitioners—the roughly three billion employed persons globally—stand to benefit the most from the knowledge that management scholarship creates. Despite this fact, management scholars somehow seem to underestimate the importance of creating knowledge that people can readily use.

Therefore, the Progress Principle serves as a positive example for the field to create actionable knowledge. Its findings, taken as a whole, suggest that the role of managers should be reframed from organizing and monitoring work to catalyzing progress by fostering better inner work lives. The book contains countless practical examples showing how a manager's actions can so profoundly affect the experience of workers and the daily progress they make, providing prescriptive insights that are evidence-based, timeless, and impactful.

The Progress Principle Moving Forward

The Progress Principle as Inspiration

The Progress Principle paved the way for a new kind of management research focused on the inner, subjective experiences of working people as they went about their ordinary—but nonetheless fascinating—days at work. For me personally, the Progress Principle was an inspiration, demonstrating that the world's best management scholars and thinkers could illuminate profound, vital insights about the lived experience of working people.

My own research investigates how workers, managers, and organizations can foster well-being through work. This endeavor includes investigating how individuals make meaning of their experiences at work, how emotions at work relate to broader judgments regarding life satisfaction, and how managers can address issues of mental health in the workplace. I am grateful that conducting this research does not make me a trailblazer but builds upon and extends the work of scholars like Amabile, who have created a space for scholars to investigate the relationship between work and well-being. The Progress Principle, in particular, shaped so much of my own thinking about how to conduct research and what to study as well as the potential of research to create positive change. Amabile's scholarship played a substantial role in shaping my interests well before we even met. In fact, I can recall completing *The Progress Principle* for the first time and bookmarking a quote at the end of the book that continues to inspire me today:

> We believe that, if management is to have enduring meaning in this world, it should improve people's lives… management should enrich the lives of people working inside the organization… (Amabile & Kramer, 2011a, p. 192)

Equally inspiring, Amabile and Kramer (2007) expanded on point and made a call to action directly to practitioners via their Harvard Business Review article:

Discovering how inner work life affects organizational performance is clearly valuable. But as researchers, we hope we have also made progress on another front. Inner work lives matter deeply to the people living them. Studies of the modern workweek show that knowledge workers today, as compared with workers of past eras, spend more time in the office and more time focused on work issues while outside the office. As the proportion of time that is claimed by work rises, inner work life becomes a bigger component of life itself. People deserve happiness. They deserve dignity and respect. When we act on that realization, it is not only good for business. It affirms our value as human beings.

Practicing the Progress Principle

Amabile provides the example of a leader who "practices what she preaches." In my own work with Amabile as both a research associate and doctoral student, I saw her live out the values and advice shared in the Progress Principle. She showed unwavering commitment to catalyzing progress in *every interaction*, removing barriers and providing support.

Amabile's reputation as an exceptional mentor is well-deserved. She has been an outstanding advisor to generations of students. In addition, she founded the Harvard Business School Organizational Behavior Lab, a flagship seminar for doctoral students well-known for its uniquely supportive culture. Students seeking useful feedback, inspiration, and encouragement to persevere through challenges consider the lab a refuge. Amabile was awarded the Wyss Award for Excellence in Mentoring in 2016, a further testament to her remarkable collaboration with students.

Before I began working with Amabile, several people informed me that she is a joy to work with and work for. I agree. Her regular highlighting and catalyzing of progress—making incremental steps on lengthy research projects—keeps me and her other collaborators engaged, enthusiastic, committed, and joyful. Indeed, I would like to thank Amabile for putting her research into practice and exceeding her own high expectations for good management that she so eloquently argued for in *The Progress Principle*. She has set an example to all that she has worked with in terms of how to implement this research in practice.

Conclusion

Amabile's scholarship was among the first large-scale studies that made the worker's thoughts, feelings, and perceptions a focus of investigation, inspiring scholars to take matters of inner work life seriously. In her current collaboration with Lotte Bailyn, Marcy Crary, Tim Hall, Kathy Kram, and me, the research team closely examines the psychological experience associated with retirement. Thus, this group of researchers is continuing this tradition of studying work as lived experience. While the legacy of the progress principle is still being written, I believe that the implications will reverberate for generations. In many ways, small and large, this principle can and has made the world a better place.

Acknowledgements I would like to thank Amabile for being such a prolific scholar, incredible mentor, and cherished friend to all her fellow researchers. I would assert that her impact is much greater than she realizes, and I, along with countless others, am excited for all that is still to come.

References

Amabile, T., & Kramer, S. (2007, May). Inner work life: Understanding the subtext of business performance. *Harvard Business Review*. https://hbr.org/2007/05/inner-work-life-understanding-the-subtext-of-business-performance.

Amabile, T., & Kramer, S. (2011a). *The progress principle: Using small wins to ignite joy, engagement, and creativity at work*. Boston: Harvard Business Review Press.

Amabile, T., & Kramer, S. (2011b, May). The power of small wins. *Harvard Business Review*. https://hbr.org/2011/05/the-power-of-small-wins.

Hackman, J. R., & Oldham, G. R. (1975). Development of the job diagnostic survey. *Journal of Applied Psychology, 60*(2), 159–170. https://doi.org/10.1037/h0076546.

Hackman, J. R., & Oldham, G. R. (1980). *Work redesign*. Reading: Addison-Wesley.

Herzberg, F. (1966). *Work and the nature of man.* Cleveland: World Publishing.

Locke, E. A. (1977). The myths of behavior mod in organizations. *The Academy of Management Review, 2*(4), 543. https://doi.org/10.2307/257507.

Mahoney, M. J. (1989). Scientific psychology and radical behaviorism: Important distinctions based in scientism and objectivism. *American Psychologist, 44*(11), 1372–1377. https://doi.org/10.1037/0003-066X.44.11.1372.

Taylor, F. W. (1911). *The principles of scientific management*. New York: Harper & Brothers.

20

Four Giant Steps Forward: A Tribute to Teresa Amabile and How She Transformed the Field of Creativity

Robert J. Sternberg

It is 1983. In this year, a Harvard professor, Howard Gardner, is about to transform the field of human intelligence with his theory of multiple intelligences (Gardner, 1983). In this same year, a *future* Harvard professor is equally about to transform a related field, the field of human creativity (Amabile, 1983a, 1983b). In this volume and her later follow-up (Amabile, 1996), Amabile will take three giant steps forward for the field of creativity, a field that until that time had specialized only in "baby steps." Her contributions would last throughout an entire career (see, e.g., Amabile, 2018).

R. J. Sternberg (✉)
Department of Human Development, Cornell University, Ithaca, NY, USA
e-mail: robert.sternberg@cornell.edu; rjs487@cornell.edu

R. Reiter-Palmon et al. (eds.), *Creativity at Work*,
Palgrave Studies in Creativity and Innovation in Organizations,
https://doi.org/10.1007/978-3-030-61311-2_20

Repositioning the Field of Creativity

Like the field of human intelligence, the field of human creativity historically has been an outlier in the broader field of psychology. At best, it has been an orphan field, with no clear historical lineage and many of the best people shying away from a field that never had had a place in mainstream psychology.

The field was revitalized by Guilford (1950) in his APA presidential address. Guilford's address was transformative, but it placed the field of creativity clearly in a psychometric tradition, and in particular, *his* psychometric tradition emphasizing fairly trivial measures of divergent thinking. It would be hard to underestimate the impact, both positive and negative, of Guilford's address. On the positive side, it helped establish creativity as a field through its emphasis on the measurement of divergent thinking. On the negative side, the main tests it spawned, the Torrance Tests of Creative Thinking (Torrance, 1974), in some respects canalized conceptions of creativity as a psychological phenomenon and made the measurement of creativity resemble that of intelligence—largely atheoretical, limited in scope, and even trivialized.

Amabile's two early books accomplished for the field of creativity what Hunt, Frost, and Lunneborg (1973) and Sternberg (1977) tried to do for the field of intelligence—to place the field in the mainstream. But whereas Hunt and colleagues and Sternberg sought to place the field of intelligence in the mainstream of cognitive psychology, Amabile tried to place creativity in the mainstream of social psychology. In an extraordinary coup, Amabile was able to place two articles on creativity in the most prestigious mainstream social-psychology journal (Amabile, 1982, 1983b), much as Hunt and Sternberg were able to place their work on intelligence into mainstream cognitive-psychology journals (e.g., Hunt, Lunneborg, & Lewis, 1975; Sternberg, 1983).

As a result of Amabile's work, the field of creativity was transformed. It was no longer merely an orphan that, at best, was peripheral even to psychometric individual differences research. It became a field that could be taken seriously because it had become a part of mainstream social psychology.

Theoretical Groundwork

Amabile made a further seminal contribution that, in large part, was the basis for her success in integrating the field of creativity into the larger field of social psychology. She recognized that, although Guilford and Torrance had developed measures of creativity, they had done so largely in the absence of any meaningful theory or model of creativity. This was in a way ironic, because Guilford was model-driven, perhaps to a fault, in his work on intelligence (e.g., Guilford, 1967). He was so model-driven that he failed to recognize that his rotations of factor analytic solutions were yielding what were largely spurious conclusions (see Horn & Knapp, 1973).

Amabile (1983b) placed creativity on a firm theoretical footing by proposing a componential model of creativity. Amabile's model had four components, three internal and one external: domain-relevant skills for expertise, creativity-relevant processes, intrinsic motivation, and the (external) social environment in which one is embedded. Other models of creativity later adopted aspects of this componential approach (e.g., Gardner, 2011; Sternberg, 1988, 2018).

Whereas the field of intelligence long had had theorists proposing rather detailed (factorial) accounts of intelligence, dating back at least to Spearman (1927), the field of creativity had grown up largely atheoretically, with the exception of some not very persuasive work of psychodynamic theorists. Amabile's work changed the field and gave rise, ultimately, to many different theories of creativity (see Kaufman & Sternberg, 2010, 2019). Some of the theories have been componential, others not. But the critical thing is that, like Amabile's, they gave rise to empirical predictions and were empirically testable.

The Role of Intrinsic Motivation

Amabile's third seminal contribution and transformation of the field was, in my view, based on her emphasis, in her work on creativity, on the importance of intrinsic motivation. Basically, she argued, if you want to encourage people to be creative, focus on promoting their intrinsic motivation to accomplish tasks, not their extrinsic motivation to receive rewards. Today most of us "know" this. It is because of Amabile's work that we know it. Lepper and Greene (1975) previously had shown that extrinsic rewards undermine intrinsic motivation. What Amabile added was that such rewards also undermine creativity more generally. Creators start to focus on the rewards rather than on the creativity of their products.

As the years went by, Amabile recognized that her initial thesis was perhaps overbroad, and that extrinsic motivators had a role to play in addition to intrinsic ones (Amabile, 2018). As an example, if university professors (including her!) were not paid a salary (clearly an extrinsic motivator), they most likely would find another line of work. But the basic point she made has remained untouched, and that is that society's preoccupation with extrinsic motivators has been largely negative for the development of creativity. Indeed, anyone who has children will have learned the same lesson the hard way as he or she watched the children become more and more focused on the rewards, such as high grades, and less and less focused on the work that leads to the grades.

The Consensual Assessment Technique

A major goal of any test-based approach is to strive for objectivity and, equally, ease of scoring. It is harder to sell tests if they are perceived as subjectively scored or as difficult to score. This is especially true when large numbers of people take the tests. The Torrance Tests, although somewhat subjectively scored, have been scored based on strict protocols for scoring, such as originality, fluency, and elaboration. Amabile (1982), in her earliest contribution to a major social-psychology journal, showed that one could obtain a quite reliable and valid measurement of creativity using what she called a consensual assessment technique (often abbreviated through the acronym CAT).

In one sense, there is nothing seemingly revolutionary in the CAT. One has creative experts (or as close as one can get to them) score creative products and one averages their ratings, obtaining an averaged score for the creativity of the various products. But in another sense, there is something revolutionary about the CAT. It adumbrated and ultimately gave rise to what is sometimes called a sociocultural approach to creativity (see Csikszentmihalyi, 2013; Glaveanu et al., 2019). The basic idea is that creativity isn't a thing that somehow resides in the head. It is a match between what resides in the head and the sociocultural demands of the environment that is doing the judging as to what is creative. From this point of view, objective scoring is not difficult but rather impossible because there is no "objective" thing that is "creative." Rather, creativity always is judged with respect to a sociocultural milieu. It is for this reason that work that is appreciated as creative in one place or one time may be viewed as pedestrian or even as uninspiringly dull in another. Some have argued that intelligence is the same way (e.g., Cole, Gay, Glick, & Sharp, 1971; Greenfield, 2020; Serpell, 2017; Sternberg, 2020)—that it can be understood only in reference to the sociocultural milieu in which it is judged.

Conclusion

In conclusion, Amabile, from early in her career, has transformed the field of creativity. Much of what we know as the field of creativity today stems from her influence. It is a pleasure, therefore, to write this brief essay recognizing the seminal contributions of a scholar who took an orphan field, found its parentage in social psychology, and made it whole again.

References

Amabile, T. M. (1982, November). The social psychology of creativity: A consensual assessment technique. *Journal of Personality and Social Psychology, 43*(5), 997–1013.

Amabile, T. M. (1983a). *The social psychology of creativity*. New York: Springer.

Amabile, T. M. (1983b). The social psychology of creativity: A componential conceptualization. *Journal of Personality and Social Psychology, 45*(2), 357–376.
Amabile, T. M. (1996). *Creativity in context: Update to the social psychology of creativity*. New York: Routledge.
Amabile, T. M. (2018). Creativity and the labor of love. In R. J. Sternberg & J. C. Kaufman (Eds.), *The nature of human creativity* (pp. 1–15). New York: Cambridge University Press.
Cole, M., Gay, J., Glick, J., & Sharp, D. W. (1971). *The cultural context of learning and thinking*. New York: Basic Books.
Csikszentmihalyi, M. (2013). *Creativity: Flow and the psychology of discovery and invention*. New York: Harper Perennial.
Gardner, H. (1983). *Frames of mind: The theory of multiple intelligences*. New York: Basic.
Gardner, H. (2011). *Creating minds*. New York: Basic.
Glaveanu, V. P., Hanchett Hanson, M., Baer, J., Barbot, B., Clapp, E., Corazza, G., … Sternberg, R. J. (2019). Advancing creativity theory and research: A sociocultural manifesto. *Journal of Creative Behavior*. https://doi.org/10.1002/jocb.395.
Greenfield, P. M. (2020). Historical evolution of intelligence. In R. J. Sternberg (Ed.), *Cambridge handbook of intelligence* (2nd ed., pp. 916–939). New York: Cambridge University Press.
Guilford, J. P. (1950). Creativity. *American Psychologist, 5*, 444–454.
Guilford, J. P. (1967). *The nature of human intelligence*. New York: McGraw-Hill.
Horn, J. L., & Knapp, J. R. (1973). On the subjective character of the empirical base of Guilford's structure-of-intellect model. *Psychological Bulletin, 80*(1), 33–43. https://doi.org/10.1037/h0034681.
Hunt, E. B., Frost, N., & Lunneborg, C. (1973). Individual differences in cognition: A new approach to intelligence. In G. Bower (Ed.), *The psychology of learning and motivation* (Vol. 7, pp. 87–122). New York: Academic Press.
Hunt, E., Lunneborg, C., & Lewis, J. (1975). What does it mean to be high verbal? *Cognitive Psychology, 7*(2), 194–227. http://dx.doi.org/10.1016/0010-0285(75)90010-9.
Kaufman, J. C., & Sternberg, R. J. (Eds.). (2010). *Cambridge handbook of creativity*. New York: Cambridge University Press.
Kaufman, J. C., & Sternberg, R. J. (Eds.). (2019). *Cambridge handbook of creativity* (2nd ed.). New York: Cambridge University Press.

Lepper, M. R., & Greene, D. (1975). Turning play into work: Effects of adult surveillance and extrinsic rewards on children's intrinsic motivation. *Journal of Personality and Social Psychology, 31*(3), 479–486. https://doi.org/10.1037/h0076484.

Serpell, R. (2017). How the study of cognitive growth can benefit from a cultural lens. *Perspectives on Psychological Science, 12*(5), 889–899.

Spearman, C. (1927). *The abilities of man.* New York: Macmillan.

Sternberg, R. J. (1977). *Intelligence, information processing, and analogical reasoning: The componential analysis of human abilities.* Hillsdale, NJ: Lawrence Erlbaum Associates.

Sternberg, R. J. (1983). Components of human intelligence. *Cognition, 15,* 1–48.

Sternberg, R. J. (1988). A three-facet model of creativity. In R. J. Sternberg (Ed.), *The nature of creativity* (pp. 125–147). New York: Cambridge University Press.

Sternberg, R. J. (2018). A triangular theory of creativity. *Psychology of Aesthetics, Creativity, and the Arts, 12,* 50–67.

Sternberg, R. J. (2020). Cultural approaches to intelligence. In R. J. Sternberg (Ed.), *Human intelligence: An introduction* (pp. 174–201). New York: Cambridge University Press.

Torrance, E. P. (1974). *Torrance Tests of creative thinking: Norms-technical manual*. Lexington, MA: Ginn.

21

Coherence, Courage, and Community: Lessons Learned from Professor Teresa Amabile

Jing Zhou

"How far that little candle throws his beams!"
—William Shakespeare

At one point or another during the formative years of their careers, many people experience an encounter that has a profound and long-lasting impact on them. I surely did. When I was a Ph.D. student trying to choose a dissertation topic, I became excited about studying the effects of

Forthcoming in Reiter-Palmon, R., Fisher, C. M., & Mueller, J. (Eds). *The Componential Theory of Creativity (Research): Uncovering New Skills, Experts, and Motivations in the Field.* London, UK: Palgrave Publishing.

This chapter is based on a talk I gave at the Creativity Conference: Festschrift in Honor of Teresa Amabile, Harvard Business School, August 14, 2019.

J. Zhou (✉)
Mary Gibbs Jones Professor of Management, Jones Graduate School of Business, Rice University, Houston, TX, USA
e-mail: jzhou@rice.edu

R. Reiter-Palmon et al. (eds.), *Creativity at Work*, Palgrave Studies in Creativity and Innovation in Organizations, https://doi.org/10.1007/978-3-030-61311-2_21

feedback on creativity. Choosing a dissertation topic was a huge decision for me. Thus, in addition to paying close attention to the guidance of my dissertation advisor and committee, I sought advice from a few senior students. They quizzed me on whether I was sure no one had studied this topic. I told them I was sure, because I had conducted a very thorough literature search. They pushed back, asking questions such as, "how do you know it's not BEING studied by somebody right now?" This question sent me into a panic mode, because I did not know whether anyone was in the process of studying it or not; I only knew nothing on this topic had been published. If someone else had started to research it already, by the time I completed my dissertation work and developed a paper for journal submission, other people could have already published a similar paper! I had to find out. But, how?

I decided to write a letter to Teresa Amabile. Though I had never met her, I knew she was the leading figure in the research area in which my dissertation idea would fall. I loved reading her book, *Creativity in Context* (1996). In the book, she presents an impressive and coherent body of work centering on contextual influences on creativity. She and coauthors had investigated the effects of a wide range of contextual factors. I figured if anyone was working on the topic of feedback and creativity, Teresa would be the most likely person. Besides, even if she was not working on this topic, she might know if someone else was working on it.

So I literally sent her a letter in which I described my dissertation ideas, and essentially asked her two questions: was she working on a similar idea? If not, did she happen to know who else might be working on the idea?

A few days after I mailed the letter to her, I actually received a response letter in the mail. Eagerly opening the envelope, I quickly realized that Teresa hand-wrote responses to my questions. She indicated that she thought my dissertation ideas were good, she was not working on a similar project, and she was not aware anybody else was working on similar ideas. When I wrote to her, I did not know what to expect and felt the chance of receiving a response was low. Thus, I still remember how pleasantly surprised I was that a famous scholar like Teresa would take the time to answer each of my questions, and how happy I was to know my dissertation ideas were indeed novel!

Perhaps it is worth mentioning that as a Ph.D. student I also wrote letters to a couple of other well-known and prolific scholars, asking them questions about research. I did not receive any response from them. They must have had demanding workloads and busy schedules. Thus, it is quite understandable that they did not have the time to write back to a student who they did not even know. What is remarkable is the fact that Teresa Amabile did take the time to answer each and every one of my questions. I don't think Teresa remembers this. Even if I reminded her, she probably would humbly say it was just a small thing to do. However, her small deed made a big difference in alleviating a student's anxiety and creating a positive and memorable experience for the student.

Before the letter-writing experience, I had enjoyed reading Teresa's work and admired her scholarship, and yet rarely connected what I read in her articles with her as a person. After that experience, I became a big fan of hers, not only because she is a prominent scholar but because she is a compassionate human being. I believe that through her trail-blazing research work and generous helping of others, Professor Teresa Amabile has offered three invaluable lessons: coherence, courage, and community. Her systematic program of research has resulted in a coherent body of knowledge that features intrinsic motivation as the primary driver for individual creativity—the generation of new and useful ideas. Using the intrinsic motivation principle of creativity (Amabile, 1996) as the anchor, this coherent body of work highlights the role of contexts in boosting or restricting creativity via intrinsic motivation. She is courageous in formulating research questions. By shifting the focus of creativity research from individual traits to the context, she has pursued a path less traveled, working on important research questions even if they are unconventional or counterintuitive. In addition to being a brilliant scholar, Teresa leads by example in making a positive difference in the academic community. I know I was not the only student who benefited from her generosity. I am grateful to have the opportunity to share some experiences on how the inspiration of coherence, courage, and community has shaped my own journey as a researcher.

Creating a Coherent Body of Knowledge

In her distinguished career, Teresa Amabile conducted a highly coherent program of research. She pioneered the research area concerning contextual influences on creativity. Prior to the emphasis on context, much psychological research had focused on studying genius or searching for traits that reliably distinguish creative people from noncreative ones. This focus on genius and traits does little to consider the influences of organizational culture, structure, processes, managerial practices, task characteristics, and the social environment in which employees are embedded. Though many employees are not geniuses, under the right conditions, they may be able to come up with new and useful ideas concerning products, services, and processes, which is the definition of workplace creativity (Amabile, 1996). On the other hand, if the work context is restrictive, even employees who have a strong natural inclination to be creative will not have the opportunity to express their creative potential.

Inspired by Teresa and other like-minded scholars, I have attempted to create a coherent body of knowledge via conducting a systematic program of research. The first aspect of this research program is using an interactional approach to reveal how individual attributes influence effects of contexts on creativity, and how contexts may boost or undermine the creativity of individuals who vary on a given attribute. My coauthors and I have conducted empirical studies in a variety of settings, from the behavioral laboratory to work organizations in different industries, to investigate interactional effects of key personal attributes and contextual factors (e.g., George & Zhou, 2001; Hirst, van Knippenberg, & Zhou, 2009; Liu, Gong, Zhou, & Huang, 2017; Shin & Zhou, 2003; Zhang & Zhou, 2014; Zhang, Zhou, & Kwon, 2017; Zhou, Shin, Brass, Choi, & Zhang, 2009; Zhou, 1998a, 2003).

Ultimately, this systematic effort to investigate personal and contextual factors contributed to the development of a typology regarding how configurations of actor–context interactions enhance or restrict creativity (Zhou & Hoever, 2014). This typology provides a novel conceptual lens for understanding how high vs. low creativity-relevant attributes interact with positive vs. negative contexts to elevate or reduce creativity. For example, a remedial type of interaction depicts the situation in which employees who have fewer creativity attributes measured by the creative personality scale (Gough, 1979) benefit more from a certain context condition (e.g., the presence of creative coworkers and absence of supervisory close monitoring) by exhibiting greater creativity in that context than employees who have more creativity attributes (Zhou, 2003). As another example, a synergistic type of interaction depicts the situation in which employees or teams who have greater natural inclinations to be creative, such as team functional heterogeneity exhibit greater creativity in a context that is specifically suited for triggering and reinforcing such natural inclinations, such as transformational leadership (Shin & Zhou, 2007). It has truly been a pleasure and privilege to work with collaborators at creating a coherent body of knowledge.

Creating a coherent body of knowledge is essential for science and practice. From the standpoint of science, doing so allows for an understanding of the complexity of organizational behavior, with employee creativity being such a behavior, in all its depth and breadth. From the standpoint of practice, doing so facilitates the design of effective and scientifically proven organizational practices that achieve both the success of the organization and the well-being of members of the organization. Unfortunately, under the pressure of landing a job or getting tenure and promotion, some researchers devote their attention and energy toward getting as a large number of papers published in top-tier journals as possible and as quickly as possible, instead of focusing on developing deep expertise in a chosen field and achieving true understanding of what is being studied. They try to get on as many projects as possible, publishing papers in various research areas or streams detached from each other. In the end, despite having a long list of published papers, they do not achieve full mastery of what they study, and consequently, their work has limited utility and impact. Teresa Amabile exemplifies the value for researchers to direct their attention and effort at building a coherent body of knowledge, instead of doing bits and pieces of work on different topics. I find her to be an inspiring role model for high-quality scholarship, and strive to conduct research by following the example she has set.

Being Courageous in Challenging Assumptions

Amabile's (1996) emphasis on creativity in context was courageous and changed the conversation about the focus of creativity research in social psychology; it also substantially influenced research into employee creativity in the field of management. I imagine it was not an easy thing to do at the beginning. When most people in the field took a person-centric approach to understanding creativity, it was lonely to advocate a context-centric approach. Yet she persevered and succeeded through thoughtful theoretical reasoning and careful empirical testing. A primary goal for conducting scientific research is seeking truth. Thus, researchers need to have courage in choosing research questions that challenge commonly held assumptions and not following the crowd.

Inspired by Teresa and other like-minded scholars, I have attempted to be courageous in choosing research questions. The second aspect of the systematic nature of my research program is investigating conditions under which dissatisfaction and negative affect facilitate creativity. My coauthor and I first revealed that job dissatisfaction and negative mood contribute to creative endeavors (George & Zhou, 2002; Zhou & George, 2001). Prior work on affect and creativity emphasized that positive affect facilitates divergent thinking. We argue that the generation of creative ideas in the workplace involves a process that goes beyond divergent thinking. The process includes problem detection, divergent thinking, and idea refinement. We highlight the positive role of dissatisfaction or negative mood in the creative process in terms of detecting a problem and sustaining effort so that the focal employee perseveres until a truly new and useful idea or solution results. We conducted a series of studies to test these ideas. Eventually, our systematic effort resulted in the development of the dual-tuning theory. It posits that negative and positive mood facilitate different aspects of the creative idea generation process, and in a supportive context, the two mood states work in concert to enhance the overall creative output (George & Zhou, 2007).

This set of systematic investigation required courage in challenging commonly held assumptions. A fundamental assumption is that high job satisfaction is good and people who express dissatisfaction are problematic. Challenging this assumption, George and I argue that coming up with creative ideas is a form of responding to dissatisfaction via voice. Sometimes real problems in organizational practices or processes cause employee dissatisfaction. Feeling dissatisfied at work, the employees may generate creative ideas to promote continuous improvements. We identify continuance commitment as a necessary condition, and theorize that useful feedback from coworkers, coworker helping, and perceived organizational support for creativity each works jointly with continuance commitment to facilitate the employees' channeling their dissatisfaction into creativity (Zhou & George, 2001).

Likewise, George and Zhou (2002) theorize that under certain conditions, negative moods foster creativity and positive moods inhibit it. This argument challenges the traditional view in research on divergent thinking and creativity, which suggested that positive moods are always beneficial for creativity. According to the mood-as-input model, individuals' mood states provide them with information (e.g., Schwarz & Clore, 2003) and the significance and consequences of the information depend upon the context (Martin & Stoner, 1996). Drawing insights from this model, we argue that the work environment provides employees with cues concerning their ongoing creative behaviors. These cues are valuable because, when employees are engaged in creative activities at work, they often have little objective information or criteria dictating when to stop. They have to decide for themselves when they have tried hard enough to come up with a new and improved procedure, or put forth enough effort to come up with a new and better way of completing tasks. Consistent with these theoretical arguments, we found that negative moods were positively related to creativity when perceived recognition and rewards for creativity and clarity of feelings (a meta-mood process) were high. We also found that under the same conditions, positive moods were *negatively* related to creativity.

The third aspect of the systematic nature of my research program is investigating the receiving side of creativity. The creativity research field has made exciting discoveries regarding antecedents of creativity. A fundamental goal for research into antecedents is to promote the generation of creative ideas. This excitement has created a momentum, directing even greater attention toward identifying even more antecedents. It took a while for the field to embrace the need to understand the receiving side of creativity (e.g., Mueller, Melwani, & Goncalo, 2012; Zhou, 1998b). To shift the field's attention to the receiving side of creativity, this programmatic line of inquiry also requires courage in asking big questions and opening new frontiers.

It started with the attempt of developing a social-cognitive account of managers' recognition of employees' creative ideas (Zhou, 1998b; Zhou & Woodman, 1999, 2003), explaining how and why a set of multilevel factors involving personal, interpersonal, and organizational variables affect the recognition of creative ideas. In a programmatic manner, my coauthors and I (Zhou, Wang, Song, & Wu, 2017) conducted four studies in which we found perceivers who were high on promotion focus perceived greater creativity in ideas that are creative. Innovation culture led perceivers to recognize greater creativity in ideas that are highly creative. Contextual cues in terms of gain-framing helped perceivers who had prevention focus to recognize greater creativity in ideas that are highly creative. Zhou, Wang, Bavato, Tasselli, and Wu (2019) provide a multidisciplinary review of creativity receiving. Together, these conceptual and empirical works help to broaden creativity research from a heavy focus on antecedents of creativity to the new research stream—the receiving side of creativity.

Making Positive Contribution to Community

During her distinguished career, Professor Amabile has not only significantly helped moving the creativity research field forward, but also generously helped many individual students and researchers. She inspires us to each find our own way of making a positive contribution to the community. A unique way that I find particularly rewarding is to give back to the research community by editing books and writing review articles. Though these outputs are not seen as "top-tier journal publications" and hence do little in the way of providing extrinsic rewards, they help Ph.D. students and researchers to survey the literature in an efficient manner. Thus, I find them meaningful and internally rewarding.

When editing books and writing review articles, I have also tried to present a coherent body of knowledge accumulated by the collective effort of researchers. In doing so, my collaborators and I recognize that edited books and review articles help advance research in unique ways. Compared with review articles published in journals, an edited book has greater flexibility in providing a platform for researchers to be bold in discussing their ideas. Accordingly, to push creativity research forward, the book edited by Zhou and Shalley (2008a) presents thought-provoking ideas revolving around workplace creativity. To facilitate cross-fertilization and integration, the book edited by Shalley, Hitt, and Zhou (2015) brings together researchers from creativity, innovation, and entrepreneurship fields to showcase their work and make connections across fields.

On the other hand, the value of a review article lies in its comprehensive review and appraisal of extant research. Accordingly, my coauthors and I invested a great deal of time in systematically developing qualitative or quantitative reviews. Zhou and Shalley (2003) provide detailed information on definitional issues, theories, research designs, and measurements. Newcomers to the creativity research area can be acquainted with the field quickly by reading this paper. Zhou and Shalley (2008b) point out new directions for expanding the scope and impact of creativity research, calling for greater attention to multilevel and cross-level theorizing and research. This paper has stimulated multi- and cross-level creativity research. Zhou and Shalley (2011) focus on the affective, cognitive, and motivational mechanisms of creativity, thereby building on and substantially extending Zhou and Shalley (2003, 2008a). It has stimulated research into the next frontier of developing a scientific understanding of creativity: to reveal different types of psychological mechanisms that explain the effects of various antecedents.

After a sufficient number of primary studies on a certain topic have been conducted, a meta-analysis is particularly suitable for taking stock of prior findings and suggesting future research. Thus, Liu, Jiang, Shalley, Keem, and Zhou (2016) conducted a meta-analytic review of motivational mechanisms for creativity. It shows the effectiveness of intrinsic motivation and creative self-efficacy as motivational mechanisms or mediators, and takes stock of their antecedents found in primary studies.

It also reveals prosocial motivation to be the least frequently investigated mechanism, suggesting that more future research is called for.

While significant advancements have been made in understanding the antecedents of creativity, research into how creative ideas are recognized, evaluated, and implemented has lagged behind (Zhou et al., 2019). To accelerate the advancement of the emergent research stream on the receiving side of creativity, my coauthors and I comb through literatures in different disciplines and provide a multidisciplinary review of relevant research conducted in arts, education, psychology, sociology, and marketing, and a small number of studies in management (Zhou et al., 2019). This review underscores the limited work that management researchers have done on this topic, and suggests potential areas in which management research on creativity receiving may benefit from other disciplines.

Finally, my coauthors and I have also crafted review articles that were published in the widely read *Journal of Management* annual review issues. Shalley, Zhou, and Oldham (2004) focus on providing a qualitative review of creativity research and suggesting new research directions. Anderson, Potocnik, and Zhou (2014) review both creativity and innovation literatures, identify synergy and inconsistencies between them, and suggest ways of integrating them. In addition, the authors provide 60 new research questions. We are grateful that both of these review papers received the *Journal of Management Best Paper Award* in 2009 and 2019, respectively. The award is based on the impact of a paper five years after its publication. Receiving this award suggests that readers in the research community find our reviews useful.

A joy of being a researcher is having the opportunity to solve puzzles—seek answers to intriguing questions. For me, another joy is having the opportunity to observe, interact with, and learn from others in the academic community. Though I have only had limited interactions with Teresa, and only one episode of exchanging letters with her, I feel her positive influence looms large. Coherence, courage, and community are three invaluable lessons I have learned from her. I am grateful to have known her as a brilliant scholar, and an extraordinary role model.

References

Amabile, T. M. (1996). *Creativity in context: Update to the social psychology of creativity*. Boulder, CO: Westview Press.

Anderson, N., Potocnik, K., & Zhou, J. (2014). Innovation and creativity in organizations: A state-of-the-science review, prospective commentary, and guiding framework. *Journal of Management, 40,* 1297–1333.

George, J. M., & Zhou, J. (2001). When openness to experience and conscientiousness are related to creative behavior: An interactional approach. *Journal of Applied Psychology, 86,* 513–524.

George, J. M., & Zhou, J. (2002). Understanding when bad moods foster creativity and good ones don't: The role of context and clarity of feelings. *Journal of Applied Psychology, 87,* 687–697.

George, J. M., & Zhou, J. (2007). Dual tuning in a supportive context: Joint contributions of positive mood, negative mood, and supervisory behaviors to employee creativity. *Academy of Management Journal, 50,* 605–622.

Gough, H. G. (1979). A creative personality scale for the Adjective Check List. *Journal of Personality and Social Psychology, 37,* 1398–1405.

Hirst, G., van Knippenberg, D., & Zhou, J. (2009). A cross-level perspective on employee creativity: Goal orientation, team learning behavior, and individual creativity. *Academy of Management Journal, 52,* 280–293.

Liu, D., Gong, Y., Zhou, J., & Huang, J. (2017). Human resource systems, employee creativity, and firm innovation: The moderating role of firm ownership. *Academy of Management Journal, 60,* 1164–1188.

Liu, D., Jiang, K., Shalley, C., Keem, S., & Zhou, J. (2016). The underlying motivational mechanisms for employee creativity: A meta-analytic examination and theoretical extension of the creativity literature. *Organizational Behavior and Human Decision Processes, 137,* 236–263.

Martin, L. L., & Stoner, P. (1996). Mood as input: What we think about how we feel determines how we think. In L. L. Martin & A. Tesser (Eds.), *Striving and feeling: Interactions among goals, affect, and self-regulation* (pp. 279–301). Mahwah, NJ: Erlbaum.

Mueller, J., Melwani, S., & Goncalo, J. (2012). The bias against creativity: Why people desire yet reject creative ideas. *Psychological Science, 21*(1), 13–17.

Schwarz, N., & Clore, G. L. (2003). Mood as information. *Psychological Inquiry, 14,* 296–303.

Shalley, C. E., Hitt, M. A., & Zhou, J. (Eds.). (2015). *The Oxford handbook of creativity, innovation, and entrepreneurship*. New York: Oxford University Press.

Shalley, C. E., Zhou, J., & Oldham, G. R. (2004). The effects of personal and contextual characteristics on creativity: Where should we go from here? *Journal of Management, 30*, 933–958.

Shin, S., & Zhou, J. (equal contribution). (2003). Transformational leadership, conservation, and creativity: Evidence from Korea. *Academy of Management Journal, 46*, 703–714.

Shin, S., & Zhou, J. (2007). When is educational specialization heterogeneity related to creativity in research and development teams? Transformational leadership as a moderator. *Journal of Applied Psychology, 92*, 1709–1721.

Zhang, X., & Zhou, J. (equal contribution). (2014). Empowering leadership, uncertainty avoidance, trust and employee creativity: interaction effects and mediating processes. *Organizational Behavior and Human Decision Processes, 124*, 150–164.

Zhang, X., Zhou, J., & Kwon, H. K. (Zhang and Zhou contributed equally). (2017). Configuring challenge and hindrance contexts for introversion and creativity: Joint effects of task complexity and guanxi management. *Organizational Behavior and Human Decision Processes, 143*, 54–68.

Zhou, J. (1998a). Feedback valence, feedback style, task autonomy, and achievement orientation: Interactive effects on creative performance. *Journal of Applied Psychology, 83*, 261–276.

Zhou, J. (1998, June 12–14). *Managers' recognition of employee creative ideas: A social-cognitive approach*. Paper presented at "The 21st Century Change Imperative: Evolving Organizations & Emerging Networks" Conference, Center for the Study of Organizational Change, University of Missouri-Columbia.

Zhou, J. (2003). When the presence of creative coworkers is related to creativity: Role of supervisor close monitoring, developmental feedback, and creative personality. *Journal of Applied Psychology, 88*, 413–422.

Zhou, J., & George, J. M. (2001). When job dissatisfaction leads to creativity: Encouraging the expression of voice. *Academy of Management Journal, 44*, 682–696.

Zhou, J., & Hoever, I. J. (equal contribution). (2014). Workplace creativity: A review and redirection. *Annual Review of Organizational Psychology and Organizational Behavior.*

Zhou, J., & Shalley, C. E. (2003). Research on employee creativity: A critical review and directions for future research. In J. J. Martocchio & G. R.

Ferris (Eds.), *Research in personnel and human resource management* (Vol. 22, pp. 165–217). Oxford, UK: Elsevier Science.

Zhou, J., & Shalley, C. E. (Eds.). (2008a). *Handbook of organizational creativity*. Hillsdale, NJ: Lawrence Erlbaum.

Zhou, J., & Shalley, C. E. (2008b). Expanding the scope and impact of organizational creativity research. In J. Zhou & C. E. Shalley (Eds.), *Handbook of organizational creativity* (pp. 347–368). Hillsdale, NJ: Lawrence Erlbaum.

Zhou, J., & Shalley, C. E. (2011). Deepening our understanding of creativity in the workplace. In S. Zedeck, et al. (Eds.), *APA Handbook of Industrial-Organizational Psychology* (Vol. 1, pp. 275–302). Washington, DC: American Psychological Association.

Zhou, J., Shin, S. J., Brass, D. J., Choi, J., & Zhang, Z. (2009). Social networks, personal values, and creativity: Evidence for curvilinear and interaction effects. *Journal of Applied Psychology, 94,* 1544–1552.

Zhou, J., Wang, X., Bavato, D., Tasselli, S., & Wu, J. (2019). Understanding the receiving side of creativity: A multidisciplinary review and implications for management research. *Journal of Management, 45,* 2570–2595.

Zhou, J., Wang, X., Song, J., & Wu, J. (2017). Is it new? Personal and contextual influences on perceptions of novelty and creativity. *Journal of Applied Psychology, 102,* 180–202.

Zhou, J., & Woodman, R. W. (1999). *Managers' recognition of employee creative ideas: A social-cognitive approach.* Paper presented at the Academy of Management Annual Meetings, Chicago.

Zhou, J., & Woodman, R. W. (2003). Managers' recognition of employees' creative ideas. In L. V. Shavinina (Ed.), *International handbook on innovation.* Hillsdale, NJ: Lawrence Erlbaum.

22

A Labor of Love: Reflections on a Research Career, with Love

Teresa M. Amabile

As I look back from this vantage point of July 2020, nearly 45 years after I began my research explorations into creativity, I am overwhelmed with gratitude and love—for the people who taught me to think imaginatively, to love science, and to do research well; the people who enabled my research to progress through their encouragement, collaboration, and day-to-day support; the institutions that generously supported my research with tangible and intangible resources; the people who trusted me to guide them in becoming creativity scholars; the people who joined me and so many friends, colleagues, and former students for the HBS Creativity Conference in August 2019; and the remarkable researchers who contributed to and edited this volume. Here, I will offer my first-person perspective on my creativity research program and its roots, as well as some difficult lessons I learned along the way. I will try, however

T. M. Amabile (✉)
Harvard Business School, Boston, MA, USA
e-mail: tamabile@hbs.edu

R. Reiter-Palmon et al. (eds.), *Creativity at Work*,
Palgrave Studies in Creativity and Innovation in Organizations,
https://doi.org/10.1007/978-3-030-61311-2_22

inadequately, to acknowledge some of the many people who helped make it happen. Caveat: None of this, of course, is as linear as this brief reflection will make it seem. There are many twists and turns beyond the few that I will recount.

Intellectual and Motivational Foundation

My father, Charles Amabile (1917–2002) loved to think creatively, he did it all the time, and he encouraged all seven of his children to do it, too. The son of impoverished Italian immigrants, he became an entrepreneur at a young age, working with his brother to build a food importing and packing business that thrived for over 60 years, employed 25 people at its peak, and supported two large families. He and our mother, Carmela (1918–2010), would engage all of us children in planning fun activities for our annual summer vacations, enthuse over the projects and reports we brought home from school, and once had all of us spend a Sunday afternoon writing advertising jingles for a local contest. (We won first prize!) Various of my siblings demonstrated extraordinary creativity in art, humor, baking, writing, and storytelling. I still remember the day that Dad excitedly read us an article he'd found in the *Buffalo* (New York) *Evening News*, about a promising problem-solving technique being developed at a local university. It was called "brainstorming." (See Osborne, 1963; Parnes, 1967.) "Let's try it, kids," Dad said. "Let's brainstorm!" Years later, two of my sisters, Carolyn and Phyllis, would assist me in running my first creativity experiment, in our Palo Alto apartment complex's community gathering room.

Lesson for future creativity researchers: Choose your parents (or parental figures) and your siblings wisely. Pay attention.

Education and Training

Never able to attend college due to the grim economic realities of the Great Depression during which they entered adulthood, both of my parents were determined that all of their children would attain at least a

Bachelor's degree. (We did.) One Christmas when I was in late elementary school, my parents gave me something I'd been begging for: a microscope. I spent hours with that thing, and soon Dad declared me "the family scientist." I liked that; it seemed to fit. When I chose Chemistry as my major upon entering Canisius College, he predicted that I'd discover the cure for cancer. (Sorry for the disappointment, Dad.)

At Canisius, my first, most influential science mentor was a young professor named Frank Dinan. With active research programs and no doctoral students, Frank and his colleagues were eager to hire any qualified undergraduates who wanted research assistantships—part-time during the academic year, full-time during the summers. That research, and being part of a bustling, productive lab, was a heady experience for me. I loved it, and I did well; in fact, my first publication was in *Chromatographic Science* (Szymanski & Amabile, 1969). By the midway point in my undergraduate program, however, I'd discovered psychology—due, in large part, to another extremely influential teacher at Canisius, social psychologist Harvey Pines. I immediately realized that I was far more interested in the behavior of humans than the behavior of molecules and, though I did finish the chemistry degree, I took four or five psychology courses and set my sights on a Ph.D. in the field.

I owe an enormous debt of gratitude to my principal scientific mentors in the social psychology doctoral program at Stanford University, Mark Lepper (recently retired) and Lee Ross (still on the active faculty), as well as the other members of my dissertation committee, Daryl Bem and Philip Zimbardo. I am also grateful to my doctoral-student colleague (and first husband) Bill DeJong, who played a major role in helping me learn to think and write like a social psychologist. But it was Mark's pioneering work on the negative effects of extrinsic reward on intrinsic motivation (Lepper, Greene, & Nisbett, 1973), and our subsequent conversations about possible performance effects, that led me to do my first experiments on how social-environmental factors can influence intrinsic motivation and creativity.

When my first experiment yielded promising results, Mark, Lee, Daryl, and Phil were all enthusiastically supportive. But their enthusiasm turned to concerned skepticism when I told them this was what I wanted to pursue for my dissertation and my initial research program post-Ph.D.; I wanted, I told them (with considerable hubris), to develop a social psychology of creativity. The pre-1975 psychological literature on creativity, a literature I had spent much time reading, was strongly focused on the personality traits and other individual differences associated with genius-level creativity. I was excited by exploring the virgin territory of how the social environment could influence everyday creative behavior. My advisors countered that creativity research had a spotty reputation in the field, due to poor methodology, a narrow focus on personality, and inadequate theoretical depth, and they counseled me to avoid the uphill battle for credibility that I would likely face should I attempt to publish even solid research in such a sketchy subfield. Needless to say, I was undeterred. Moreover, my case was buttressed by an outstanding article that appeared in *JPSP* around that time, by Dean Keith Simonton, using (for the first time in print, to my knowledge) the term "social psychology of creativity" (Simonton, 1975). To my relief, my Stanford advisors ended up fully supporting my early empirical efforts, providing invaluable counsel.

The Stanford psychology department was a rather peculiar place at that time. Walter Mischel, a prominent personality psychologist, had recently called into question the very concept of stable personality traits, focusing more on the important influence of stimuli in the environment. Daryl Bem, a prominent social psychologist, was publishing a study that demonstrated the utility of using personality traits to predict behavior—but only under certain conditions. Phil Zimbardo had recently completed his scandalous, groundbreaking Stanford Prison Experiment, which demonstrated that apparently normal young men, randomly assigned to the role of prisoners or guards in a simulated prison, could become cringingly submissive or aggressively dominant simply by dint of those roles and the external environment in which they were enacted.

The overall Zeitgeist of the psychology department was, essentially, hostile to personality-based explanations of behavior; social-situational explanations of behavior dominated; and the experimental method reigned supreme. I realized only later that I had been so strongly imprinted with this attitude that it had become an unthinking bias.

That bias led me to disdainfully dismiss previous interview, observational, clinical, and assessment-instrument-based personality studies of creativity, some of them quite well-done (e.g., MacKinnon, 1965), in my first attempts to publish the dissertation—an attitude that did not sit well with my reviewers and editors. Only after I had moderated my stance did I gain publication traction (Amabile, 1979). Before long, not surprisingly, I incorporated personality into my first theoretical model of creativity (Amabile, 1983a, 1983b).

Lesson: Learn well from your mentors; become a sponge. But beware of the inevitable attitudes/prejudices you'll soak up from them. I hope my own students have seen through mine.

Experimental Research, the Intrinsic Motivation Hypothesis, and the Componential Model

When I arrived in the psych department at Brandeis to take up my first job, armed with extensive plans for experiments on the effects of the social environment on children's and adults' creativity, I was embraced by a powerful mentor and role model (and still a close friend), attribution researcher Leslie Zebrowitz. As the first social psychologist to have been promoted to tenure in that department, Leslie served as a strongly positive model of a creative, productive experimentalist; an enthusiastically supportive colleague; an engaged member of the broader profession (serving, for example, as Associate Editor of *JPSP*); and a working mother devoted to her two very young sons. Supported, too, by my great friend and peer, developmental psychologist Mick Watson, who was also interested in children's creativity (though from a very different perspective), I dove into—and began publishing—my new creativity experiments. Simultaneously, I began developing and writing my paper on creativity assessment (the Consensual Assessment Technique (Amabile, 1982)) and my creativity theory—version 1.0 (the Componential Model of Creativity (Amabile, 1983a, 1983b)). I thrived during my 18 years at Brandeis, buoyed by my colleagues, my students, and (eventually) significant research funding from foundations and federal institutes (particularly the National Institute of Mental Health).

But it would be untruthful to say that I arrived at Brandeis determined to follow my passion to develop a social psychology of creativity. Or even that I planned to focus exclusively on creativity. During my first years at Brandeis, I felt that I was still casting about for a professional identity, a truly programmatic approach to research. I published papers on attribution theory and human inference (e.g., Amabile & Kabat, 1982; Ross, Amabile, & Steinmetz, 1977) and what I called a "negativity bias" in evaluations made under intellectual insecurity (Amabile, 1983c; Amabile & Glazebrook, 1982).

As I look back on that time, I realize that a significant turning point was meeting Beth Hennessey, a doctoral student who became as fascinated by creativity as I was. She also became my great friend, my most frequent creativity research collaborator (by far) across the past three-plus decades (e.g., Amabile, Hennessey, & Grossman, 1986; Hennessey & Amabile, 1998, 2010; Hennessey, Mueller, & Amabile, 2020), and an internationally renowned creativity scholar in her own right (e.g., Hennessey, 1989, 2004; Hennessey & Zbikowski, 1993). Together and separately, Beth and I (sometimes with other doctoral students, like Karl Hill) were amassing a growing body of evidence that supported my initial hunch: intrinsic motivation is crucial for creativity; extrinsic motivation triggered by the social environment is inimical to it. We began referring to this as "the intrinsic motivation hypothesis of creativity."

Lesson: Much uncertainty can mark even seemingly single-minded research careers. Eventually, things begin to fall into place, often with the help of people who come from unexpected directions—a student unsure of what she wants to study, for example, or a colleague with a different set of interests. But beware the smug assumption that the uncertainty has come to an end.

Unexpected Results, Irritating Colleagues, and a Major Revision

Beth and I were taken aback when studies we'd done with adults and children showed that, under certain conditions, the extrinsic motivator of contracted-for reward did not undermine creativity. In fact, it seemed to enhance creativity (Amabile et al., 1986). To me, this unexpected pattern initially felt like a failure. I'd been wrong—or at least not quite right—about something fundamental to my theory. My original "intrinsic motivation hypothesis of creativity"—the most novel and, I felt, important element of my theory—asserted that intrinsic motivation has positive effects on creativity, and extrinsic motivation has negative effects. Period.

As so much good research has shown (e.g., Lord, Ross, & Lepper, 1979), people try to reconcile anomalous information with their preexisting ideas; I was no exception. But the internal pressure I experienced to reconsider had already been mounting. During the wine-and-cheese reception after a talk I'd given on my theory and its empirical evidence in the Stanford psych department, the renowned cognitive psychologist Amos Tversky quite literally backed me into a corner of the room while arguing, vocally and persuasively, that extrinsic motivation had to be an essential stimulant to creativity. In the early 1990s, behavioral psychologist Robert Eisenberger began publishing a series of papers calling into question the negative effects of reward on intrinsic motivation and creativity (e.g., Eisenberger & Cameron, 1996). And, when I spent a sabbatical year at Harvard Business School in 1992–1993, my office-suite mate Michael Jensen, the famed Chicago-School financial economist who held that humans are simply reward ("utility") maximizing creatures, became my main intellectual irritant (Fama & Jensen, 1983; Jensen & Meckling, 1976). Mike was an enjoyable conversationalist who seemed, to me, to be highly intrinsically motivated in his work; yet, he claimed that intrinsic motivation didn't even exist.

Seeing the possibility that extrinsic reward might add synergistically to intrinsic motivation and, thus, creativity (at least under some circumstances), Beth and I designed an experiment with children that demonstrated just that (Hennessey, Amabile, & Martinage, 1989). Her later research upheld the discovery that children could be "immunized" against the negative effects of reward on intrinsic motivation and creativity and that, under certain conditions, reward could actually boost creativity (Hennessey & Zbikowski, 1993). During that sabbatical year at HBS, I wrote and published a major revision of the intrinsic motivation hypothesis, as part of a theory of "motivational synergy" (Amabile, 1993). It turned out to be only the first of many times I revisited and revised my previous work (e.g., Amabile, 1996; Amabile & Mueller, 2008; Amabile & Pratt, 2017).

Lesson: Your biggest failures and your most vocal critics can be your most powerful intellectual stimulants.

Adventures beyond the Laboratory

When the Center for Creative Leadership (CCL) invited me to their 1982 "Creativity Week" conference, I had no inkling that it would lead my research in an entirely new direction. Already, I'd been feeling some dissatisfaction with the fact that, although I could now enumerate several environmental conditions that can undermine intrinsic motivation and creativity—evaluation, surveillance, reward, competition, and restricted choice—I had no idea to what extent these factors might play a meaningful role in creativity outside my lab. During that week, I had several exciting conversations with Stan Gryskiewicz, an organizational psychologist who was then leading up CCL's major educational and research programs on creativity in R&D. He ended up asking if I'd come to CCL as a guest instructor in one of his programs. Though nervous at the prospect of teaching R&D managers, which I suspected might be a bit different from teaching undergraduates and doctoral students, I agreed—and asked if, in return, he would allow me to interview participants about their experiences doing creative work inside their organizations. This led to a years-long collaboration, in which Stan and I interviewed R&D scientists in a number of companies, analyzed those interviews, and wrote several papers and chapters based on that research.

At the start of these research ventures outside my laboratory, I felt intellectually nauseous—sometimes, viscerally nauseous, too. I'd had a great deal of success with the experimental method, I loved the smug sense that I could confidently draw causal inferences from my data, and I still had the hangover of disdain for nonexperimental, non-quantitative methods from my Stanford days. Yet I was too curious about what *actually* happens out there in the real world to resist. Over the next several years, I collaborated separately with Stan, his wife Nur (also an organizational psychologist), and my Brandeis doctoral student Regina Conti, to conduct a series of studies, using interviews and survey assessments, on factors that appear to support or inhibit creative work in organizations (e.g., Amabile & Conti, 1999; Amabile, Conti, Coon, Lazenby, & Herron, 1996; Amabile & N. Gryskiewicz, 1989; Amabile & S. Gryskiewicz, 1987). I am immensely grateful to CCL and my collaborators on this early work environment research for helping me learn how to talk and listen to managers—and helping me do the research that gave me something interesting to say to them.

Another new pathway opened unexpectedly when, after that sabbatical year at HBS, the School—starting with my dear colleagues Howard Stevenson and Mike Beer—recruited me to join its tenured faculty in the Entrepreneurial Management unit that was just forming. A pivotal moment came my first year there (1995), when I presented my findings on creativity and organizational work environments at a research workshop; I ended by saying that I had a new dissatisfaction. Although I felt that we now understood a great deal about how general work environment factors, such as supervisors' support, could stimulate organizational creativity, we understood quite little about how that sense of support—or, indeed, how any other work environment perception—arises. What is it that supervisors say and do, at the nitty-gritty, day-to-day level, that can lead people to perceive supervisory support and, ultimately, impact the psychological states that can result in higher levels of creativity? Among the 20 or so doctoral students and faculty in the room, one voice boomed out immediately. "Well, why the hell don't you go ahead and find out?"

It was Richard Hackman, and his rather startling comment got me thinking. Now that I was at HBS—an institution with the resources to support even a large-scale, long-term study, and with access to a wide array of organizations (for which I am deeply grateful)—I figured that I could—that I *would*—go ahead and try to find out. That day, Richard was, as he had often been to me, a friendly (if outspoken) intellectual irritant. As I designed my research program, he gave much useful advice.

With that study, which collected daily diaries over several weeks from 238 professionals engaged in their companies' most important innovation projects, I fully embraced qualitative methods, incorporating several quantitative survey measures, as well. Several practitioners, who had become friends or acquaintances, helped me and my research associates find our way through—and actually collaborated in—recruiting companies and participants, designing and testing the methods, collecting the data, and trying to figure out what the early results might mean: Lynn Miller, Candis Cook, Mel Marsh, Tom Wojcik, Paul Odomirok, and Chelley Patterson.

When I again became nauseated about my research—this time, about the volume of data we'd ended up with (nearly 12,000 separate daily diary entries, each including an "event of the day" story)—I got rescued by Leslie Perlow, who taught me rigorous qualitative analysis, and by Jennifer Mueller, who started as a summer doctoral assistant on the project and ended up being one of my key collaborators throughout the course of the research program (as well as a good friend). Former student (and, now, good friend) Connie Hadley became an important collaborator over several years on this project, as did Giovanni Moneta; doctoral student Sandra Cha helped very early on, offering insightful perspectives. Sigal Barsade and Barry Staw were instrumental in completing that stage of my continuing education, working with Jen and me on perhaps the most important paper to come out of the diary study (Amabile, Barsade, Mueller, & Staw, 2005).

But of all of my wonderful collaborators on that massive 15-year diary research program, the most important was Steve Kramer. Not only did he end up publishing more papers with me than anyone else, ever (e.g., Amabile, Schatzel, Moneta, & Kramer, 2004), but he coauthored the book that came out of this study (Amabile & Kramer, 2011). And the dear man stayed married to me through it all!

Here's the thing about me and collaboration: As a hyper-detail-oriented, high-need-for-control perfectionist, I never much liked it. I avoided it, if I could, unless it was with an undergraduate or graduate student. But, as my early graduate-student collaborators became prolific, highly-skilled professionals with exciting research ideas of their own, I gradually realized that I could enjoy—and benefit from—letting others run the show. At least as importantly, I realized that I would probably still be stuck in an experimental lab, never having learned the scary, demanding, but highly satisfying ways of qualitative research, had I not been enticed by so many colleagues to venture forth.

Lesson: Don't be afraid to leave your comfort zone, in preferred working style, favorite methodology, research questions, or even academic home. And don't be afraid to let other people be part of—even run—the research show. If you play your cards right, many of them will propel your work forward, and become close friends in the bargain.

Revising the Model, Embracing New Perspectives on Creativity

The diary study did, indeed, illuminate much about the managerial actions and other workplace events that can influence psychological state and creativity. In doing so, it yielded some surprises. For one thing, not only can day-by-day fluctuations in intrinsic motivation make a difference for creativity, but so can day-by-day fluctuations in positive affect (Amabile et al., 2005). And, of all the workplace events that can spark positive affect and intrinsic motivation, the single most prominent, by far, is making progress in meaningful work—even seemingly incremental steps forward. In the new light of these revelations, I saw that my creativity theory was, once again, inadequate, even in its revised state. Not only had I revised it by theorizing about motivational synergy (Amabile, 1993), but—prodded by *Research in Organizational Behavior* editor Barry Staw—I had also elaborated the original model to include organizational influences on individual and team creativity, as well as effects of individual and team creativity on organizational innovation (Amabile, 1988). I had altered some terminology and the figural representation of the model to better fit empirical findings (Amabile, 1996). More recently, Jen Mueller and I had revised parts of the theory so as to include positive affect (Amabile & Mueller, 2008).

Nagged by the sense that all of this piecemeal revision required a major overhaul of the theory, and that the overhaul should also include our findings about progress in meaningful work, I was daunted by the prospect. Moreover, fully aware of the research on our human tendencies to anchor on our own prior ideas, I suspected that I might find it difficult to modify pet elements of the theory. So I sought a peer collaborator who had a clear interest in creativity but had never collaborated with me or my coauthors, who was not principally a creativity researcher, whose work was superb, and whom I knew well enough to be confident we could figure out a way to collaborate effectively. I found such a collaborator in Mike Pratt (Amabile & Pratt, 2017). Not only did we collaborate effectively on this quite difficult task, but we had a wonderful time doing so.

I don't think that, when I first formulated my creativity theory in the early 1980s, I could have imagined all the ways in which I've ended up modifying it over the years. If I *had* imagined that, I would have certainly been exhausted by the prospect. Yet the theory, and my thinking, have been expanded and enriched immeasurably not only by my students and collaborators, but also by the creativity researchers who have been opening new pathways, publishing groundbreaking papers, and training their own generations of students since that time—among them Markus Baer, Lucy Gilson, Francesca Gino, Adam Grant, Jack Goncalo, Spencer Harrison, James Kaufman, Nora Madjar, Babis Mainemelis, Mike Mumford, Paul Paulus, Jill Perry-Smith, Gerard Puccio, Roni Reiter-Palmon, Bess Rouse, Mark Runco, Christina Shalley, Pam Tierney, and Jing Zhou.

In recent years, my work on creativity has taken yet more unexpected turns. My doctoral advisees/colleagues Michele Rigolizzo and Sujin Jang got me thinking about creativity and adult learning, and the influence of cross-cultural experience on creativity, respectively. At the insistent prodding of my wonderful student Johnathan Cromwell, I seriously considered the ways in which, and conditions under which, constraints might facilitate creativity. Eventually, we published a paper on some of John's ideas (Cromwell, Amabile, & Harvey, 2018), and he has since taken the work much further in his growing research program on creativity and invention. My amazing former student Colin Fisher led Julianna Pillemer and me in an extensive qualitative exploration of intra-organizational help for complex creative work, yielding new insights about how committed "deep help" by senior-level employees can make a difference (Fisher, Pillemer, & Amabile, 2018). And, in my current research program, a fantastic group of senior colleagues—Lotte Bailyn, Marcy Crary, Douglas T. (Tim) Hall, and Kathy Kram—are collaborating with me to explore (among many other things) how creative activity at work and outside of work might impact professionals' satisfaction with their retirement transitions. Not only is this research fascinating, but it is also highly self-relevant (Amabile & Hall, 2019). All of these more recent colleagues have also become good friends.

It's both dazzling and dizzying, as I consider how these recent projects have led me so much farther from where I began. I see now that I evolved, in fits and starts, from an experimentalist viewing creativity solely as a dependent variable, an individual behavior influenced negatively by the extrinsic motivators and constraints I so carefully manipulated in my laboratory, to a multi-method researcher considering both positive and negative effects of a range of factors, including reward, and viewing creativity not only as an individual outcome, but also as a team and organizational outcome—and, most recently, as a context and an independent variable, too. As I learn more about creativity, I realize how far we have come. But I also realize how little, really, I (and we) know.

Lesson: Hang on. Researching creativity is likely to be a wild ride.

A Closing Thought: Confident Humility

I am acutely aware, these days, of the many unanswered questions we still have about creativity. Here are just a few I've been considering recently: What are the functions of creative activity in the lives of older adults, before and after retirement, and how do they think about it? How, and for whom, might engagement in creative activity facilitate the retirement transition? (Amabile, 2019a). How might (and should) existing knowledge about human creativity shape the development of artificial intelligence, to the point where truly autonomous machines can produce highly novel yet appropriate ideas and other outputs? (Amabile, 2020).

What roles do various forms of constraints play in creativity, and what are the processes by which they operate?

At the end of our long interview in the current retirement study, we ask participants if they feel they have left (or hope to have left) a legacy through their work. I know it's quite unlikely that my creativity theory will continue to be used indefinitely, unaltered, even in its new and improved form. And I realize that at least some of my empirical findings may be overturned by subsequent research. That's the way it should be, in science. I hope that my legacy, what really endures, is the excitement about understanding creativity, the determination to rigorously unlock its mysteries, and the passion to bring that understanding to people who can make a difference in the world (Amabile, 2019b).

I'm grateful that, all those years ago at Stanford, my mentors didn't laugh outright when I expressed my hope of working to establish a social psychology of creativity. I'm grateful for the many mentors, collaborators, students, intellectual irritants, and inspiring researchers I've encountered along the way—and to the great institutions that have supported my work. And I'm even grateful for the many misbegotten ideas, research failures (all those file-drawer studies that my students and I undertook), and unexpected—even unwelcome—findings. Without them, I wouldn't have taken some of the twists and turns that ended up being so enjoyable and fruitful. Some of the lessons were very hard, but I'm glad for them, and I hope other researchers can learn from some of them.

Lesson: Adopt a stance of confident humility. Be confident enough to pursue the research questions that you really believe are most interesting and important, even when others cast doubt. And be confident enough to develop theory about what you think is going on. But be humble enough to realize that you probably won't get it right the first time, or even the second. Be willing to question and revise your prior work, and be grateful when others do the same. Finally, just be grateful—for the work and the colleagues that have graced your life.

References

Amabile, T. M. (1979). Effects of external evaluation on artistic creativity. *Journal of Personality and Social Psychology, 37,* 221–233.

Amabile, T. M. (1982). The social psychology of creativity: A consensual assessment technique. *Journal of Personality and Social Psychology, 43,* 997–1013.

Amabile, T. M. (1983a). The social psychology of creativity: A componential conceptualization. *Journal of Personality and Social Psychology, 45,* 357–377.

Amabile, T. M. (1983b). *The social psychology of creativity*. New York: Springer Verlag.

Amabile, T. M. (1983c). Brilliant but cruel: Perceptions of negative evaluators. *Journal of Experimental Social Psychology, 19,* 146–156.

Amabile, T. M. (1988). A model of creativity and innovation in organizations. In B. M. Staw & L. L. Cummings (Eds.), *Research in organizational behavior* (Vol. 10). Greenwich, CT: JAI Press.

Amabile, T. M. (1993). Motivational synergy: Toward new conceptualizations of intrinsic and extrinsic motivation in the workplace. *Human Resource Management Review, 3,* 185–201.

Amabile, T. M. (1996). *Creativity in context: Update to the social psychology of creativity*. Boulder, CO: Westview Press.

Amabile, T. M. (2019a). Understanding retirement requires getting inside people's heads: A call for more qualitative research. Guidepost commentary. *Work, Aging, and Retirement, 5*(3), 207–211.

Amabile, T. M. (2019b). Educating leaders who make a difference in the world. *Perspectives on Psychological Science, 14,* 7–11.

Amabile, T. M. (2020). Creativity, artificial intelligence, and a world of surprises. *Academy of Management Discoveries, 6*(3). https://doi.org/10.5465/amd.2019.0075. Published online October 29, 2020.

Amabile, T. M., Barsade, S. G., Mueller, J. S., & Staw, B. M. (2005). Affect and creativity at work. *Administrative Science Quarterly, 50*(3), 367–403.

Amabile, T. M., & Conti, R. (1999). Changes in the work environment for creativity during downsizing. *Academy of Management Journal, 42,* 630–640.

Amabile, T. M., Conti, R., Coon, H., Lazenby, J., & Herron, M. (1996). Assessing the work environment for creativity. *Academy of Management Journal, 39,* 1154–1184.

Amabile, T. M., & Glazebrook, A. H. (1982). A negativity bias in interpersonal evaluation. *Journal of Experimental Social Psychology, 18,* 1–22.

Amabile, T. M., & Gryskiewicz, S. S. (1987). *Creativity in the R&D laboratory* (Technical Report Number 30). Greensboro, NC: Center for Creative Leadership.

Amabile, T. M., & Gryskiewicz, N. (1989). The creative environment scales: The work environment inventory. *Creativity Research Journal, 2,* 231–254.

Amabile, T. M., & Hall, D.T. (2019, April 30). The undervalued power of self-relevant research: The case of researching retirement while retiring. *Academy of Management Perspectives*, published online.

Amabile, T. M., Hennessey, B. A., & Grossman, B. S. (1986). Social influences on creativity: The effects of contracted-for reward. *Journal of Personality and Social Psychology, 50,* 14–23.

Amabile, T. M., & Kabat, L. (1982). When self-descriptions contradict behavior: Actions do speak louder than words. *Social Cognition, 1,* 311–335.

Amabile, T. M., & Kramer, S. J. (2011). *The progress principle: Using small wins to ignite joy, engagement, and creativity at work.* Boston: Harvard Business Review Press.

Amabile, T. M., & Mueller, J. S. (2008). Studying creativity, its processes, and its antecedents: An exploration of the componential theory of creativity. In J. Zhou & C. E. Shalley (Eds.), *Handbook of organizational creativity.* New York: Lawrence Erlbaum Associates.

Amabile, T. M. & Pratt, M. G. (2017). The dynamic componential model of creativity and innovation in organizations: Making progress, making meaning. In B. Staw & A. Brief (Eds.), *Research in Organizational Behavior, 37,* 157–183.

Amabile, T. M., Schatzel, E. A., Moneta, G. B., & Kramer, S. J. (2004). Leader behaviors and the work environment for creativity: Perceived leader support. *The Leadership Quarterly, 15*(1), 5–32.

Cromwell, J. R., Amabile, T. M., & Harvey, J.-F. (2018). An integrated model of dynamic problem solving within organizational constraints. In R. Reiter-Palmon, V. Kennel, & J. Kaufman (Eds.), *Individual creativity in the workplace* (pp. 53–82). San Diego, CA: Elsevier.

Eisenberger, R., & Cameron, J. (1996). Detrimental effects of reward: Reality or myth? *American Psychologist, 51,* 1153–1166.

Fama, E. F., & Jensen, M. C. (1983). Separation of ownership and control. *The Journal of Law and Economics, 26,* 301–325.

Fisher, C. M., Pillemer, J., & Amabile, T. M. (2018). Deep help in complex project work: Guiding and path-clearing across difficult terrain. *Academy of Management Journal, 61*(4), 1524–1553.

Hennessey, B. A. (1989). The effect of extrinsic constraints on children's creativity while using a computer. *Creativity Research Journal, 2,* 151–168.
Hennessey, B. A. (2004). The social Psychology of creativity: The beginnings of a multi-cultural perspective. In S. Lau (Ed.), *Creativity: When East meets West* (pp. 201–226). Hong Kong: World Scientific Publishing.
Hennessey, B. A., & Amabile, T. M. (1998). Reward, intrinsic motivation, and creativity. *American Psychologist, 53*(6), 674–675. Lepper, Greene, & Nisbett, 1973.
Hennessey, B. A., & Amabile, T. M. (2010). Creativity. *Annual Review of Psychology, 61,* 569–598.
Hennessey, B. A., Amabile, T. M., & Martinage, M. (1989). Immunizing children against the negative effects of reward. *Contemporary Educational Psychology, 14,* 212–227.
Hennessey, B. A., Mueller, J. S., & Amabile, T. M. (2020). Consensual assessment. In M. Runco & S. Pritzker (Eds.), *Encylopedia of creativity* (Vol. 1, 3rd ed., pp. 199–205). Elsevier, Academic Press.
Hennessey, B. A., & Zbikowski, S. M. (1993). Immunizing children against the negative effects of reward: A further examination of intrinsic motivation training techniques. *Creativity Research Journal, 6,* 297–307.
Jensen, M. C., & Meckling, W. H. (1976). Theory of the firm: Managerial behavior, agency costs and ownership structure. *Journal of Financial Economics, 3,* 305–360.
Lepper, M., Greene, D., & Nisbett, R. (1973). Undermining children's intrinsic interest with extrinsic rewards: A test of the "overjustification" hypothesis. *Journal of Personality and Social Psychology, 28,* 129–137.
Lord, C. G., Ross, M., & Lepper, M. R. (1979). Biased assimilation and attitude polarization: The effects of prior theories on subsequently considered evidence. *Journal of Personality and Social Psychology, 37*(11), 2098–2099.
MacKinnon, D. W. (1965). Personality and the realization of creative potential. *American Psychologist, 20,* 273–281.
Osborne, A. (1963). *Applied imagination: Principles and procedures of creative thinking.* New York: Scribner's.
Parnes, S. (1967). *Creative behavior guidebook.* New York: Scribner's.
Ross, L. D., Amabile, T. M., & Steinmetz, J. (1977). Social roles, social control and biases in social perception processes. *Journal of Personality and Social Psychology, 35,* 485–494.

Simonton, D. K. (1975). Sociocultural context of individual creativity: A transhistorical time-series analysis. *Journal of Personality and Social Psychology, 32,* 1119–1133.

Szymanski, H. A., & Amabile, T. (1969). The use of proteins to remove water from GLC samples. *Journal of Chromatographic Science, 7,* 575–576.

The manufacturer's authorised representative in the EU is Springer Nature Customer Service Centre GmbH, Europaplatz 3, 69115 Heidelberg, Germany. If you have any concerns regarding our products, please contact ProductSafety@springernature.com

Printed and bound by CPI Group (UK) Ltd, Croydon, CR0 4YY
22/09/2026
02221066-0005